LIVING WITH ONE'S PAST

LIVING WITH ONE'S PAST

Personal Fates and Moral Pain

Norman S. Care

ROWMAN & LITTLEFIELD PUBLISHERS, INC.

ROWMAN & LITTLEFIELD PUBLISHERS, INC.

Published in the United States of America
by Rowman & Littlefield Publishers, Inc.
4720 Boston Way, Lanham, Maryland 20706

3 Henrietta Street
London WC2E 8LU, England

Chapter 4 "On Living with Others" contains material previously published as
book reviews of J.R. Lucas, *On Justice* (Oxford: Clarendon Press, 1980)
appearing in *Nous* 17, 4 (November 1983) and Vinit Haksar, *Equality, Liberty,
and Perfectionism* (New York: Oxford University Press [Clarendon], 1979) in
Nous 17, 2 (May 1983). Material is used by permission of author and publisher.

British Cataloging in Publication Information Available

Library of Congress Cataloging-in-Publication Data
Care, Norman S.
Living with one's past : personal fates and moral pain / Norman S. Care.
p.   cm.
Includes bibliographical references and index.
1. Ethics.   2. Agent (Philosophy).   3. Pain—Moral and ethical
aspects.   I. Title.
BJ1031.C36   1996   170—dc20   96–15160   CIP

ISBN 0–8476–8236–6 (cloth : alk. paper)
ISBN 0–8476–8237–4 (pbk. : alk. paper)

Printed in the United States of America

∞ ™ The paper used in this publication meets the minimum requirements of
American National Standard for Information Sciences—Permanence of Paper
for Printed Library Materials, ANSI Z39.48–1984.

For Barbara

Contents

Preface

In what follows, my general subject is moral psychology and, hence, the moral experience of individuals. My special interest is in the moral sensibility involved in one's recognition of and response to moral-emotional low points in oneself and others. The low points I have in mind often involve, for those who suffer them, extreme moral pain—in the forms, for example, of guilt, shame, regret, or remorse—and such low points are sometimes accompanied by serious losses in self-confidence and capacity for action. In the fortunate case these negative aspects of such experiences motivate one to "recover" or "get past" or "go on from" the low points; the suffering and losses can also, through the work of memory and imagination, help us identify certain contrasting positive states (e.g., serenity, a reasonable ambition, a certain inner togetherness) by which one can measure one's recovery efforts. Recovery is not always achieved, however, even when it is strenuously sought. In fact, one emphasis of my discussion is that people do not always recover from moral-emotional low points; another emphasis is that in some cases people are not able to recover from them, even when we think they can and should.

When moral theory and political philosophy came alive again in the early 1970s with the publication of John Rawls's *A Theory of Justice*,[1] the object of attention, by and large, was not the direct moral experience of individuals, which is what I wish to understand. It was instead what Rawls called "the basic structure of society."[2] My concern is not society's structure but the moral psychology of the individual moral agent, that is, the moral sensibility of a person living in, with, and under the many practices that constitute ordinary moral life. When I say "moral sensibility" here, I have in mind the forms of thought and feeling, laced as they are with maxims and concern for responsibility, of these individual participants—in some cases participants willy-nilly—in ordinary moral life. My discussion is thus located mainly in, as it were, the moral psychology section of the wing of moral philosophy concerned with individual responsibility.

While moral psychology is a respectable part of moral theory, the negative moral-emotional experience that I attempt to write about perhaps makes me vulnerable to being found laughable, boring, tiresome, or objectionable by some professional intellectuals, for the "low points" I am concerned about are also the subject of pop psychology, advice columnists in newspapers and magazines, television soap operas and talk shows, and psychological counselors, and some members of the intellectual world show little enthusiasm for any of these. Still, one must be careful about what one disdains. The forms of experience in question are also the concern of fine novelists and sensitive filmmakers, of genuinely close friends, of associates and colleagues who respect one another, and of members of families if or when they care about one another. I see no reason in principle for excluding such experience—in particular, the sensibility of moralized low points—from philosophical attention.

I should say that it is not an aim of my discussion to propose a radically new way to live. From the angle of an interest in how to live, I suppose my writing will seem tentative and exploratory at best and probably ordinary—even banal—in many places. Even though the experience I write about will seem personal in places, my aim is not the relief of confession or therapy for myself or others but an understanding of some of the moral practices embedded in our lives as persons among other persons. From the angle of an interest in moral philosophy, the discussion as a whole constitutes a challenge to a familiar received conception of moral agency, namely, the conception that treats the individual human being as possessed of a unitary capacity for choice, giving him or her a running chance at being a master of his or her fate. I argue that this conception, when generalized across persons as we know them in ordinary life, is importantly wrong.

My discussion contains many short sections which I have collected into five chapters. The discussion begins and ends with remarks about *peace of mind*, which I think is one of the important values susceptible to disturbance by the occurrence of moral-emotional low points. In the first group of these sections, I am concerned with *the problem of living with one's past* when one's past contains one's own moral wrongdoing and one is unable, or chooses not, to ignore or explain away the wrongdoing. This leads me, in the second group of sections, to explore what I call *persona moralism*, that is, the stereotyping and judging of others and ourselves that we enter into when we participate in ordinary moral life and on the basis of which we hold others and ourselves to account and engage in accusing and blaming others or ourselves for what they or we do. In a third group of sections I discuss *problematic agency*, by which I mean in particular the difficulties we and others have in the world as a result of diminished will or personality deficits (or what others tell us are deficits) or constitutional misfortune resulting in reduced agency in some form. Here I say what I can about depression, fear, anger, anxiety, and certain sorts of personal incapacities when these are for those who bear them something more than, and deeper than, the moods or failings of the moment. Perhaps I need to say, in this connection, that I am no psychologist, psychiatrist, or therapist, but, again, my writing is not about how to understand or cure diseases or compensate for syndromes or even get through a stressful day. My interest is in the ordinary facts of diminished, flawed, or reduced agency—facts that I realize are difficult for many to acknowledge or tolerate—and in the implications of these ordinary facts for an understanding of persons and ordinary moral life. I argue that there is a certain risk of unfairness to persons (others and ourselves) involved in the everyday moral thinking we engage in and that even for conscientious individuals the effort to live a moral life is, as a matter of practical necessity, itself morally hazardous.

These matters collectively push me on in the fourth chapter to the problem of *living with others*. The sections in this chapter concern what morality requires of us in a world of individuals, some or many of whom suffer diminished, flawed, or reduced agency. In the final chapter I treat the problem of *recovery and self-protection*. The discussion in these sections concerns—in a way that I hope is philosophical—one actual recovery program, namely, the famous Twelve-Step Program of Alcoholics Anonymous. My reasons for attempting an interpretation of the AA program are both personal and theoretical; the latter consideration is that this program has had some success with alcoholics who have suffered moral-emotional pain of the sort I am concerned with, yet it also acknowledges that recovery may not occur for some alcoholics who attempt to follow it, and it thus recognizes that agency may be constitutionally blocked, that is, diminished, flawed, or reduced; this latter notion I find of great theoretical interest.

My overview of my discussion runs as follows. In *A Theory of Justice*, Rawls said that his conception of justice as fairness, as a set of principles for the basic structure of society, allows its members a collective form of reconciliation to the human condition: "should it be truly effective and publicly recognized as such, [it] seems more likely than its rivals to transform our perspective on the social world and to reconcile us to the dispositions of the natural world and the conditions of human life."[3] In an earlier work,[4] I explored a conception of individual responsibility ("shared-fate individualism") that might operate to reconcile the individual as such (apart from whatever conception of justice guides the basic structure of his or her society) to a human condition riddled (as ours is) with destitution and inequality. In the moral-psychological discussion I undertake here, I explore a conception of moral agency that might serve to reconcile one internally, that is, to oneself, as represented to one by one's understanding of one's own history and, in particular, its negative impact on those one cares for. My general view is that an important part of living the life of a human being is dealing somehow with these different reconciliation problems.

I have had much help in the preparation of this manuscript from Karen H. Barnes of Oberlin College. My departmental colleagues at Oberlin—Daniel D. Merrill, Robert H. Grimm, Peter K. McInerney, George W. Rainbolt, David A. Love, Ira S. Steinberg, and Alfred F. Mackay—have been most helpful. George Rainbolt gave me a written page-by-page critique of my manuscript that has been invaluable to me. David Love and I have discussed the issues I explore here for years, and it is a troubling thought for me that all the good ideas in my discussion may derive from him. Thomas Van Nortwick, an Oberlin colleague in the classics department, and William E. Hood, an Oberlin colleague in art history, have been extremely helpful to me in discussion, teaching, and the challenges of friendship. S. Frederick Starr read my manuscript while President of Oberlin College, and I was much taken by his insightful response to it. A number of people saw an early version of the sections concerned with the problem of living with one's past, and many of them responded with encouragement and, in some cases, with detailed comments; let me acknowledge the help of Owen Flanagan, Charles Landesman, Andrei Straumanis, Phyllis Morris, Alisa Carse, Claudia Card, Lynne McFall, Richard Garner, Barbara Horan, Harry G. Frankfurt, Kristin Shrader-Frechette, John R. Thompson, Ernest LePore, Michael Stocker, and Laurence Thomas.

My discussion of problematic agency grows out of comments on Claudia Card's excellent paper, "Responsibility and Moral Luck," presented at the Colloquium in Philosophy at the University of North Carolina at Chapel Hill in October 1990. Parts of the discussion of living with others are drawn from my review of J. R. Lucas, *On Justice* (Oxford: Clarendon Press, 1980), in *Nous* 17:4 (November 1983); and from my review of Vinit Haksar, *Equality, Liberty, and Perfectionism*

(New York: Oxford University Press [Clarendon], 1979), in *Nous* 17:2 (May 1983).

Time for writing in 1991–92 was made possible by a Research Status Appointment awarded by Oberlin College. I am very grateful for this support.

Finally, let me express my appreciation to Jennifer Ruark (acquisitions editor), Deirdre Mullervy (production editor), and Debbie Greinke (copyeditor) at Rowman & Littlefield for their very welcoming, efficient, and careful treatment of my manuscript.

Chapter 1

On Living with One's Past

Lingering perdition—worse than any death
Can be at once—shall step by step attend
You and your ways; whose wraths to guard you from, —
Which here, in this most desolate isle, else falls
Upon your heads,—is nothing but heart-sorrow
And a clear life ensuing.

The Tempest

I wanted to forget the past, but it refused to forget me; it waited for
sleep, then cornered me.

Margaret Atwood, *Lady Oracle*

Sometimes this awful past which was his and yet not his was a subject
about which he could almost calmly reflect. Sometimes it came upon
him suddenly as a painful incomprehensible jumble against which he
had no natural defence; it penetrated into his body, making him feel
fear and remorse and shame, and mingled, as it did now, with some
quite other anguish.

Iris Murdoch, *Nuns and Soldiers*

I get tired of digging around in other people's dirty laundry. I'm
sick of knowing more about them than I should. The past is never
nice. The secrets never have to do with acts of benevolence or good
deeds suddenly coming to light. Nothing's ever resolved with a
handshake or a heart-to-heart talk. So often, humankind just seems
tacky to me, and I don't know what the rest of us are supposed to
do in response.

Sue Grafton, *"E" is for Evidence*

Peace of Mind and Effective Agency

If peace of mind is an intrinsic personal good, then it is something we
can have an interest in for its own sake, but it is also something that has

1

value through its connection with agency, for when peace of mind is threatened or lost, agency is often diminished. For many of us it then becomes a struggle to conduct our lives in such a way as to take reasonable initiatives, deliberate efficiently, and, in general, keep one's mind on what one means or needs it to be on. In what follows I am concerned mainly with the value that peace of mind has through its connection with agency.

The term "agency," as used here, is common in philosophical texts but not common in ordinary discourse. I use it as a sort of shorthand, referring to one's capacity to live one's life so that what takes place in it is seen by one as flowing from or resisting what one views as one's own choices and decisions. Agency in this sense is manifest when one takes reasonable initiatives and deliberates efficiently, as suggested above; it is also manifest when one takes reasonable initiatives, only to have them frustrated or defeated, or deliberates efficiently but has the result rejected or ignored. Agency can be displayed in productive work (even when its aim is unrealized), in following through on one's projects (even when they fail), in attempting to protect oneself physically and emotionally (even if to no avail), and in meeting one's responsibilities (even when the final results of doing so are other than expected). The term "agency" refers, then, to our capacity to control the content in our lives, but in this discussion it is important that the term does its referring through the sense we have (when we have it) that we are, as we sometimes think, in control of our lives.[1]

Of course, this sense of control is hardly a constant of our moral-psychological condition. There are many different cases that one might try to distinguish. Sometimes—perhaps often—the events in our lives are such that we do not have this sense that we are in control. Sometimes we have the sense that we are in control, but we are mistaken. Sometimes we have the capacity to control the content in our lives, but we cannot exercise it for reasons that we may or may not understand, and so we have no sense of control. Sometimes (perhaps most mysteriously) we *are* exercising the capacity but have no sense that we are in control of the relevant events in our lives. Sometimes we have some sense of control relative to the content of our lives, but it seems only partial, or a matter of degree, and our hold on our lives seems precarious. The idea of agency is philosophically difficult to treat, especially, I believe, if (as here) one is concerned with understanding the role of the sense of control in the human being's efforts to live.[2]

When we are agents, of course, we are not always or thereby moral agents. We can have the sense that we are in control of what happens in our lives without striving to meet moral principles we respect or to cultivate in ourselves the habits of virtue. Immanuel Kant viewed moral agency as something we achieve with effort and, sometimes, struggle.[3] This seems essentially right to me. We do not have or achieve moral agency by merely exercising agency or being agents.

How separate, though, are the notions of "agency" and "moral agency"? We can be agents without being moral agents, but can we ever be moral agents without being agents? This is difficult to imagine, but some candidate cases come to mind.

In the first case I might, for example, do nothing in response to a troubling moral problem, and let us suppose that in this case doing nothing is in fact—by relevant moral principles—the right thing to do. Shall we say that I did the right thing, but that I did not "exercise agency" in doing so? Here one might reply that I did exercise agency in the sense relevant to the issue if in fact my did-nothing response flowed from thought and deliberation about the troubling moral problem I faced. I may not have moved my body, made any promises, or uttered any words; but still, via the thought and deliberation, I exercised agency, and, as a result, I made the right response—so in this case when I was a moral agent, I was an agent. Suppose, however, that I did nothing, and this was *not* the result of thought and deliberation about the problem I faced. What I did (viz., nothing) just happened to be, or be in effect, the right thing. Was I then a moral agent but not an agent? I think not, for surely in this case I was not a moral agent at all. What I did was not the right thing to do in the circumstances (even if it looked the same as the right thing to do), for what I did was no response to the problem I faced at all.

Another, more difficult case comes to mind. Suppose I am one of many, and the result of our collective activities over time is that you and yours are hurt and damaged. Perhaps you are disadvantaged or disenfranchised or made destitute through practices to which I am a party.[4] Suppose further that I am not aware that the practices to which I am a party work out in such a negative way. It is not my intention or desire to hurt or damage you and yours. I have not really thought much about the fact that I am a party to the activities that produce these negative results. In these circumstances you might view me as a moral agent: you might think of me as someone doing wrong; you might hold me to account, or charge me with responsibility for what is happening to you and yours, and you might think of me in this way, and judge me accordingly, even though I have no sense that I am an agent relative to the damaging practices that you hold me responsible for engaging in.

The situation I describe here is common enough, but is it a situation in which I am a moral agent but not an agent? Not in any interesting sense, I think. After all, should rational communication between us ensue, the notion that I am a moral-agent-but-not-an-agent could not be sustained; for if, through the communication, I see your point about what I am doing, then I am a moral agent doing wrong, and if I continue to be a party to the damaging practices, I am very much an agent, for I now recognize what I do for what it is, and I continue to do it. Alternatively, if, through the communication, I meet your criticism, or defend against it effectively, then while I may be an agent regarding what I do, the characterization of what I do is not, or is no longer, such that I am a moral agent doing wrong. Once we get together, through communication, we cannot both hold the view that I am a moral-agent-but-not-an-agent.

There is a third case that is of a very different sort and that seems to me more interesting and less easy to dismiss. This is the case in which I have done wrong—perhaps a great deal of wrong over time—but when I have done wrong, I have been under the influence of chemicals, e.g., alcohol. Suppose that I, when drunk, have harmed you or damaged my own children. Suppose further that I have done this often over the years. I then reach the point in my life at which I hit bottom, sober up, perhaps enter treatment, and begin to recover, that is, learn to live dry, and seek to rejoin my community and repair my personal relationships with family members and others. The going might be hard for me internally, in terms of my own desires and cravings, and it might also be confusing for me externally, in terms of my reception by others. I might be met with accusation and distrust or with condescension or with pity. Some might think of me as a moral agent with a long record of wrongdoing; others might view me as morally weak; and still others, with a different understanding of the role of chemicals in my life, might view me as an addict or, now, a recovering addict, that is, someone whose makeup is such that he or she is, or was, a victim of sorts.

Is there application in this third case for the notion of moral-agency-without-agency? Not for those who confront me with accusation and distrust. For them I am a moral agent—I have done wrong—and I am very much an agent. Here, the notions of moral agency and agency do not separate. There also is no application for this notion for those who look down on me as morally weak. For them I am a moral agent—one who has given way to the impulses and desires of various moments—and I am an agent: I just haven't tried hard enough to keep myself under control and to do what I ought to do. For those who approach me with pity, however, perhaps there is an application for the notion of moral-agency-without-agency. These observers or judges see me as a victim of my physiology, environment, family background, or all of these. For them, yes, I have done wrong, that is, I did indeed perform the hurtful and damaging acts, and I am morally responsible for doing so, yet somehow I was not really an agent relative to those acts. In the view of these people, I cannot deny that I did wrong, for what I did was wrong; yet what I did flowed from my nature as chemically dependent, that is, it flowed from factors in my makeup by virtue of which I count as a sort of addict and over which my control is nil or controversial. In this view I might be said to be a moral agent but not an agent. What would be meant, I suppose, is that I am morally responsible for what I did, but what I did resulted from elements in me that I was stuck with despite myself.

Of the candidate cases thus reviewed,[5] the third case, involving addiction, is the most confusing. We may well be unclear whether it is a case of moral-agency-without-agency. I will return to it later.

No doubt the term "peace of mind" has a variety of associations, including those of laid-back emotional states. Here I am concerned with the aspect of peace of mind that involves being at ease with one's moral record. When one lacks peace of mind in this respect, one is vulnerable to different forms of moral-emotional pain, for example, depending on different factors in different cases, regret, remorse, shame, guilt, despair, and perhaps in some cases mortification. When one suffers such pain, one's agency is, or risks being, negatively affected, and this is so, I think, even if there are other aspects of one's life or selfhood unrelated to one's moral record regarding which one finds oneself satisfactory or better.

In what follows I discuss the backward-looking difficulty one can have when one's past, or a part of it having moral content, is so upsetting or distressing that one's peace of mind is disturbed or, in extreme cases, destroyed. I focus in particular on those parts of one's past that involve wrongdoing but in respect to which the ascription of agency and, hence, responsibility is in some way or to some extent controversial. These are among the parts of one's past that one is stuck with, and typically they contain actions or even states of mind that one did not mean. I wish to discuss this difficulty as a subject for moral philosophy and moral psychology rather than as a problem for psychology, psychiatry, or the theory of counseling. The aim is to offer an interpretation of some cases in which this difficulty is experienced, to throw light on the nature of the suffering (the moral pain) that occurs, and to consider what is involved in being or becoming entitled to go on with one's life from the low point involved in the experience of the backward-looking difficulty. The discussion thus gives some attention to the problem of recovering or regaining one's agency when that agency has been diminished or disrupted by one's understanding of one's own history. My thought is that in some cases this regaining of agency is, as a matter of practical fact, no easy task. Some individuals seem never to succeed at it; others do succeed at it, in some instances rather too easily. My discussion, though, is restricted to the philosophical problem of being entitled to go on with one's life and does not consider the problem of overcoming an obsession with one's past wrongdoing.

Hume, Falk

David Hume recognized the importance we attach to being free of the backward-looking difficulty.

> Inward peace of mind, consciousness of integrity, a satisfactory review of our own conduct—these are circumstances very requisite to happiness, and will be cherished and cultivated by every honest man who feels the importance of them.[6]

W. D. Falk speaks of the human being as one who has a "stake in the kind of self-preservation which requires that one should be able to bear before oneself the survey of one's own actions."[7] To make a beginning, let us treat these points from Hume and Falk in the following manner. Assume that the idea of peace of mind includes, as a part, the idea of being able to make a "satisfactory review of our own conduct" or being able to "bear before oneself the survey of one's own actions." When these ideas are connected in this way, then one's peace of mind is harnessed to one's view of one's past: it becomes a condition of one's having peace of mind that one's moral record be such that on review one finds it satisfactory or bearable.[8] (A certain form of caring about the past is then built into the possession of peace of mind.) When these ideas are thus connected, if one does not find one's moral record satisfactory or bearable, one is in moral trouble with oneself, and this may be manifest in one's experiencing certain of the negative moral emotions I referred to above.

Of course, nearly anyone can cite events or situations from his or her past that get in the way of that person easily making a satisfactory review of his or her conduct. Peace of mind would be rare indeed if it were a condition of a satisfactory review that one believe that one never did anything wrong. I do not think peace of mind is all that rare, so Falk's phrase "bear before oneself the survey of one's own actions" becomes helpful: we may suppose that peace of mind requires not so much a past that one sees as a tabula rasa in respect of wrongdoing as it does a past that one can live with. Perhaps for a fortunate few a review of the past may be open to Hume's word "satisfactory"; but for others the review available, more in line with Falk's words, may be only tolerable or just bearable. In what follows I focus mainly on cases in which the agent has great difficulty in living with or tolerating his or her past. Even a conscientious individual—a person who aspires, and has always aspired, to principled conduct and who takes seriously, and has always taken seriously, the difficulties of principled conduct—can have a past containing parts that are, to say the least, problematic.[9]

When the Past Is Problematic

Problematic parts of one's past might be episodic or relatively long-term. In cases of the latter sort a very problematic section of one's past might extend over many years and have internal stages and subparts all its own. Whether episodic or long-term, problematic parts of one's past may not only haunt one, they can leave a mark, in the form, for example, of a change in one's personality, loss of self-confidence, restriction on ambition, or paralyzing bad feeling about oneself.[10] It understates the point to say that in these cases one's past may command one's attention in a way that seems coercive. Apart from things such as personality effects and bad feeling, one's view of one's past in these cases may indeed dominate one's thoughts and even prevent one's giving reasonable attention to current projects and future plans.[11] Again, one's agency is at stake. It may become urgent, if one is to go on at all, that one come to terms with the past and somehow overcome it or somehow move beyond it.

We may acknowledge that in some cases what one has done may not seem to others to be serious or a genuine matter for concern at all, and one's being pained by it or finding it difficult to live with may appear to others and, perhaps, in time to oneself more like self-indulgence or self-pity than anything else.[12] The suffering in such cases seems out of proportion to the seriousness of the wrong done. In other cases the wrong done was, or becomes, something that occurred so long ago that others find themselves impatient with the continued suffering or suspicious that the suffering is mere posturing. In still other cases one may find it difficult to live with something in or about one's past that clearly does not involve one's own agency at all, for example, having been born illegitimate. Others may fail to see how or why it is that this fact is disturbing, but one nevertheless finds it to be so, perhaps because one is vulnerable to the thoughts of people caught in the ideologies of an earlier period.

There are thus different cases in this subject-area, and sometimes a case of suffering over one's past may seem faintly or not so faintly spurious; but on the other side it seems that there are cases in which we find it plausible to suppose that morality does not allow a person to overcome his or her past, for in these cases what the person has done is so awful that his not being pained by it, her finding it easy to go on as though nothing had happened, his being able to ignore it after awhile, or her forgetting what happened seems outrageous. Clearly, when Jones has committed mass murder or betrayed us all to the enemy, we do not find ourselves hoping he will soon, or ever, overcome or move beyond the dark actions in his past. In fact, we think he should not find the survey of his past bearable. We not only have difficulty forgiving him; we also expect him to have very serious difficulty forgiving himself.[13] If Jones is not ever able to forgive himself, well, perhaps we find that to be neither unfortunate nor regrettable, but simply appropriate.[14] In a case of this kind if Jones were to find his past tolerable or better, we would be outraged and perhaps frightened.

Some Cases

For the purposes of my discussion let me sketch some features of four examples of individuals facing the problem of living with their past.

Example 1

Consider first the following brief newspaper account[15] of a terrible accident:

> For Air Force Maj. Bruce L. Teagarden, nightmare became a reality a week ago when he lost control of his crippled jet fighter near Indianapolis International Airport and ejected, leaving the plane to crash into a hotel lobby, killing nine people.
> Preliminary investigations appear to exonerate Teagarden of any implica-

tion of negligence. He seems to have done all he could have to steer the plane toward an open field before he ejected into a parking lot. His aircraft's single engine had quit and Teagarden, an accomplished pilot without a previous accident, was unable to restart it as the plane descended in poor visibility.

There have been heroic tales of military pilots staying with their doomed planes, steering them away from schools, hospitals, houses and other places where casualties might be heavy. There is no evidence that, in choosing to eject, Teagarden traded his life for those on the ground. He said later he thought the plane was headed away from the hotel and that it took a spin toward the building after he got out.

The Air Force, of course, wants to save the lives of its valued flight crews. That is why it equips its planes, where practicable, with ejection seats. The public supports such a policy.

The relatives of the Indianapolis victims may, in time, accept the randomness of their loss. It is the pilots who, when their own fate becomes linked in a disastrous way with that of others in their path, are left to reproach themselves. That such tragedies are rare may only deepen their inconsolability.

Teagarden may very well be stuck with a very problematic event in his past in the aftermath of this accident. People may come forward to emphasize to him that what happened was an accident and that he must set it aside and go on, but we can recognize that Teagarden might have difficulty absorbing this point.[16] That the event in question was an accident, that what happened was not intentional or voluntary on the part of the pilot—these are important aspects of the situation, and they raise philosophical questions about individual responsibility and the conditions of its possibility. What most concerns me here, however, is how one lives with an event such as this in one's past. I think we could understand Teagarden's having difficulty living with the event described no matter how much or how often its accidental, nonintentional, and nonvoluntary character is emphasized. We (or the pilot) may gloss the connection between the pilot and the tragic event in the most agency-minimal vocabulary we can find; it remains that the pilot finds himself to have been a party to the deaths of other human beings, and that may indeed be very distressing and difficult for him to live with.

Example 2

The next case is less easily set out, since the subject it involves is controversial in certain ways. Suppose Alan Severance is an alcoholic—a practicing alcoholic—and has been one for many years.[17] Suppose too that during those years Severance does not know much about alcoholism; he possesses on the subject only some bits and pieces of general opinion that, when collected together, are inaccurate and confusing in their tension with one another. (Some of the bits and pieces, for example, view alcoholism as a moral weakness rather than a disease; other bits view it differently.) It is easy in such circumstances for Severance to be relatively ignorant of, or at least unhelpfully informed about, his own condition. He does not, as we might say, understand himself as an alcoholic, and he does not interpret his experience in a way that makes much connection between his problems in life and his patterns of drinking. Of course, as Severance progresses through his life, he may become increasingly alarmed about what is happening to himself. He may then engage in what recovery counselors regard as denial that he has a problem with alcohol. Perhaps he finds ways to rationalize, explain away, or disguise to himself if not to others his condition, as in fact it takes its toll on him physically, emotionally, and spiritually. Suppose further that during many years of incremental deterioration, increasing bewilderment, and loss of self-esteem, Severance somehow manages to pursue a career, make and lose friends, marry, and help raise a family. He does his work and, in general, does his best to meet his responsibilities as he understands them. People regard him as a decent person. He thinks of himself as essentially a good person, even as he slowly self-destructs.

Finally, we may imagine that Severance's alcoholism worsens to that point (different in its details for different victims) at which his own perception of his condition is no longer bearable. In the vocabulary of Alcoholics Anonymous, Severance hits bottom and thus finds himself in physical, emotional, and spiritual distress that has embedded in it a sense of defeat that he cannot evade. If Severance survives this experience in such a way as to make a start on a program of recovery—perhaps involving a period of hospitalization, treatment, and therapy, followed by a commitment to total abstinence (under the guideline "one day at a time") supported by, say, several AA meetings per week, plus time for reading and reflection, plus support from sponsors and understanding friends—he may well come up against the fact that his past indeed contains some very problematic parts. I will limit attention here to one such part, overwhelming in the pain it carries for Severance when he reviews his life now: Severance has the sense that he damaged the moral personality of his children.

Obviously, how the term "moral personality" is to be interpreted will be controversial among philosophers, but here we need not enter far into controversy. In broad terms, we may consider moral personality to be or centrally involve the various capacities that allow one to develop and enjoy self-respect and to be capable of respect for others.[18] Moral personality thus includes those capacities for rationality, sensibility, and judgment that, when exercised, allow us to formulate and pursue the individually defined projects of choice associated with self-realization and to contribute in a positive way to our evaluations of ourselves as being worth something in our own eyes. We may assume that Severance, now in recovery, hears that children in families of practicing alcoholics are at risk of damage to moral personality.[19] As Severance attempts to retrieve his position in life, including his position in his own family, he comes to see that the moral personalities of his children are damaged and to believe that this seems connected with his years of drinking. Severance is devastated. It may only make matters worse when he realizes that whether he in fact caused such damage may not be ascertainable. At this point Severance may or may not view alcoholism as a disease. Whatever interpretation of his condition he finally arrives at will in any case not change, settle, relieve, or ameliorate his pain over his children's fate. The perception of his condition as a disease, for example, does not itself make his children undamaged. For his children to become better, as indeed may be possible,[20] they may require special counseling within a time-consuming program of recovery of their own[21]; but that their lives should need to be tied up in this way may only add to his pain.

We can understand, so I believe, how the recovering alcoholic (whose recovery we may wish to encourage and support) could find it very distressing and difficult to live with his own drinking history, that is, a very problematic many-yeared section of his past. In a deep sense of a sad word, Severance, now sober, may be in despair.

Example 3

The third case I have in mind involves divorce and its aftermath. It differs from the cases above insofar as it does not involve either accident or the controversies about disease or weakness that can arise in cases of alcoholism. In the third case, C and E divorce, and the separation is at C's initiative and for reasons that C regards as perfectly sound. After eighteen years of marriage and raising children, C finds herself no longer in love with E and no longer able to bear the increasing strain of maintaining the relationship with E. This is not a case in which C abandons her family or acts hastily, crudely, or irresponsibly. It is not a case in which C's initiative is based on actions by E that were harmful, embarrassing, or hurtful to C. It is not a case in which C all of a sudden hates E or has lost respect for him, and it is not a case in which she is fed up with her children, her work, life in general, or anything else. It is not a case in which C is captivated by a shallow or spurious feminism. It is a case in which C is suffocated by the marriage in ways she can explain and feels are important, and part of the course of happiness for C requires release from the marriage. Let us also suppose that in this case the breakup of marriage and family will cause no special material hardship for those involved.

It is a major factor in this case, however, that the breakup of the marriage is recognized by C to be a severe loss to E. E's anguish is genuine, extreme, and pervasive. His energy is gone, and the blow to his self-esteem is very deep and lasting. We might say, following the earlier language, that in this case too C's action leaves her with the sense of having damaged E's moral personality. E's capacities for rationality, sensibility, and judgment are seriously affected, and C is aware of this. It remains, however, that even though it grieves C deeply that her release from the marriage carries with it such costs, all things considered, the course of happiness for her is plain. Terminating the marriage is for C in that way justified. We may, of course, find ourselves irritated by the apparent self-regarding nature of the justification that moves C—it is also easy for us to be irritated, for our lives are not at stake—but even if we are sympathetic to C's justification, the aspect of the case that is of interest here is that C finds it massively troubling to live with the fact that her action had such a deep negative impact on E. She may be aware of other cases in which the impact of divorce on the parties to it is not so great, but in this case the negative impact on E was very great. C thus finds herself stuck with a part of her past that is indeed very problematic for her.

Example 4

The last case I will sketch is provided by Rousseau in *The Confessions*.[22] It is the story of his own "cruel memory" of his falsely accusing a young servant—Marion—of stealing a small item from the household in which he was residing when, in fact, he stole the item himself. Rousseau speaks of the false accusation as a "terrible" and "heinous" deed (also as the "sole offense I have committed"), and he says that it "has rested till this day on my conscience without any relief." This deed, he says, "was cruel in every respect" and, so Rousseau thought, contained among its "possible evil consequences" substantial damage to the young woman's moral personality: "Who can tell to what extremes the depressed feeling of injured innocence might have carried her at her age? And if my remorse at having perhaps made her unhappy is unbearable, what can be said of my grief at perhaps having made her worse than myself?"

Rousseau's remorse and grief do not preclude his offering certain excuses for his false accusation.

> Never was deliberate wickedness further from my intention than at the cruel moment. . . . When afterwards I saw her in the flesh my heart was torn. But the presence of all those people prevailed over my repentance. I was not much afraid of punishment, I was only afraid of disgrace. But that I feared more than death, more than crime, more than anything in the world. . . . If I had been allowed time to come to my senses, I should most certainly have admitted everything.

Also, "my age . . . should be taken into account . . . really my crime amounted to no more than [a young person's] weakness."

Despite all his minimizing, however, what he has done stays with Rousseau. It is quite clear that he wishes to remove the cruel memory: "I can affirm that the desire to some extent to rid myself of it has greatly contributed to my resolution of writing these *Confessions*." At the end a striking measure of the sheer weight of the cruel memory is taken:

> If this is a crime that can be expiated . . . it must have been atoned for by all the misfortunes that have crowded the end of my life, by forty years of honest and upright behaviour under difficult circumstances. Poor Marion finds so many avengers in this world that, however great my offense against her may have been, I have little fear of carrying the sin on my conscience at death. That is all I have to say on the subject. May I never have to speak of it again.[23]

Self-Conception and Self-Doubt

If these sketches are enough to remind us of what it is for a person to have difficulty living with his or her past, we may ask next why we have, or are vulnerable to, such a difficulty. Notice that in each of the cases above it is open to the person involved to realize intellectually that something blocks or interferes with viewing his or her situation as falling easily or without qualification under a description involving a simple conjunction of agency and wrongdoing, for example, a description of the form "I did x and x was wrong." (1) In the case of the pilot, the fact that the event was an accident blocks the "I did x" part of the conjunction, and in the other part the term "wrong" might be replaced by "tragic," "sad," or "unfortunate." (2) In the case of Severance's alcoholism and its effects on Severance's children, understanding the situation as involving alcoholism at least raises issues about whether the judgment "I did x" requires qualification. (There are competing accounts of what alcoholism is.) (3) In the case of divorce, the alleged justificatory self-regarding reasons involved in the situation tend to preclude—for C, at any rate—the conjoining of "I did x" with "x was wrong." (If C was justified in doing x, then x was not wrong; if x was wrong, then what C did, which she was justified in doing, was not x.) (4) Even in the case of Rousseau's "cruel memory," the pressure of circumstances (Rousseau was stampeded, if we take certain of his excuses seriously) and his extreme fear of disgrace seem to make Rousseau at least less than satisfied with the accuracy of the unqualified judgment "I did x"; but even when the simple conjunction of agency and wrongdoing is blocked or made controversial in our understanding of these cases, nevertheless, enough sense of responsibility for what happened in the agent's past seems to be remaindered in the agent's perception of the situation to allow moral pain to flourish. How can that be?

In the first place, even if the direct application of a simple conjunction of agency and wrongdoing is blocked or controversial in these cases, it remains that the individuals in them are stuck with something in their past that is, or appears to them to be, a manifestation of "self" that does not really fit who or what they think they are. The point about self-identity might be put in this way: insofar as one's life is something one leads,[24] in rather the way in which a story is something one authors, I take it that one leads it according to some sort of conception of oneself that is in part normative in character. This is to say that living a life is something one does to some extent under a view of oneself as being a person of a certain kind or having a certain character, with certain desires, hopes, aspirations, and fears, and possessed of certain principles, policies, and strategies for living.[25] Notoriously, however, such self-conceptions are often indeterminate or in the process of change; thus, if indeed one's life is construed as a story one authors, it is so with the special complication that one's own makeup as combined author-character is not always clear.

Perhaps for many of us the collection of normative elements in a self-conception is a miscellany. For others the collection might be quite structured or systematic. For some of us self-deception regarding the elements in the collection is a recurring threat. These differences amongst us do not matter, however, for present purposes. One's conception of oneself may not be fully worked out, with all its elements ordered appropriately relative to each other and to some more general aims; it may not be conscious to the mind; it may undergo frequent revisions; and, perhaps most important, it may contain inaccuracy and be lacking in wisdom; but apart from the indeterminacy and in-process revision of self-conceptions, it is the fact of their presence in our lives that makes it possible for there to be cases in which there is a mismatch between a part of my past and me, that is, that idea of myself in terms of which I understand, with whatever roughness or degree of inaccuracy, who or what I am.

The fact that a problematic part of one's past is out of line with one's conception of oneself is not by itself, however, enough to explain the existence of that remaindered sense of responsibility that makes it possible for moral pain to flourish. The fact itself is not that rich. My thought is that in some cases there is something more at work, something over and beyond a mismatch between the problematic stretch of my past and my conception of myself. This something more is, I think, a belief, perhaps experienced initially as worry, that my conception of myself might be importantly inaccurate, plus the further belief, perhaps experienced as suspicion, that I might in fact be a person of the kind that the out-of-line behavior fits. The notion that one might not be as one's conception of oneself portrays one, but rather the darker sort of person suggested by the problematic section in one's past, may be forceful (increasingly so over time) in one's moral psychology. When one ends up living with not only conduct that is a direct, clear expression of one's understanding of oneself but also with conduct that it appears one may have to acknowledge as one's own but that suggests or fits a conception of oneself that one disavows or finds objectionable, then one might indeed become suspicious of the accuracy of one's conception of oneself.

These remarks outline, then, a sort of slide into self-doubt to which we are vulnerable. What is at stake here are conduct and character and the role of self-conception in inferences from the former to the latter. Interestingly, when I make a judgment about the character of a stranger, I may find myself inferring quickly from "you lied" to "you're a liar." Nothing, in the case of the stranger who lies to me, stands in the way of a quick move from conduct to character. It would take the recognition of special contexts or circumstances, principled tolerance on my part, or perhaps an unusual native generosity for me to presume, in the absence of counterevidence, that "you lied, but you're not necessarily a liar."

When I am judging myself or a friend, however, I am less inclined to move quickly from "I (you) lied" to "I'm (you're) a liar." In the case of judgment of a stranger, what we have to go on is conduct, and so, by default and in the absence of special contexts or circumstances or, indeed, our own tolerance or generosity, the connection between conduct and character seems pretty tight. In the self-judgment case, however, or the case involving judgment of a friend, what I have to go on is not just behavior. In these cases known self-conceptions enter in. Part of what I have to go on in my own case, at any rate, is my idea of the kind of person I am. If my behavior is or was out of line with that idea, I do not immediately infer that my character is not that specified by the idea. The self-conception provides, as it were, a measure of protection against hasty inference from objectionable conduct to distressing conclusions about character. Still, despite all this, the fact seems to be that my self-conception does not always or automatically win out in a clash with evidence from the past regarding what my character is. The worry—that I am not really the essentially good person I think I am—may in some case still arise.

Why does it arise when it does? Different answers may be possible in different cases. Perhaps, for some of us, self-conceptions are, as it were, weak in us or in their hold on us, perhaps by reason of confusion within them in some cases, and even limited counterevidence from the past simply, by its clarity, overwhelms them. For others, self-conceptions may be reasonably strong, but nevertheless give way in the face of lots of counterevidence from the past. In another kind of case, involving, say, a practicing alcoholic, a strong self-conception might be effectively challenged—"broken" might be a better term—by an organized intervention conducted by family members, friends, employer, and so on under the direction of counselors from a hospital's chemical-dependency treatment center. There may be, too, some people who live in fantasy relative to their self-conceptions, so that their self-conceptions are so strong as never to be shaken by counterevidence from the past.

Examples 2, 3, and 4 sketched in the previous section seem open to interpretation in the terms of the brief account I have just given, though other readings of them might become possible should other factors be added to the cases. This is to say, in summary form, that in each of these cases:

(1) The agent's past contains wrongdoing of a sort that people are blamed for when they commit it deliberately, voluntarily, intentionally, and so on.

(2) The wrongdoing is serious insofar as it involves damage to the moral personality of another—damage that may or may not be retrievable.

(3) The wrongdoing is negatively out of line with the agent's self-conception, such that (a) the agent believes he or she might be a person of the objectionable kind suggested by the wrongdoing, even though (b) there is something in the situation (e.g., a personal condition, sound self-regarding reason, special circumstances, certain personality factors) that makes controversial any direct connection between agency and wrongdoing in the case.

I should add that I do not intend that this account should be considered to apply to all cases of difficulty in living with the past. The makeup of moral pain can be different from what I am concerned with here, namely, suffering constituted by a combination of beliefs experienced as worry and suspicion that one is not as one's self-conception portrays one. In example 1 in the previous section, for example, we can imagine that while an account that runs in the terms sketched above may seem to the pilot to fit his case (he may feel that it does) in the early aftermath of the accident, its applicability will probably not be, or probably should not be, lasting in the long term. If the case is clearly one of accident, then the damage to the victims is tragic or sad but not the result of the pilot's wrongdoing. The pilot does not have an entitlement problem in going on with his life, though that is not to say that he will be free of emotional pain. If the pilot continues to have difficulty in living with his past, then his suffering must be understood as being constituted in some way other than that suggested by the account above.

Deliberate Wrongdoing; Blackouts

I should take steps to keep two sorts of cases separated from those cases that fit the account given just above, for while cases of these other sorts are cases in which one may have difficulty living with one's past, they do not involve any remaindered sense of responsibility and, hence, no questions need arise concerning the accuracy of one's conception of oneself.

In cases of the first sort, it is considered to be true without qualification or special explanation both that one did *x* and that *x* was wrong, and one must now live with that. In these cases the wrongdoing is fully intentional and deliberate. For example, I stole the money from my friend's wallet, and I did so deliberately and in full awareness that what I was doing was wrong—and there is nothing further to say. Some philosophers argue that, strictly speaking, the case thus characterized is impossible and that some qualification or special explanation in connection with either agency or wrongdoing is required as a condition of the intelligibility of their conjunction. Fortunately, we do not have to take up this conceptual problem here.[26] It is enough for this discussion that the alleged case—if it is possible—is not one involving any remaindered sense of responsibility or worries about the accuracy of one's conception of oneself. There is nothing in such a case that is puzzling or baffling for the person involved. Any difficulty one has in living with the situation envisaged (if it can be real) is not that of coming to terms with past action that is out of line with one's conception of oneself such that doubts about the latter arise but, rather, that of coming to terms with the fact that one's character countenances wrongdoing. That, of course, might (or should) be a difficulty, unless one cares nothing for morality, but as such its makeup is different from the difficulty sketched in the account in the previous section.

Cases of another sort also need separating from those that fit the account in the section above. Imagine the situation in which Severance—again a practicing alcoholic—steals money from his friend's wallet while in a blackout. Now, blackouts are temporary periods in which the victim (who may or may not be an alcoholic) functions, that is, looks and acts more or less all right, but later has no recollection of what he or she did.[27] Severance may thus have to be told what he did. It is not that he then remembers and that the missing part of his past is somehow brought back. He may never have the sense of control involved in agency—that direct, unqualified "I did it" sense about an event to which one is a party—relative to the episode in question (though indeed we may suppose that Severance has this sense relative to at least some of his non-alcohol-influenced conduct, that is, he does know from experience this form of agency). We may note that actions performed in a blackout can be quite discontinuous with the character the victim projects in conduct in line with his or her self-conception. In fact, these actions may be strikingly out of character. (They, of course, may not be: one may act in character in a blackout, though one will still not recollect what one did.) These actions are not, however, out of character in the way I described as out of line in the account above. In the blackout situation Severance did x, yes, but his doing x is quite foreign to him.[28] What Severance did may not be known to him, and he may even have to be informed of what he did to become aware that it is in his past. My thought here is that in this case the action does not express, or even purport to express, Severance's self under any conception at all. When it is realized that Severance acted in a blackout, then the question of what his reasons were for what he did is cut short. In a sense Severance was not there and, thus, he had no reasons for what he did. No question about Severance's character, construed as a problem about what conception is applicable to him, is addressed by study of what he did, though of course we may be puzzled or astonished by Severance's being in a blackout or worried about him for being in it if he is so regularly and we care about him. We may have watched Severance do x, but—rather literally, from Severance's point of view—he thinks "it wasn't me" who did x. In this case, any difficulty Severance has in living with the relevant chunk of his past—and it may be considerable—is different again from what is under discussion above. It is not a matter of coming to terms with the darker but possibly more accurate conception of himself suggested by what he did (namely, stealing the wallet). It is more a matter (experientially very frightening) of his now being required to live with what another has done in his name when he was not around. To give the point a slight metaphysical edge: it is as if Severance must now live with a little of someone else's life stuck in his past, without knowing much of anything about who or what that someone else is. (Beyond this living-with problem, Severance may also, if his blackouts are no longer isolated occurrences, have to face the fact that he is the sort of person who is vulnerable to blackouts when he drinks.)

To forestall certain objections, let me add two comments about this last case. First, I hope it is plain that I am speaking of the experience of blackout from, as it were, the inside, that is, from the perspective of the victim of a blackout in the period following the blackout. It is worth noting that from a more detached perspective, blackouts can occur throughout the lengthy drinking history of a real alcoholic, though they may bunch up and occur more often at certain points within such a history. In recovery, it is not uncommon for alcoholics to be dismayed ("horrified" is perhaps a better term) by the fact that their addiction prevailed through many years of drinking despite their familiarity with blackouts. On the surface it somehow seems, to them as well as others, as if they were fools in connection with alcohol or too dumb to learn their lesson when they had so often had bad experiences with the drug. At this point, it is tempting to the alcoholic in the early weeks of recovery to see his or her situation as one in which he or she faces the problem of coming to terms with another, darker, and very strange "self."[29] The notion that alcoholism is, or is like, a "disease" is sometimes helpful in therapy to counter this devastating possibility to some extent.[30]

The other comment is that I do not wish to assimilate the case of the alcoholic to the case in which the pilot's accident results in the deaths of innocent people. Clearly, when the alcoholic in a blackout steals money from his friend's wallet, it is not the case that the money comes to be stolen as a result of an accident. I am not prepared by research or training to offer the sort of account of alcoholism that could with confidence provide an answer to the question of whether alcoholism is a disease. To view alcoholism as, in turn, a disease, an illness, an addiction, a moral weakness, or an unfortunate way of life is to move through a series of conceptions of it that are, as it were, structurally different, and these conceptions carry with them different implications for the appropriateness of holding the agent accountable for what he or she does when under the influence.[31] Perhaps I should add as well that from the fact that I do not wish to assimilate the cases of the pilot and the alcoholic, it does not follow that I hold any particular view, or any view at all, on the matter of how responsibility and blame are to be ascribed in the case of the alcoholic.[32]

On What to Do

In line with the discussion above, suppose the following: (1) that one's life is led, in important ways, according to a conception, as per the sketch in the previous sections; (2) that a part of one's past is out of line with that conception; (3) that that part of one's past involves one's having done things that resulted in damage to the moral personality of another person; (4) that part of one's past seems to one to lie within the region of one's life that is, or is supposed to be, governed by that conception[33]; and (5) that insofar as one's character is not experienced entirely as a matter of choice but in some cases (times of test, for example) as a matter of discovery, that part of one's past seems to suggest a conception of oneself as other than the conception one intends. When such conditions are fulfilled or satisfied (there are doubtless further conditions) and the alien conception of oneself is an object of worry and suspicion, then one may very well face the problem of living with one's past that I have in mind. If one in fact has such a problem, what is one supposed to do about it?

Now, I wish to respond to this question in a way that is philosophical: the aim is not to propose general advice or counsel, but to exhibit the structure of an all-too-familiar difficulty many people have, a difficulty whose importance is wrapped up in its invasion or disruption of peace of mind, and then to take the measure of its seriousness. (Not all difficulties, or even moral difficulties, that people have are serious matters.) Particular cases differ, and what techniques or forms of therapy would help you or me to overcome the past I am not able to say. (Of course, a problematic past is not the only thing capable of invading or disrupting peace of mind.)

In some cases one may be able to explain away the notion that what one did in fact caused damage to someone's moral personality. It is easier to do this if the alleged victim is no longer around. I have even heard it said that a person cannot really damage the moral personality of another, that we do not have that much power over one another; but given the understanding of moral personality briefly suggested above, it seems that this extreme claim is not plausible. On that understanding moral personality is a set of capacities for rationality, sensibility, and judgment, and there appears to be no a priori reason to suppose that such capacities cannot be damaged by others. Some of us may be tougher than others in the matter of keeping moral personality intact, but we are hardly invulnerable to each other.[34] Of course, if we do have it within our power to damage the moral personalities of others (as I believe), when in fact such damage has been done, how deep it is, or to what extent it can be ameliorated—all these questions may be difficult or practically impossible to answer.[35] I assume here that in some cases damage to moral personality is done, and the problem of living with one's past cannot be solved honestly by simply explaining away such damage. Similarly, in cases of the sort I sketched in "Some Cases" above the admonitions "Forget it" or "Ignore it" are not relevant. For the individuals involved in these cases, the problematic parts of their pasts are such that they are not entitled to obey such instructions. (Perhaps one can imagine cases in which a person in fact forgets or ignores, or comes to forget or ignore, a very problematic part of his or her past, but such in-fact forgetting or ignoring is not the same as fulfilling an entitlement to follow the admonitions in question.)

In many cases in which people have difficulty living with their past, the imperative "Make amends" is thought to be appropriate, and so it may be in many cases, for in those cases it may be that something can be done toward putting things right. In the cases sketched above, however, in which the individual suffers a past in which he or she is a party to damage to the moral personality of another, it is not clear either that amends can be made or even what would count as making amends.

Suppose my damaging your moral personality is the mental, emotional, and spiritual analog to my causing you to lose a limb; in either case whether amends can be made or what counts as making amends is unclear. If the alcoholic, the person who seeks divorce, or Rousseau were to do what they can for the damaged person, in whatever ways circumstances now permit, that may be a fine thing, but it will not change the past, and the extent to which its being a fine thing makes the past bearable may be minimal. Similarly, even if they are forgiven by those who are damaged, that will not gain them a past that might allow the satisfactory review to which Hume refers, and, notoriously, other-forgiveness is not sufficient for self-forgiveness.[36] Putting things right, in the sense either of correcting the past or making up the past, may in many cases not be possible, and even in cases in which making amends makes sense, doing so may not affect the moral-psychological difficulty in living with one's past much at all.

In the literature associated with Alcoholics Anonymous, recovering alcoholics are urged to understand their powerlessness over alcohol but then to admit their past, that is, to acknowledge responsibility for what they have done to others and themselves and to make what amends they can without harming others or further harming those they hurt. They are also urged to take certain steps in the famous Twelve-Step Program whereby they resolve to turn over their will and lives to the care of a higher power, with no theological or denominational interpretations required, and also to help other suffering alcoholics. The program of recovery calls as well for a rigorous and continuing moral inventory of oneself, focusing on the recognition and removal of defects of character. In general, relative to our immediate purposes here (I will discuss the AA program in more detail later), this approach to the problem of living with one's past involves a resolute letting go of the past—a confessional distancing from one's own problematic history—combined with new attitudes toward one's powers of control over one's life and a firm forward-looking commitment to service to others. This form of practical advice seems to me direct and straightforward, and there is evidence that it has been helpful in allowing many people to move forward in their lives from low points of very great pain and very great despair.[37] Again, however, and this time with some regret, one must notice that for a person stuck with a past that is painful to contemplate in the manner I have described, even this advice will not yield the satisfactory review of which Hume speaks.

In the end, then, regarding the latter three of the four cases I sketched in "Some Cases" above, a common pattern emerges:

In the alcoholism case (example 2):

(1) Severance damages his child's moral personality.
(2) He does so when he is in the grips of addiction (in this case, alcoholism).
(3) The damage to the child's moral personality may or may not be so deep as to be irretrievable. (It is difficult or impossible to tell, either way.)
(4) Making amends may gain the child's expression of forgiveness, but it will not set things right. In fact, there is no way to set things right.

In the divorce case (example 3):

(1) C damages E's moral personality.
(2) C does so as a consequence of acting on what seems to her to be sound self-regarding reasons for breaking up her marriage with E.
(3) The damage to E may or may not be retrievable.
(4) Again, there is no way to set things right (even if C gains an expression of forgiveness from E).

In the Rousseau case (example 4):

(1) Rousseau damages Marion's moral personality.
(2) Rousseau's doing so happens when he finds himself accused in circumstances that are confusing to him and in which he seems threatened by disgrace (which he "fears more than death").
(3) The damage to Marion may or may not be retrievable.
(4) Again, there is no way to set things right (even if Marion expresses her forgiveness of Rousseau).

In each case an important life question arises for the person involved: how am I (Severance, C, Rousseau) to live with my problematic past?

My view, after reflection on cases of the sorts I sketched, is a very simple one. It is that for many of us Hume's satisfactory review—that "requisite of happiness," he called it—is not in the cards. In the end, the lives of many of us simply turn out, with no malice on our part, to have in them very problematic parts whose survey we are unable to bear; and then, insofar as our lives contain these problematic parts, we are left with the worry and suspicion that we do not fit the conceptions of ourselves by which we mean to govern ourselves. For the very different sorts of considerations displayed in the cases I sketched, one's control of one's life seems somehow to have failed, and one simply ends up with a past that does not contribute positively toward the sense one intends one's life to have or make.[38] If lives exist that through good moral luck get retrospectively justified,[39] so there are lives that through bad moral luck get retrospectively flawed. In fact, the latter phenomenon, relative to first-person moral sensibility, is probably the much more common one. In slightly more dramatic language, the human condition is such that many of us are or will be condemned by our pasts to be without peace of mind.

One may ask at this point, however: so what? That is, suppose indeed that I am without peace of mind, in the sense that I am not able, honestly, to make a Humean satisfactory review of my life. Does the moral pain thus incurred matter? Should it matter? After all, one does not want to be gratuitously hard on oneself.[40] (1) Should one go on anyway, perhaps via a serious effort to absorb the advice afforded by something like the AA Twelve-Step Program and force oneself as much as possible not to look back? (2) Should one suffer with the fact that one is not entitled to peace of mind? (3) Should one, indeed, commit suicide for such reason as that latter fact affords?

Now, I consider these to be legitimate and very serious questions, but I am not at all sure how to respond to them. It is not clear to me how, if at all, the great moral theories (e.g., utilitarianism, Kantianism) speak to them. For my own part: regarding (2), all I can say is that people do suffer with the fact, though they do not want to; they also ordinarily do not want others to suffer with the fact, though they often understand if others do. Regarding (1), all I can say is that people want sometimes to go on anyway, but they often fail to force themselves not to look back. Regarding (3), all I can say is that I hope one is not supposed to commit suicide over the fact in question, but—again, with regret—I can understand how one's difficulty in living with one's past might be too painful, and one might be inclined to take the prospect of suicide very seriously. Of course, these "all I can say" responses hardly constitute a theory. In fact, what a theory in this matter would be like is not plain to me.

My view, in the end, remains the meager one that there may be cases in which living with one's past is a problem without a solution. This seems to me so, at any rate, if "solution" is construed as involving something like possession of peace of mind, and that notion in turn is construed (as may be suggested by Hume and Falk) as being conditioned by one's being able to make a satisfactory review of one's past or "bear before oneself the survey of one's life." As a last observation in this section, I would note that the problem of living with the past seems to me to be without solution most clearly in cases in which what one has done links up somehow with what I have called "damage to the moral personality of another." In other sorts of cases—for example, cases in which the damage is to, say, material goods, political power, or even reputation—solutions (usually in the form of making amends) typically seem available for the problem of living with one's past. If this is sound as an observation about moral sensibility, then it reflects the interpretation of morality according to which morality's most precious good is moral personality itself—and damage to moral personality is presumed unpardonable.

On Unmanageable Internal Factors

My line of thought perhaps raises a familiar sort of philosophical objection that there is something trivial about my claim that peace of mind is not really possible for those whose pasts are flawed by very problematic episodes or sections, especially insofar as these involve damage to the moral personality of another person; for if the idea of peace of mind is defined as requiring a satisfactory review or bearable survey of one's past and if damage to the moral personality of another is assumed to be incompatible with a review or survey being satisfactory or bearable,[41] then of course peace of mind is not available to those whose pasts are flawed by very problematic episodes or sections. It appears that I am attempting to derive a substantive moral claim from a definition of terms.

My response to this objection is to see its point but then to look beyond it. What matters is the special normative question it raises: should the idea of peace of mind be construed in such a way that a condition of its application is that one be able to make a satisfactory review or bear a survey of one's past? It seems to me clear that the idea of peace of mind is often construed in that way, both in the philosophical literature and in real life; but perhaps the discussion above suggests that this construal itself should be reviewed. The remarks that follow are exploratory and focus on one matter that should, I believe, figure in such a review.

Let me say first that I do not have an alternative definition of peace of mind to propose. Even if I did, I can see that there is reason to retain the partial definition suggested by the Hume-Falk approach,[42] for if it denies peace of mind to people whose pasts are flawed in the way I have been examining, as a moral practice it may nevertheless encourage (to the extent people pay attention to it) the constraining of the will of individuals in a way that is productive of good moral order. That is, by making a satisfactory review or bearable survey a condition of an individual's being morally at ease with himself or herself, we keep a certain pressure on ourselves to avoid damaging the moral personalities of others. My discussion has nevertheless made me somewhat skeptical of the retention of this received approach to the idea of peace of mind. My reasons are in part self-regarding ones, and I suppose they appear self-serving: (1) I have problematic parts in my own past, (2) I believe many other people do as well, and (3) there is for me and others great pain involved in this fact. It may be that such reasons, insofar as they are self-serving, should be set aside in a philosophical discussion. Perhaps a philosophically more legitimate, or at least interesting, reason for skepticism about the received view is that it may ascribe to individuals more power and control—more management capability—over their lives than in fact the human condition ordinarily permits.[43] Let me briefly explore this matter at this point (I will offer more discussion of it in chapter 3).

We may begin with the commonplace that our efforts to lead our lives according to the self-conceptions we work out for ourselves in some cases run up against factors that block or frustrate those efforts. Sometimes these factors are external, for example, spurious labels or stereotypes imposed on us by others or simply others' dim opinions of our merit or character; against such factors our self-conceptions may, with struggle, remain intact or, in the unfortunate case, begin to give way. Escape from such factors or adjustment to them (e.g., through resignation) may be difficult in certain circumstances. However that may be, though, the cases I have been concerned with in this discussion do not center on such external factors. They are indeed cases in which people suffer a form of moral pain involving doubt about their self-conceptions, but their distress that their self-conceptions are inaccurate or misleading is the result in these cases not of external factors but of the implications of problematic events in their individual histories, and, of course, these are not any problematic events. There is a special character to these events—a self-referential aspect to them—that I find difficult to pin down philosophically. As a rough approximation: the events I have been concerned with are problematic events (e.g., wrongdoings) that come to be in a person's past not cleanly as a function of his or her will (they are not deliberate wrongdoings) and not cleanly as a function of the will of others (they are not coerced wrongdoings) but more nearly as a result of collisions between (1) factors internal to the person but over which his or her control is either nil or, at best, controversial, and (2) the moral personalities of others. Escape from these factors, or a healthy adjustment to them, may in some cases be as or more difficult than their analogs in the cases involving external factors mentioned above.

In the *Foundations* Kant observed that one may be "inexperienced in the course of the world" and "incapable of being prepared for all its contingencies."[44] I wish to suggest that one of those contingencies, in regard to which a person may be "incapable of being prepared," might be the flawed past he or she has as a result of the development of internal factors over which his or her control is nil or controversial and whose subsequent unmanageability in certain circumstances places others at risk (e.g., of damage to moral personality). This point suggests the following, when applied in interpretation of the three cases that especially interest us. If Severance is a real alcoholic, then he cannot help being so, even though, epistemically and emotionally, he may deny that he is one, not believe that he is one, and honestly feel that next time he can be in control of his consumption of alcohol. If C is a person who considers herself to have sound self-regarding reasons for divorcing her spouse, it may be that C is the kind of person for whom reason of that sort is compelling, and C cannot help being that way. If Rousseau was stampeded by circumstances and fear of disgrace, it may be that Rousseau is that kind of person (stampedable and disgrace-fearful in the extreme) and that Rousseau cannot help being that way. From this perspective, all these people suffer moral pain when their surveys of their pasts focus on events that flow in part from factors in them over which their control is nil or controversial. The lives of these people are, in effect, unmanageable in certain respects, and, of course, the unmanageability takes its toll on others who are caught in its path as a result of circumstances, personal relationships, or even love. The unmanageability here must be construed, of course, in such a way as to be compatible with a robust sense of recovery: Severance remains an alcoholic when he finally abstains and pursues his Twelve-Step Program in AA (indeed, AA will teach him that he must not forget that), but the sense in which he cannot help being alcoholic does permit the latter course of recovery. There should be analogs to this point for the cases of C and Rousseau.

According to this perspective on the cases that interest us, those in them who face the problem of living with their pasts cannot help being the kinds of persons they are, or, less sweepingly, they cannot help being the ways they are in respect to certain features of their personalities or characters. In this view, some elements in the nature of a person may be relatively settled or fixed. This view need not hold that these elements are the same in everyone or that no change in them will ever occur. What may be fixed in me may not be fixed in you. What it may be possible for you to change with effort and time may not be similarly possible for me. Taking this view seriously raises a special question about peace of mind as it is understood by the approach I derived from the remarks of Hume and Falk: why should the peace of mind of the individuals in the cases I sketched be in jeopardy if indeed the problematic parts of their histories are a result of what I have called fixed elements of character?

Of course, the question remains: are there in fact fixed elements of character? I suspect that there are, though I have little idea of how to prove that there are. The facts do not speak for themselves. There are cases in which a person has apparently altered his or her character and other cases in which, despite strenuous effort, change was not realized. In another sort of case one may find it not worthwhile all things considered to try to change, so whether one can change remains unsettled. I do not mean to suggest that parts of character are determined in any sense that is interesting for philosophy. I mean rather, and simply, that there are aspects of character that are so salient in one's makeup, so fixed as a matter of practical fact, that the prospect of changing them (at any rate, to the person involved) is tantamount to the prospect of changing one's identity at the deepest level. At some point, in the matter of personality or character, most of us come somehow to a position regarding who and what we are. Even if I have no idea of how to prove that there are fixed elements of character, it at least seems to me plain enough, from real life, which must include one's own difficulties with oneself as well as one's sensitivity to others' difficulties with themselves, that the elements of character are not smoothly and uniformly open to alteration.

In general, the view suggested by the remarks of Hume and Falk harnesses my peace of mind to my past, and when my past is seen to be flawed (it contains wrongdoings by me) and amends are not feasible (in some cases not even possible), peace of mind is pushed out of reach. To what extent, though, should my possession of peace of mind be canceled by the presence in my past of something that I can now do nothing about and that is in any case grounded in elements of character that are such that perhaps my control over them was nil or controversial? It may be that some people are able to meet the conditions of the backward-looking index of peace of mind and that in any case its pressure in our lives operates in a general way to promote good moral order. Given the discussion above, however, I am inclined to think it important to note that pasts can come to be flawed in many different ways, including (1) as a function of the agent's will, (2) as a function of the agent's reactions to what emanates from the will of others, and (3) as a function of what I have called collisions between what flows from factors in the agent's makeup over which his or her control is nil or controversial and the moral personalities of others. My suggestion here, then, is that the received backward-looking index can be misused. One might fail to distinguish cases (1), (2), or (3) or be too narrow in what one allows to count as unmanageable internal factors for the purposes of cases of type (3). When the index is misused, people may be left without peace of mind insofar as their lives come to be flawed via contingencies grounded in factors over which their control was nil or controversial. In certain cases a person may suffer a deep loss of peace of mind involving the pain not only of bad feeling over particular actions but also of distress over the kind of person he or she apparently is. In such cases the problems of recovery, of going on with one's life, can be formidable. My thought is that we should be careful not to deny ourselves peace of mind through uncritical application of the backward-looking index. We often, I think, cannot help being the kinds of persons we are. A serious respect for the responsibilities that members of the moral community have to and for each other should be tempered with a certain generosity toward individuals, given the degree to which the perspective on the human condition that suggests that there are fixed elements of character seems plausible.

In chapter 4 I explore how this recommendation of generosity is to be understood. Before that, however, I explore in more detail the issues raised by the complicated idea that some elements in the personality or character of a person—but different elements for different persons—may be fixed.

Chapter 2

Persona Moralism

People want to believe in an ordered, regular world, of faithful married couples, legitimate children, normal sex, legal behaviour, decent continuity, and they will go to almost any lengths to preserve this faith. Any suggestion that "real life" is otherwise tends to be greeted as "melodramatic" or "implausible". . . . Solicitors know better. The police know better. Social workers know better. . . . Dark blotches spread. Life is more like an old-fashioned, melodramatic novel than we care to know.

Margaret Drabble, *A Natural Curiosity*

When a man has reflected much he is tempted to imagine himself as the prime author of change. Perhaps in such a mood God actually succeeded in creating the world. But for man such moods are times of illusion. What we have deeply imagined we feign to control, often with what seem to be the best of motives. But the reality is huge and dark which lies beyond the lighted area of our intentions.

Iris Murdoch, *An Accidental Man*

We are all the judges and the judged, victims of the casual malice and fantasy of others, and ready sources of fantasy and malice in our turn. And if we are sometimes accused of sins of which we are innocent, are there not also other sins of which we are guilty and of which the world knows nothing?

Iris Murdoch, *Nuns and Soldiers*

People Are Different

At the end of chapter 1 I suggested that we often cannot help being the kinds of persons we are. There are two thoughts here. One is that some elements of personality or character may be fixed; the other is that

31

elements fixed in the personality or character of one person may be different from those fixed in the personality or character of another person. People may thus be stuck with elements of personality or character that they cannot budge (even despite strenous effort) such that, in ordinary life, what one person can do or do easily may be, for another person, difficult or impossible. In another vocabulary, people may be powerless over themselves in certain respects, and they may differ from one another in what it is in themselves that they are powerless over.

This is to say at least that people are different from one another. At one level this is, of course, not news, even though I think it is important for moral theory. People are different in many ways—not just in their circumstances but in their makeup as persons. If we think of, for example, the physical properties of persons, their talents and skills, or even their powers of intelligence and insight, then the difference thesis is hardly controversial. Of course, people are powerless over themselves in different respects, if we have in mind these qualities. I cannot run as fast as an Olympic contender or swim as well as my daughter, and these facts about me, grounded in my physical abilities, are for all practical purposes fixed. If they are changeable at all, the change will be within such a limited range as to make no real difference to the point. In many cases there is little pain lurking in the recognition of such differences, and one doesn't much mind ranking in the lower regions of the relevant scales. Perhaps one experiences some resentment or envy, but, in the fortunate cases, this pain is not debilitating; it does not interfere with one's life; indeed, the resentment or envy is manageable and may alternate with a detached sort of admiration of the other person's prowess or strength.

At another level, the difference thesis becomes more controversial. The idea that people are powerless in different respects, when extended to some constituents of personality and character, becomes in certain contexts less easy to accept—at any rate, this appears to be so when one reflects on some of our common attitudes and practices; indeed, in certain contexts (some of which I explore below) when we are asked to apply the idea that other persons are different from us in certain ways and cannot help being so, we are in different cases baffled, suspicious, or even angered. Our judgments about others and about how those people relate to what they have done seem threatened. In particular, the important practice at the center of our form of moral life, namely, holding others to account, risks misfiring or at least being thrown into confusion when in particular cases it is controversial whether the idea in question applies; and since the judgments we make as participants in this practice affect what we do in response to those we hold accountable, the misfiring or confusion may have great practical importance.

It is interesting to note the exasperation and irritation drawn by some applications of the idea in question. Ann Landers began one of her newspaper columns[1] with this short letter from "J.E.G.":

> I am a physician with 20 years of experience in general practice and have worked in jails and psychiatric hospitals. My heart bleeds for the thousands, yea, tens of thousands of men and women in our penal and psychiatric institutions and on the streets who did somthing terrible in a moment when they lost control.
>
> Actually, many people live on the edge of losing it and then, under the influence of alcohol, a mind-altering drug or a stressful situation, they suddenly slip over the edge. I know what I'm talking about because for most of my life I have lived on the edge myself. Shouldn't we have mercy and compassion for these folks, Ann? What do you say?

Ann Landers responded:

> Dear J.E.G.: I am all for mercy and compassion for the emotionally unstable who have run afoul of the law, but I am more concerned with the victims and their families. These borderline folks must be aware that their psyches are somewhat fragile. When they go over the edge and assault or kill innocent people, they must pay the price for their anti-social behavior. Too many people are judged temporarily insane when they knew very well what they were doing.

There is an uncharacteristic streak of moralism in Ann Landers's treatment here of those she calls "borderline folks." The moralism lies in the judgmental "they know better" involved in her response to J.E.G. In fact, of those who are insane or seriously emotionally ill, some are and some are not "aware that their psyches are somewhat fragile." When Ann Landers's response to J.E.G. smooths out the mixed facts (some are aware, others are not) in favor of the notion that "they knew very well what they were doing," she does so in line with a normative premise about how persons are that is itself a priori or, at any rate, not immediately readable off the facts.[2]

The thesis I am concerned with suggests not only that people are different, but also that difference can be solid at a deep level of the self. The thesis could be taken to suggest, in Ann Landers's vocabulary, that we are all, albeit in different respects, "borderline folks," though the results of this being so will be evident only in different contexts or settings for different people. When I say that we are all borderline folks, I do not mean that we are all insane or emotionally ill in the manner suggested by extreme images associated with those powerful words. I do mean two things: (1) that our psyches are fragile in ways that show up in our failings to meet the sometimes interestingly different and sometimes conflicting terms of how persons are given by the variety of conceptions of persons associated with the practices (including moral practices), institutions, ideologies, and general theories that structure our common life; and (2) that these failings are sometimes traceable to fixed elements in personality or character, that is, elements over which our control is nil or controversial.[3] When this is so for us and our circumstances make us vulnerable to the judgment of others, we may be the target of the persona moralism (as I call it) of the sort transparent in Ann Landers's response to J.E.G. above. We may thus incur blame as a result of being held to account for our failing.[4]

Assumptions about Persons

Insofar as our common life requires us to participate in practices and institutions, that is, to think and act in those contexts or settings in which what we do is given structure by terms (e.g., rules, principles, policies), we are not rarely but in fact regularly and often subject to conceptions of how persons are. How we fare relative to these conceptions can become very important when our not doing what, according to those terms, ought to be done carries with it liability for blame or even punishment.

To mark the point, consider an extreme example: soldiering. In the case of the military trial of Lt. William Calley resulting from the so-called My Lai Massacre during the Vietnam War, the judge said:

> Soldiers are taught to follow orders. . . . [But] the obedience of a soldier is not the obedience of an automaton. A soldier is a *reasoning agent*, obliged to respond, not as a machine, but as a person. The law takes these factors into account in assessing criminal responsibility for acts done in compliance with illegal orders. The acts of a subordinate done in compliance with an unlawful order given him by his superior are excused and impose no criminal liability upon him unless the superior's order is one which a man of ordinary sense and understanding would, under the circumstances, know to be unlawful. . . .[5]

The judge offered the following illustration of what a "reasoning agent" is: "A reasonable man, for instance, ought to know that murdering children who are only standing around is a crime even if no one has taken the trouble to explain that fact to him."[6] Kurt Baier comments on these words in a way that exhibits a concern for fairness in connection with how practices and institutions impose terms on us that we may fail to meet.

> But is it fair to say that Calley was "criminally responsible" simply on the grounds that a "man of ordinary sense and understanding" would have known that the order was unlawful? Surely a person should be declared criminally responsible only if he *should* have known that such an order was unlawful. But from the fact that a man of ordinary sense and understanding *would* have known, it does not follow that every type of person *should* have known.[7]

Baier adds:

> If Calley was not a person of that type—and much of the psychiatric evidence produced during the trial casts doubt on whether he was—then it would be necessary to show, in addition, either that it was Calley's fault (not someone else's) that he was not such a person, or that he should have known better, even though he was not such a person. No such evidence was produced. . . . the available evidence tends to place the blame for this ignorance elsewhere. . . . A society prepared to turn men like Calley into officers incurs an additional responsibility to make clear to them the distinctions they are supposed to draw particularly if society seriously intends later to charge them with failure to do so.[8]

The concern for fairness (it might be called "accusation fairness") can be extended to our fate under other practices and institutions, I think, though, of course, the point of doing so may not always have the importance it had in the Calley case. Soldiering assumes certain things about those involved in it, and this assuming bears on what responsibilities soldiers are thought to have and, hence, on what liability for blame and punishment they have. Similarly, other positions, roles, and offices that persons hold, occupy, and play assume certain things about people as they negotiate their lives in or under the overlapping, nested, or otherwise related institutions and practices that constitute their society, and these assumptions bear on our construals of people's responsibilities and their liability for blame and punishment. If education is a practice, then it assumes that persons are educable, at any rate, up to a point at which noneducability is shown.[9] If society is bureaucratic, then it assumes that its members are capable of bureaucracy, that is, that they are reading, writing, form-understanding, and form-manipulating beings. Many persons, of course, do not meet these terms, and others meet them only minimally and incur great discomfort in struggling to do so.[10] At a very basic level, society, as a network of institutions and practices, rests on a foundational practice—call it "living-in-society"—that assumes of its members elementary capacities for hygiene and care of the person. Even regarding participation in this foundational practice, some people do not meet its terms.[11]

If practices as various as education, soldiering, bureaucracy, and living-in-society all make assumptions about how persons are that some people do not or cannot meet and others meet only with great difficulty, it is no surprise that the practices in our form of moral life also make assumptions about those who participate in them. Friendship, according to some philosophical accounts,[12] requires self-disclosure of a deep kind, and one immediately thinks of cases of people who cannot so disclose or can so disclose only with enormous difficulty. These people find it hard or impossible to be friends. Promising also makes its assumptions about us—in particular, that we are capable of construing our own futures in such a way as to be able to self-impose the forfeiture of certain options regarding future conduct in favor of commitment to other options.[13]

If friendship and promising are moral practices that make different assumptions about persons, they nevertheless have the idea of duty connected with them. Whatever one's analysis of duty and however one sorts out the differences among duty, supererogation, permission, and so on, the notion that persons have duties to perform is also a practicelike conception (call it "duty-performance" or "duty-meeting") that carries with it certain assumptions about those to whom it is applied. Here we are ferreting out assumptions about persons of a very general sort. Stanley Bates writes that among the relevant general assumptions of morality and human nature are these:

> that morality is actual, that moral distinctions are real distinctions, and that the propositions expressing moral judgments and the ascription of moral responsibility are capable of truth and falsity. Let us also assume that men are capable of choosing among alternatives, the alternatives themselves often being limited by factors which are out of the control of particular individuals. It may seem grotesque to call these "assumptions," since they seem to be clearly true and to be common features of everything that can be called "moral." Indeed, they seem to be preconditions of the meaningfulness of moral language, not merely of its applicability. Note also that they are not assumptions about the correctness of a particular moral view, but rather assumptions about morality itself and about human nature.[14]

These remarks are reminiscent of the Kantian view whereby anyone who takes morality to be real and not chimerical must assume that those to whom it is applied are rational and free (in senses of those terms that Kant labored to explain).[15] In discussion of a distinction between moral ideals (action aspiring to which is admired by us but not required of us) and moral duties (action in line with which is required of us but not admired by us), A. M. Honoré reports another very general assumption of duty-performance or duty-meeting: that "moral duties are pitched at a point where the conformity of the ordinary man can reasonably be expected."[16] This point, too, is reminiscent of a Kantian theme, namely, that "ought implies can," though now in Honoré's hands the point is accompanied by the notion that this implied "can" is not itself free of qualification: what morality requires (as distinct from what it might allow or even encourage) is what it is reasonable to expect from ordinary persons. We can allow our interest in the difference thesis and, hence, in the extent to which real people fit the assumptions made by practices and institutions, to alert us to the difficulties generated by such degree notions as reasonable and ordinary. *J*'s view, line of thought, or interpretation regarding *x* might be more or less reasonable, and *J* himself or herself can be more or less ordinary, and what we expect as more or less reasonable of more or less ordinary persons may itself vary from case to case, given different particulars about persons and their circumstances. All this suggests at a minimum that the point at which "can" merges into "cannot" is not easily stated.

In more detail, consider the moral imperative to preserve integrity, a mainstay in the moral education many parents offer to children and some friends offer to friends and the violation of which can give rise to the problem of living with one's past discussed earlier.[17] This imperative—rather sophisticated in what it requires of us—assumes in part that we think of ourselves as enduring selves, that is, as forward looking in certain respects and as persisting unchanged (except in extraneous ways) through time.[18] Consider these passages from John Rawls's *A Theory of Justice*,[19] in which Rawls portrays a theme of the moral-credentialing reasoning of hypothetical "parties to the original position" that emphasizes the enduring-individual assumption.

> [T]he guiding principle [is] that a rational individual is always to act so that he need never blame himself no matter how things finally transpire. Viewing himself as one continuing being over time, he can say that at each moment of his life he has done what the balance of reasons required, or at least permitted.

Therefore any risks he assumes must be worthwhile, so that should the worst happen that he had any reason to foresee, he can still affirm that what he did was above criticism. He does not regret his choice, at least not in the sense that he later believes that at the time it would have been more rational to have done otherwise. This principle will not certainly prevent us from taking steps that lead to misadventure. Nothing can protect us from the ambiguities and limitations of our knowledge, or guarantee that we find the best alternative open to us. Acting with deliberative rationality can only insure that our conduct is above reproach, and that *we are responsible to ourselves as one person over time*. We should indeed be surprised if someone said that he did not care about how he will view his present actions later any more than he cares about the affairs of other people (which is not much, let us suppose). *One who rejects equally the claims of his future self and the interests of others is not only irresponsible with respect to them but in regard to his own person as well. He does not see himself as one enduring individual.*

Now looked at in this way, the principle of responsibility to self resembles a principle of right: the claims of the self at different times are to be so adjusted that the self at each time can affirm the plan that has been and is being followed. The person at one time, so to speak, must not be able to complain about actions of the person at another time. This principle does not, of course, exclude the willing endurance of hardship and suffering, but it must be presently acceptable in view of the expected or achieved good. From the standpoint of the original position the relevance of responsibility to self seems clear enough. Since the notion of deliberative rationality applies there, it means that the parties cannot agree to a conception of justice if the consequences of applying it may lead to self-reproach should the least happy possibilities be realized. They should strive to be free from such regrets.

Now, given our concern about assumptions that institutions and practices make about persons, we may ask how far the assumptions of the maxim of self-responsibility enjoining the preservation of integrity are satisfied by persons in real life as we know it. In particular, how far is the assumption that Rawls's remarks focus on, namely, that persons think of themselves as "enduring individuals," in fact commonly applicable to real people? This question is important, I think, for in Rawls's view (and the views of Hume and Falk mentioned earlier) it seems plain that the ideas of integrity and self-responsibility are closely linked to the idea of being a moral agent. How closely people fit the assumption that persons do or can see themselves as enduring individuals is then a matter that bears on our understanding of morality, its applicability to us, the seriousness of its pressure on us, and, in general, its place in the lives of people as we know them.

Some theorists have seen the enduring-individual assumption in a different way from that suggested by Rawls's discussion. An example is the treatment of it by Edward Banfield in *The Unheavenly City*.[20] For whatever it may be worth,[21] Banfield treats the construal of and respect for oneself as an enduring individual as a characteristic of higher social class—or at any rate not a characteristic of low social class: "the more distant the future the individual can imagine and can discipline himself to make sacrifices for, the higher is his class."[22] Norman E. Bowie reports that Banfield's view is that "what puts a person in one class rather than another is the individual's orientation to the future."[23]

Banfield himself wrote:

> At the present-oriented end of the scale, the lower class individual lives from moment to moment. . . . Impulses govern his behavior either because he cannot discipline himself to sacrifice a present for a future satisfaction or because he has no sense of the future. He is therefore radically improvident: whatever he cannot consume immediately he considers valueless. His bodily needs (especially for sex) and his taste for "action" take precedence over everything else—and certainly over any work routine. He works only as he must to stay alive and drifts from one unskilled job to another, taking no interest in the work. The lower class household is usually female based. The woman who heads it is likely to have a succession of mates who contribute intermittently to its support but take little or no part in rearing the children. The lower class individual lives in the slum and sees little or no reason to complain. He does not care how dirty and dilapidated his housing is either inside or out nor does he mind the inadequacy of such public facilities as schools, parks, and libraries: indeed where such things exist he destroys them by acts of vandalism if he can.[24]

Banfield's summary (a gloomy one for social reformers) is given in these words.

> So long as the city contains a sizable lower class, nothing basic can be done about its most serious problems. . . . The lower class forms of all problems are at bottom a single problem: the existence of an outlook and style of life which is radically present-oriented and which therefore attaches no value to work, sacrifice, self-improvement, or service to family, friends, or community. Social workers, teachers, and law-enforcement officials cannot achieve their goals because they can neither change nor circumvent this cultural obstacle.[25]

Now, I doubt that Banfield's generalized characterization of members of lower economic classes as "radically present-oriented" is accurate, but apart from that issue, it seems plain enough that his characterization fits some people, whatever their economic class, and this, in the context of our concern for the assumptions of practices and imperatives, is enough to raise a number of questions. (1) To what extent is the familiar injunction to preserve integrity merely a part of middle-class culture rather than something more objectively a part of morality? (2) If certain people seem not to fall under the enduring-individual assumption, are we supposed to introduce it into their lives, if they are able to meet its terms? Is it a duty to do so? If not a duty, does morality gives us permission to do so? If neither duty nor permission, is to do so paternalism of an objectionable kind? (3) Is falling under the enduring-individual assumption a matter of degree, or is it an all-or-nothing matter? If the former, what could help to make a person fit under the assumption better or more fully? (4) If not everyone does or can fall under the enduring-individual assumption of the integrity maxim, what follows for the standing of the latter qua moral imperative? (5) If someone does not or cannot fall under the enduring-individual assumption, how are we to respond to him or her?

Stereotyping and Judging

In general, the fact that some people do not or cannot fit cleanly under the assumptions of certain practices or institutions or can fit under them only with great difficulty generates an issue that has this form.

> We treat *J* as falling under our positively valued institution, practice, or policy *P*.
> *P* assumes persons to be *a*, *b*, and/or *c*.
> *J*, though, is not *a*, *b*, and/or *c*.
> It is unclear or unknown (to us) whether *J* can or cannot be *a*, *b*, and/or *c*.
> So: ——— What?
> Should we punish *J*?
> Should we make *J* be *a*, *b*, and/or *c*?
> Should we exclude *J* from *P*?
> Should we investigate *J*'s not being *a*, *b*, and/or *c* to determine whether *J* should be excused from *P* or required to meet the terms of *P*?
> Should we do nothing, that is, just tolerate, accept, or somehow live with *J*'s not being *a*, *b*, and/or *c*?
> And so on.

In this discussion my attention goes to hard cases, that is, cases in which when we treat *J* as falling under *P* and *J* fails to meet the assumptions of *P*, it is unclear or unknown whether *J* can meet the terms of how persons are that are associated with *P*, *and*, too, there is something in the way of a positive valuational rationale for *P*. For example, if *P* is a moral practice, perhaps it operates to keep order among people, or perhaps it encourages people to exercise what Kant called their "fortunate natural gifts"[26] and thus fosters self-realization and enhances self-esteem, or perhaps it simply gives people one way among others to meet what Rawls called "the Aristotelian Principle."[27] It is cases of this sort that invite what I call persona moralism. I am not concerned here with the case often discussed by moral theorists—namely, the case in which *J* could meet *P*'s assumptions but refuses to do so—so I am not concerned now with the principled dissenter from ordinary morality (a sort of Nietzschean, say) or the "sensible knave" (driven entirely by self-interest and prudence) whom Hume discusses in the conclusion of his *Enquiry Concerning the Principles of Morals*,[28] or even the "uncaring man" whom Phillippa Foot has in mind in this passage.

> We are, naturally, concerned about the man who doesn't care what happens to other people, and we want to convict him of irrationality, thinking that he will mind about that. Outside moral philosophy we would not think of the cool and prudent, though wicked, man as specifically irrational in his conduct; outside philosophy we also know that there is nothing one can do with a ruthless amoral man except to prevent him from doing too much damage. . . . To say that since his conduct is immoral we can tell him of some reason why he should change it, or that he necessarily has reason to alter his ways, seems yet another case of keeping up a pretense. We speak as if there were an authority in the background to guarantee that wickedness is necessarily foolishness, though the "binding force" of morality is supposed to be independent of such an appeal. Would it not be more honest either to change the language or else to recognize that the "should" of moral judgment is sometimes merely an instrument by which we (for our own very good reasons) try to impose a rule of conduct even on the uncaring man?[29]

Persona moralism is not merely what I am vulnerable to in your treatment of me. It is also something I do to others—pretty nearly unavoidably so, given the demand of the human condition that we live with others.[30] From the standpoint of one who commits persona moralism, it is a sort of stereotyping of the people one deals with; it consists in uncritically imposing on them the terms of how persons are that are associated with certain practices and institutions and then judging those who do not meet those terms in a negative or adverse fashion. All this can take place quite innocently and without explicit awareness that stereotyping and judging have occurred, for the conceptions of persons we thus wield at others and ourselves are typically the conceptions assumed by the most familiar of the practices and institutions that structure our everyday lives. Persona moralism infects our life with others: we might characterize it as insidious, and wonder whether anything can, or should, be done about it.

On Legal Punishment

The theme in the discussion above was that the practices and institutions that structure our common life carry with them certain assumptions about those who live with and under them and that, since people are different in myriad ways, when we participate in these practices and institutions, and thereby treat other participants on the terms specified by these assumptions, we risk committing persona moralism. In this and the next several sections I explore this matter further. I examine the connections between some views of how persons are and the institution—very important to our common life—of legal punishment. In particular, I examine the claim of a philosophical account that these views about how persons are form a part of the justification of the institution of legal punishment. I explore this claim, then reflect on it in certain ways, and finally suggest that the philosophical account's recommended construal of the logical character of these views and of how they figure in the justification of punishment is mistaken. I must be careful not to exaggerate the point of the discussion that follows. Its upshot is not that there is no justification for legal punishment, for there is much that is not touched on in my discussion here that would be required for that conclusion. The discussion casts doubt, however, on a type of claim that is often made as part of a justificatory argument for legal punishment, for my thesis is that the justification of legal punishment, if there is one, does not involve or rest on general facts about persons in any central way. The justification of punishment is essentially normative regarding how persons are in a manner I attempt to make clear. The main purpose of the small inquiry into legal punishment conducted in these sections is to throw more light on the character of what I have called persona moralism.

The philosophical account I have in mind concerning the way in which the justification of legal punishment involves views about how persons are is this.[31]

[W]e should note that there are some very general assumptions of fact . . . upon which any justification of the practice of punishment must rest.

The first of these assumptions is that men are capable of calculating their own interest; and that in general they will. Obviously the efficacy of the threat contained in a criminal law rests on this assumption.

The second assumption is that, in general, men are able to govern present impulses by the thought of future consequences. If they were not, the threat of punishment would be useless.

Third, it is assumed that it is possible to find "evils" which are more or less universally dreaded. If there were no general desire to avoid fines or jail, then these "evils" would not be eligible as punishment. But unless the legislator can find some "evil" which qualifies, the institution of punishment fails; or is modified to allow judges complete discretion in the choice of punishment. Whether this would still be punishment and this "judge" a judge are open questions. Certainly a door would be left ajar for radical abuse of power.

To the extent that any of these assumptions . . . [is] false, the case for legal punishment breaks down. We shall not argue for them, but simply assume their truth.[32]

In this account, then, the acceptability of legal punishment is construed as resting in part on certain propositions about persons, and these propositions are construed as being factual in character. These factual propositions about persons are thought of as forming a main part of what is referred to as a justificatory case for the legal practice of punishment, if not a conclusive argument for it.[33] Overall, this case for punishment has three parts to it: (1) certain factual propositions about persons and about society; (2) a moral assumption about the disvalue of misery, namely, that "survival in conditions not merely miserable, and with some hope of happiness, is a value worthy of protection";[34] and (3) a view to the effect that various alternative means of social control are neither more efficient nor more acceptable, by criteria of justice and humanity, than legal punishment. In what follows I am concerned with just the first part of this case for punishment and of that, just the subpart involving the general factual claims about how persons are.[35] As the quoted remarks above indicate, among these claims about persons are the following:

(a) that persons are calculators in terms of their own interests
(b) that persons can govern present impulse by the thought of future consequences
(c) that persons dread certain evils, such as fines, imprisonment, or death[36]

Basic Individuals and Social and Historical Particulars

I propose first to challenge the view that such claims as these are factual generalizations about persons and then to show how the challenge, insofar as it is successful, affects the proffered case for legal punishment. To develop my challenge I employ a distinction between persons as basic individuals and persons as social and historical particulars. I do not suggest that challenging the view that the claims in question are factual generalizations about persons requires exactly this terminology, but the distinction at stake is nevertheless interesting, and it helps to fill out the challenge in such a way as to give it philosophical content.[37]

The distinction I have in mind is as follows. Consider what persons are in respect of their actual involvement in the circumstances and activities of everyday life. That is, consider them as we know them to be, or, as I sometimes put it, as social and historical particulars. Persons are indeed different from each other in many ways when considered from this perspective. They typically vary in styles of appearance; talents; capacities; opinions; intelligence; types of family background; the interests they have; the social positions they occupy; the physical, emotional, and spiritual difficulties they experience; their status in the economic system; and in many other respects. There may, of course, be similarities among persons viewed from this perspective, but most of these seem to be simply partial overlappings among some persons, and many seem conventional in character: a certain style of appearance, bearing, or attitude may prevail among some persons, a common opinion on some subject among others; a shared social position, background, or set of interests may lead us to group some or many persons together; a high or low level of intelligence as measured by certain tests or perhaps a special kind of intelligence (the sort displayed in dance, say), may put others together. Even persons who can be grouped together in respect of some characteristic differ, however, from each other in respect to a dozen others, and as a group they differ from other persons who do not have that characteristic at all or who do not have it in the same way, degree, or extent that they do.

In daily life, then, when we deal with persons as social and historical particulars, we deal with them primarily as individuals or groups that differ from each other in the familiar ways I have just alluded to. My phrase, "persons as social and historical particulars," emphasizes the perspective on persons familiar from engagement in life, the ordinary perspective from which individuals and groups typically differ from each other, despite partial, sometimes important overlaps and conventional similarities. If, however, persons as social and historical particulars typically differ from each other, it does not follow that persons are not basically the same in some ways of interest to moral theory, political philosophy, and jurisprudence. Let us consider the idea that persons are the same in some way of interest to philosophy, despite the evident differences among them as social and historical particulars.[38] In doing so we raise the perennial philosophical question: what are persons by nature or qua persons?

This question, thus expressed, may, however, be unclear. In an effort to clarify at least my interest in it, I propose to distinguish between the following two questions:

(1) What are persons basically?
(2) What are persons as basic individuals?

I wish to argue that these questions can be treated or interpreted differently, even though it is not uncommon to find answers to them run together in certain contexts of philosophical inquiry, such as that concerning the case for legal punishment that I indicated earlier.

We may think of the first question as a question about persons as social and historical particulars. The more familiar answers to this question that come to mind (setting aside whether any such answers are true) may then be thought of as generalizations across the class of persons as we know them. Think of general propositions expressing facts about persons as we know them: "persons suffer pain"; "persons have needs for food and shelter." Sometimes such propositions involve degree or extent-qualifiers, perhaps to make them go more easily or more completely across the class of persons as we know them: "persons are to some degree self-interested"; "persons are to some extent concerned about reputation." Many natural answers to this first question seem best elucidated in the vocabulary of capacity, perhaps, again, to make them go more easily or more completely across the class of persons as we know them: "persons are rational," that is, they are capable of foreseeing and acting in accordance with the consequences of what they do; "persons are characterized by natural sympathy," that is, they are capable of being affected, troubled, or touched by pain, suffering, or lack of well-being in others.

Some theorists might argue that, aside from factual generalizations about persons as social and historical particulars, there are also propositions about persons that are, or are more nearly, conceptually true and, hence, that definitionally apply to all persons. These would be propositions that would stand as constitutive of the concept of person rather than merely contingently general across the class of persons as social and historical particulars. "Persons are motivated by what they perceive to be in their own interest" and "persons aspire to a sense of self-respect" might be proposed as candidate conceptual truths about persons.

Whether there are conceptual truths about persons as social and historical particulars is a difficult philosophical question, and I have no worked-out answer to it.[39] I avoid the issue here, as it is in any case not central to my purposes, but speak as though conceptual truths about persons as social and historical particulars are possible. What is central to my purposes here is to note that the factual generalizations I mentioned above, plus conceptual truths, if there are any, apply to persons as social and historical particulars, that is, to persons as we know them. Our neighbors, colleagues, friends, enemies—these are the persons such propositions are about.

In the case of answers to the second question—what are persons as basic individuals?—however, the situation is different. In this case the propositions are not directly about persons as we know them, though this does not mean that they are irrelevant to persons as we know them. My discussion requires that I characterize propositions about basic individuals to some extent, though I find this difficult to do. What I offer here is very sketchy.

To begin, we may notice that historically the tradition of the doctrine of the social contract is explicitly a source, though hardly the only source, of propositions about basic individuals. The theorizing in the social-contract tradition that is devoted to persons as they are in the state of nature in fact often contains a mix of answers to the two questions I wish to distinguish. My thought is that there are different sorts of propositions in such accounts and that it is important to distinguish among them.

Those answers to the first question, about what persons basically are, that are of the character of factual generalizations would in principle be shown to be true by our observing that some person or persons have a certain characteristic, then that some others do, and then that still others do, until we become confident that all or very nearly all persons have that characteristic. It would be an inductive matter. In the other case, in which the answers seem more nearly conceptually true, I presume that we would not establish such propositions by inductive procedures. In general, how a proposition is to be shown to be conceptually true is a difficult problem, but one common way of testing a proposition for conceptual truth, or internal necessity, is by posing counterexamples to it. We may, however, note about answers to the second question, about what persons are as basic individuals, that they cannot be arrived at in an inductive way from a steadily enlarged sampling of persons as we know them nor will they survive testing by ordinary counterexamples invoking some or many persons as we know them. My suggestion is, thus, that the basis for these propositions is not simply or only persons as we know them; there is something else involved.

In *Leviathan*, Thomas Hobbes thought that persons qua basic individuals are equal to one another. He also thought that they are death fearing, self-interested, and vain, and it may be that he believed that they are these latter things to the same degree or extent. He thought too that as basic individuals, persons have natural right, which is the liberty to do whatever they individually see to be in line with preserving themselves.[40] In the *Second Treatise*, John Locke also thought that persons qua basic individuals are equal to one another, and he thought too that they are free "to order their actions and dispose of their possessions and persons as they think fit" within the bounds of the laws of nature,[41]—though he did not call this freedom a natural right. Locke differed from Hobbes in that he did not make any claims about the psychological character of basic individuals, but he did view them as each one equally in possession of the laws of nature via their capacity for reason and each one equally an "executioner,"[42] that is, enforcer, of the laws of nature.

Something important about the logical character of propositions about persons as basic individuals emerges at this point. Again, such propositions are not arrived at inductively from persons as we know them—at any rate not entirely so—and they cannot be regarded as conceptual truths, for there are counterexamples to them; rather, they are normative in logical character, and this suggests that they can be viewed as issuing from decisions about how persons as basic individuals should be viewed. Let me add, and emphasize, that to see them in this light is not necessarily to think of them has having no rational basis. If these propositions issue from decisions about how it would be best, wise, or prudent to view persons as basic individuals, then we can of course ask after the reasons that back up such decisions—reasons that appeal to other than the facts about persons as we know them—and we may examine those reasons for cogency and strength.

The importance of these few remarks about the logic of propositions about persons is in their bearing on how we go about judging the adequacy of those parts of philosophical accounts that involve views about what persons are by nature or qua persons. To summarize: such accounts might involve factual descriptions of what persons basically are, that is, inductive generalizations across the class of persons as social and historical particulars. Such accounts might also involve something more like conceptual truths elucidating the very idea of person, that is, the idea that applies to persons as we know them. Such accounts might, however, involve normative propositions about what persons are as basic individuals, that is, propositions which are the results of decisions concerning how persons should be viewed. In this last case we must recognize that we are then operating in a framework in which the question of adequacy, that is, the question of the acceptability of the claims, is different from what it would be in a straight inductive factual framework or in a purely analytic or conceptual framework.[43]

Normative Assumptions

So far I have set forth a catalog of some types of propositions that might figure in an account of how persons are basically. There might be inductive generalizations, conceptual truths, or normative propositions representing a theorist's decisions about how it would be best, wise, or prudent to view persons for the purposes of the inquiry. At this point I assert my belief that the very general assumptions of fact about persons said by the philosophical account I indicated earlier to be centrally involved in the case for legal punishment are not factual assumptions at all. They are neither inductively establishable propositions about what persons basically are nor conceptual truths elucidating the very idea of person. In the terms of my catalog they seem rather to be normative propositions about what persons are as basic individuals. Let me now discuss briefly why I place these propositions in this part of my catalog.

The propositions in question, again, are that persons are calculators in terms of their own interests, that they in general are "able to govern present impulses by the thought of future consequences," and that they dread certain evils such as fines or imprisonment. Now, I am not suggesting that such claims about persons do not characterize any persons as we know them. They are not wildly irrelevant to persons as social and historical particulars, but, nevertheless, they do not fit persons as we know them as cleanly as they must if they are to function as independently knowable facts in something like—and something as important as—a justificatory case for legal punishment. We may notice, first, that we all know some persons who do not fit under such descriptions and, second, that we all know many other persons who fit under them only with considerable strain, that is, the facts about these latter persons are such that the propositions in question are too simple and uncluttered—we would need to qualify the propositions in different ways for different individuals to make the propositions fit.

Consider the first of these propositions, the one that claims that persons are calculators from and on behalf of their own interests. We have it on Jeremy Bentham's authority that this first proposition is indeed true.

> When matters of such importance as pain and pleasure are at stake, and these in the highest degree (the only matters in short that can be of importance) who is there that does not calculate? Men calculate, some with less exactness, indeed, some with more: but all men calculate. I would not say, that even a mad man does not calculate.[44]

On the other hand, we have it on the authority of certain psychiatrists and criminologists that this proposition, and perhaps by inference the others we are concerned with as well, when considered to be factual generalizations across the class of persons as we know them, are not true: "The indifference of the criminal to the penalty that is ahead of him, even if this penalty is death, is more the rule than the exception."[45] Now, the very fact that the propositions in question are even controversial in this way, together with the retention of them as true by the theorist of punishment,[46] is evidence that those propositions, as they figure in the case for legal punishment, operate there as normative propositions about persons as basic individuals, rather than as factual generalizations or conceptual truths about persons as they basically are. A decision has been made concerning, as I put it, how it is best, wise, or prudent to view persons.

Apart from the evidence supplied by this phenomenon of retention-in-the-face-of-controversy, if we were simply to appeal to the facts as they are about persons as we know them, the propositions that persons are calculators in terms of their own interests or that persons dread certain evils and so on are just too simple. Some of us, no doubt, are creatures of a steady calculative bent and regularly manage to govern present impulses by thoughts and worries about future consequences. Others of us, however, calculate rather less steadily and are more regularly creatures of impulse, habit, and feeling. There may be still others of us who calculate only rarely and more typically react to the social environment in which we must live, containing such obstacles and stimuli as it does. It is not plain to me that Bentham's proposition, or the others, covers us as we actually are very cleanly at all.

Perhaps it would be said against this line of thought that the move toward viewing the propositions in question as normative is too hasty. Perhaps it is enough for the case for legal punishment that these propositions be roughly factually true. Bentham's view may be extreme, but then perhaps that of the psychiatrists and criminologists is too; indeed, it may be that individuals differ from each other in respect of the steadiness of their calculative disposition. When all is said and done, however, enough persons calculate steadily enough to make Bentham's view factually serviceable for the purposes of the case for legal punishment.

This reply will not do. If the facts are that some of us calculate and some do not, and of those who do some are steady but others are less so, then those facts do not by themselves imply or even suggest that we must or should take the proposition "persons calculate in terms of their own interests" to be our assumption of fact in the justification of legal punishment. If the facts are messy and mixed, as they are in this matter, then they are messy and mixed; there is no logical warrant in messy and mixed facts for smoothing them out in one way rather than some other.[47] If we do proceed to smooth them out in one way rather than another, then we are engaging in normative work: we are deciding, in this case, how persons are in a certain context, and, as I have said, our decision may be understood as the result of certain considerations (principles, ideologies, convictions) we have about how it is best, wise, or prudent to view persons. I have not argued that we should not view persons in the way suggested by the propositions in question, for it may be that the persona moralism involved in doing so is, in this case, justified. I have attempted so far to make clear only in a general way what sort of thing logically is involved in incorporating such propositions in that case for legal punishment.

Sources of Normative Assumptions

It would be natural to proceed next to consider whether there are reasons that would support the view that we should construe persons the way the propositions in question suggest, but before doing this let me first make a suggestion about how these normative propositions may in fact be related to the view that legal punishment is a justified form of social control.

Imagine for a moment that we are in the odd but nevertheless coherent position of being in possession of the system of legal punishment but not being aware of to what or to whom it applies. We have the system of punishment, and we are searching for beings of a kind that fit under it. If in our search we were to find in our midst a group of beings who were uniformly calculative, were governors of present impulse by thoughts of future consequences, dreaded fines or imprisonment, and now and then disrupted our general cooperative scheme for mutual benefit (i.e., our society[48]), we might determine that these beings fit under our system of punishment quite well. We might discover that by that system we could keep order, that is, minimize the disruption of our social scheme that these beings cause, quite efficiently. If we learned more about them—for example, that they are possessed of a sense of justice—we might even go so far as to believe that the members of this group have a right to have their disruption responded to by punishment rather than by, say, medical therapy, for in the former case the control they undergo is appropriate to their nature as rational calculators with a sense of justice, whereas in the latter case the control does not recognize or take account of their nature as such: in the latter case their behavior is not viewed as disruptive such that they have done wrong in performing it, are to be blamed for it, or are thought to be guilty of it; rather, it is viewed as symptomatic of a disease they have and with respect to which they are victims.[49]

Notice that it would not immediately follow that we would think we should subject beings who disrupted our scheme but who were not rational calculators or governors of present impulse by thoughts of future consequences and so on to our system of punishment, for we would not necessarily see beings who were not characterizable in the manner we are concerned with as fitting under the system.

On the other hand, let us imagine the situation in which we do not have the system of legal punishment in hand and in which we are searching for a system of social control to prevent disruption of our general cooperative scheme that would fit us as in fact we are. That is, we are searching for a system of control that would suit a group of beings, some of whom calculate steadily, but others of whom calculate a little but are more regularly creatures of impulse and feeling, and still others of whom calculate very little or never but more typically react to the more or less hostile environment in which they find themselves. My point is that it is at any rate not plain that we would hit on or immediately recognize, logically or even naturally, the system of legal punishment as a reasonable general mode of social control on the basis of such facts. The mix of facts about persons as we know them, as social and historical particulars, just does not directly point in a justificatory way to legal punishment.

At this point I offer the speculation that the propositions that interest us seem more like statements of the conditions of the possibility (in something like the Kantian sense) of legal punishment than anything else. That is (and to imitate the Kantian way of putting such points[50]), if legal punishment is real and not chimerical, that is, if it is applicable to certain beings, then those beings must be thought of as of a steady calculative disposition, governors of present impulses by thoughts of future consequences, and dreaders of such evils as fines and imprisonment. In short, it is more nearly correct to view the propositions in question as, logically, assumptions of the system of legal punishment than it is to view them as forming independent assumptions of fact in a case for legal punishment. That is, it is the system of punishment itself that prompts us, or at least encourages us, to think about persons in the manner those propositions indicate.

Independent Sources?

Let me briefly give some attention to the difficult question of whether there is independent reason to view persons in the manner indicated by the propositions we have been considering. This is to ask (given the discussion in "Normative Assumptions" above) whether there is reason to decide that persons be so viewed. It is also to ask (given the discussion in the previous section) whether there is reason that is independent of or importantly separate from the system of legal punishment itself.

To elaborate slightly on the question before us, the logic of my line of thought to this point appears to be this. The propositions about persons that we have been considering are neither inductively sound general factual propositions about persons nor conceptual truths about persons. I suggested that they are normative propositions representing decisions about how it would be best, wise, or prudent to consider persons for the purposes of the formulation of a justification for legal punishment. I also speculated that the propositions in question may state conditions of the possibility of legal punishment and that if that were so, they would in that case be derived from, rather than justificatory of, acceptance of the system of legal punishment. Now, finding independent reason for accepting the view of persons that propositions express might consist in locating something other than the system of legal punishment itself that similarly prompts us to accept these propositions (i.e., it has what those propositions express as conditions of its possibility) and then determining that that something other is itself desirable, acceptable, practically necessary, or in some very important way attractive. We must note, too, in connection with this scenario, that the something other we attempt to locate must occupy a suitable level of generality and importance: we could, after all, note that, for example, many games, such as chess, are such that if these games are real and not chimerical, then persons must in the appropriate ways be calculators in their own interests, governors of present impulses by thoughts of future consequences, and dreaders of certain evils (checkmate against one's king, for example); but I think we would agree that the desirability or acceptability of chess and relevantly similar games is not strong enough to move us to accept the view of persons that they project for purposes of confirming the acceptability of legal punishment.

Two possibilities come to mind, though here I am making suggestions more than arguing.

The first possibility is that the conception of society as "a cooperative venture for mutual advantage" may, when it is thought to be "real and not chimerical," carry among the conditions of its possibility something like the view of persons expressed by the propositions in question. That is, it may be required of the beings who conduct their society as a cooperative scheme for mutual benefit that they be appropriately calculative in their own interests, governors of present impulse, and so on. I find it tempting to say that the conception does require this and also to say that it is attractive, but I will be content here merely to note that this conception of society is itself normative in the sense I have in mind in this discussion: it is a result of a decision about how society should be viewed. After all, the conception of society in question is neither an empty platitude nor a necessary truth. There are other ways of characterizing society at this level of generality, and the decision to construe it in the way in question is, in effect, to take a stand on what the good society is. It is to reject, for example, the coherent possibility of viewing society in theological terms as an instrument of God's purposes; it is to reject, too, the possibility of viewing society in an Aristotelian or Marxist manner such that society is an instrument of moral or intellectual self-realization; it is also to reject the possibility of viewing society as a utility device *simpliciter*, such that the maximization of well-being, by some criteria of well-being, is the only point of society. If my line of thought in this discussion is correct, these alternative conceptions of society might very well make assumptions about persons that are different from those made by the conception according to which society is thought to be a cooperative venture for mutual benefit. We should note here, too, that not only is it not necessary to view society as a cooperative mutual-benefit enterprise, it is also true that for many of the members of societies that aspire to the cooperative mutual-benefit idea, or ideal, the reality has turned out to be very distant from the ideal.[51]

The second suggestion is that morality itself may in some general way require that persons be viewed in the manner expressed by the propositions in question. If this is so, it may also be so that this consideration figures among the reasons for deciding to view society as a cooperative venture for mutual advantage in the first place. I am not prepared, however, to demonstrate such linkages among concepts. All I can say about this suggestion is that if our reason for viewing persons as calculators is grounded in our thinking about what morality is, I do not see that this gets us to facts about persons. If morality in some large-scale sense views persons as calculators, it does not follow that, in fact, they are. Even morality in this large-scale sense may commit persona moralism. If the claim is instead that morality's normative assumptions about persons are best, wise, or prudent, then we may note that this is what is in question in this discussion.

Summary

Let me state what I take to be the main results of the discussion in the previous five sections.

1. In the vocabulary I introduced, the view of persons as calculators in their own interest, governors of present impulse by thoughts of future consequences, and dreaders of certain evils (e.g., fines, imprisonment, death) is a view of persons as basic individuals rather than of persons as we know them, that is, as social and historical particulars. The view as such, then, is not a set of factual propositions or a set of conceptual truths about persons as they basically are, though it is presented in the philosophical account I discussed as being the former. The view is normative in character and may be thought of as the result of a decision about how persons should be viewed—in this instance for the purposes of an understanding of the justification of legal punishment.

2. I suggested that an appeal to the actual facts about real people, that is, about persons as social and historical particulars—messy and mixed as such facts are—does not point directly to legal punishment as a central and general form of social control. The view of persons in question simplifies and smooths out these facts in one among different possible directions, and as a result it leaves out rather than covers certain persons as we know them or needs qualification relative to other persons as we know them.

3. I also suggested that rather than seeing the view in question as setting out independent factual propositions about persons that could figure in a case for legal punishment based on how persons are, it might instead be seen as stating conditions of the possibility of legal punishment and, as such, might be seen as a many-part assumption of the system of legal punishment itself.

4. Finally, I very briefly explored two possible independent avenues to the acceptance of the view of persons in question, that is, two ideas we have that are independent of the system of legal punishment itself but that might also require as conditions of the possibility of their application that persons be viewed in the manner of the propositions we have been considering. As I suggested, though, how these two very general ideas (of society and morality) are to be interpreted, that is, what clusters of practices, institutions, and principles are to be considered to constitute them, is controversial, and the interpretation one comes to itself involves normative decisions about how it is best, wise, or prudent to regard persons. Interpretations[52] of these very general ideas carry with them normative assumptions about persons, and choosing among them is not facilitated by simple appeal to facts about persons.

The general message of what I have offered is again not that the institution of legal punishment cannot be justified. It is rather that the case for legal punishment does not involve nor does it rest on general facts about persons in any central way. The proposed case I have discussed is essentially normative regarding how persons are. When we think about the people around us in the terms suggested by the view of how persons are that is suggested by the philosophical account of the case for legal punishment I have discussed, we willy-nilly engage in stereotyping and judging some of the people we thus think about. We—perhaps despite ourselves—commit persona moralism regarding them.

Persona Moralism Self-Imposed

Perhaps the discussion above suggests that persona moralism is something we do or have done to us through our participation in or acquiescence to what I have called practices and institutions. This needs to be broadened and also to be self-referentially supplemented: there are other vehicles for persona moralism, and our targets can be ourselves. Persona moralism is committed not only through the practices and institutions we participate in; we also commit it through what are sometimes called ideologies and through our reliance on or recourse to, perhaps in times of life crisis, very general views concerning salient features of human life. The self-referential point is simply that we can and do commit persona moralism to or on ourselves: for example, we may, with little or no awareness of the fact, impose a stereotype on ourselves and judge ourselves by it, and if we fail to meet its terms, we may indeed suffer.

An example that exhibits a tragic self-imposition of a conception of persons associated with an ideology of sorts is provided by the fate of Willy Loman, the central figure in Arthur Miller's play *Death of a Salesman*.[53] My purpose in the following few remarks is not to offer criticism of Miller's play or to suggest an interpretation of it. My attention goes directly to the fact that Willy is a victim of his own understanding of the American Dream. Willy is an ordinary person,[54] a man with a wife and two grown sons, a failed career, and little or no future in terms of time or projects. In the end Willy commits suicide, and this act, while it has its instrumental point (it moves money into the hands of his son), is also an acknowledgment by Willy that his life has failed, that is, he has not been able to meet the terms of the American Dream as he understood it, and these terms included, for Willy, being a person of a certain sort.

Any portrait of Willy must capture such features of his makeup as the following:

(1) Willy thought of himself as a man who had a strategy for living: "That's just the way I'm bringing [my boys] up, Ben—rugged, well liked, all-around."[55] "[I]t's not what you do, Ben. It's who you know and the smile on your face! It's contacts, Ben, contacts!"[56] "Be liked and you will never want."[57] "It's not what you say, it's how you say it—because *personality* always wins the day."[58]

(2) Along with his strategy for living, Willy was occupied with two sorts of dreams—one official, the other unofficial. The official dream, of course, was the American Dream. "Why didn't I go to Alaska with my brother Ben that time! Ben! That man was a genius, that man was success incarnate! What a mistake. He begged me to go. . . . There was a man started with the clothes on his back and ended up with diamond mines!"[59] The unofficial dream—the dream that was somehow closer to Willy's soul, all things considered, but that he never allowed to stand in primary place in his life—was very quiet, close to the ground, pervaded by serenity and good humor, and completely lacking in the striving and overcoming so prominent in the official dream.

[Willy gets up from the table. Linda holds his jacket for him.]
Willy: . . . Gee, on the way home tonight I'd like to buy some seeds.

Linda [laughing]: That'd be wonderful. But not enough sun gets [to our yard]. Nothing'll grow any more.
Willy: You wait, kid, before it's all over we're gonna get a little place out in the country, and I'll raise some vegetables, a couple of chickens . . . .
Linda: You'll do it yet, dear.
[Willy walks out with his jacket. Linda follows him.][60]

(3) In quiet moments with Linda or with himself, Willy was very much a creature of fears—fears of ridicule, of inability to provide for his family, of dependency, of increasing incompetence. In these moments Willy could move in an instant from bravado to vulnerability, isolation, and helplessness.

Oh, I'll knock 'em dead next week. . . . I'm very well liked in Hartford. You know, the trouble is, Linda, people don't seem to take to me. . . . They seem to laugh at me. . . . they just pass me by. I'm not noticed. . . . I joke too much! . . . I'm fat. I'm very—foolish to look at, Linda.[61]
   I get so lonely. . . . I get this feeling that I'll never sell anything again, that I won't make a living for you, or a business, a business for the boys.[62] Christ's sake, I couldn't get past Yonkers today! Where are you guys, where are you? The woods are burning! I can't drive a car![63] I can't throw myself on my sons. I'm not a cripple![64]

(4) Finally, there is Willy's own view of meaningful work, a view that sets out to prescribe the hard, tough individualism of the American Dream but wanders in the elucidation of it to the warmth of close positive relationships. Willy makes no effort to resolve the tension that is then evident. (Few of us would know how.) He is left in frustration and resentment.

Oh, yeah, my father lived many years in Alaska. He was an adventurous man. We've got quite a little streak of self-reliance in our family. I thought I'd go out with my older brother and try to locate him, and maybe settle in the North with the old man. And I was almost decided to go, when I met a salesman in the Parker House. His name was Dave Singleman. And he was eighty-four years old, and he'd drummed merchandise in thirty-one states. And old Dave, he'd go up to his room, y'understand, put on his green velvet slippers—I'll never forget—and pick up his phone and call the buyers, and without ever leaving his room, at the age of eight-four, he made his living. And when I saw that, I realized that selling was the greatest career a man could want. 'Cause what could be more satisfying than to be able to go, at the age of eighty-four, into twenty or thirty different cities, and pick up a phone, and be remembered and loved and helped by so many different people? Do you know? When he died—and by the way he died the death of a salesman, in his green velvet slippers in the smoker of the New York, New Haven and Hartford, going into Boston—when he died, hundreds of salesmen and buyers were at his funeral. . . . In those days there was personality in it. . . . There was respect, and comradeship, and gratitude in it. Today, it's all cut and dried, and there's no chance for bringing friendship to bear—or personality. You see what I mean? They don't know me any more.[65]

Ultimately, what is important to Willy, despite his official line, is neither selling nor the results of selling; rather, he prizes the human side of salesmanship. Willy is a relationship person—a people person—caught up in a man's world demanding individualist strength, self-interested calculating energy, impersonality, and an appetite for competition, and what he does in these life circumstances is impose on himself the man's-world view, including, in particular, the conception of person that goes with it. (Not entirely so, of course. Willy does what most of us do: he shuffles back and forth between conceptions of person; but he never distances himself from the individualist conception that he cannot realize in himself and so he never gains perspective on its demands.[66]) Finally, at the late point in his working life that we find him, when it is clear enough to all, even Willy, that he is not the person he thinks he is supposed to be, he moves to suicide.

> Willy: A man can't go out the way he came in, Ben, a man has got to add up to something. . . .
> Ben: It's called a cowardly thing, William.
> Willy: Why? Does it take more guts to stand here the rest of my life ringing up a zero?[67]

In this case, then, Willy commits persona moralism on himself. He takes on himself the conception of person associated with the loose and vague ideology he called the American Dream, and this conception of person was one whose terms he did not or could not meet. In Willy's case, the self was not constituted in the way the American Dream prescribes for selves. Willy suffered with this fact, and he did not know quite what to do or think about it. He ended up defeated by life, and, according to the view I have suggested, the instrument of the defeat is a self-imposed persona moralism via Willy's uncritical participation or acquiescence in the popular ideology of his (and our) day. Willy was, in effect, victimized by the power he allowed his dream to have.[68] Many of us commit persona moralism on ourselves in this fashion, via the Dream that Willy had or some analog to it. Our fate in this connection may not end in suicide, but it may well contain the confusion, frustration, and resentment so apparent in Willy's struggle with himself. Persons are vulnerable at the extreme to their own interpretations of themselves.[69]

On Death

If we commit persona moralism through the practices and institutions we participate in and also through ideologies, we do so as well through our reliance on or recourse to certain very general views concerning salient features of life. Perhaps these general views are themselves rather like ideologies; I think, though, that we do not ordinarily think of them as such, for they feel closer to experience and do not seem at all abstract. I have in mind here our strategies for coping with certain facts of life that most of us face whatever the content of our social and historical particularity turns out to be. In general, these facts of life are structural features of the human condition that we typically experience through, for example, anticipation or apprehension as needing a conceptual-cum-normative response. As such, these features form a basic problematic of life that pretty nearly everyone must deal with or accommodate somehow. Let me elaborate slightly on this basic problematic. (1) The structural features I have in mind are not the surface-level rules of law or society that we must negotiate as a part of daily life; rather, they are rooted in natural facts about persons, even though as structural features in our lives they are confronted by us (embedded as we are in our social and historical particularity) only as filtered through the grid imposed on such facts by the many artifacts of social contingency, including custom, tradition, law, politics, and even the canons of literature and philosophy. Some facts about persons—for example, that they breathe—seem natural to common sense but present no problematic; they do not, for most of us, call for a conceptual-cum-normative response.[70] Most of us just breathe—we do not have to work out any particular understanding of ideas, assess candidate principles, or quarrel with tradition in order to respond to the natural facts in question. Most of us can deal with or accommodate these facts without conceptual preparation. (2) The list of structural features, rooted in natural facts and social contingency, needing a conceptual-cum-normative response in my life may not be exactly the same as the corresponding list in your life, though I suspect that certain features would appear on the lists of most people. Death seems to be one of these structural features of human life; work, sexual union, and children seem to be others.[71]

In the few remarks that follow, I focus on death. The aim is not to offer a full-blown theory of death or even to recommend any particular interpretation of death over others. My interest remains what it was in the discussion above: persona moralism. My thought is that even our responses to structural features of the human condition are conceptually loaded with assumptions about how persons are, and sometimes, perhaps without thinking, we impose these on others or ourselves. Even regarding the ground-level problematic of life, our ideas invite us to commit persona moralism.

Death indeed comes to us all, but what is it to be the sort of creature that is thus stuck with mortality? It is many things, of course, but, among the most of important of them, in the human case, is that it is to be a creature who typically is able to be aware that its life will end.[72] I live now under the premise that sooner or later I must die. What is it to live under the prospect of death? I suggest some features.

In the first place, the prospect of death functions in one's life somewhat like one's own promising: it influences options, usually by closing them. I do not mean here the obvious point that the occurrence of death closes options. The prospect of death leads me, at age fifty-four, *not* to undertake to learn Chinese, for there is too little time for the expenditure of effort I would have to make to yield a reward. It leads me, at age sixty-five, not to have a child, for there is not time enough for the duties of parenting to be carried through. It leads me, at age fifty, to spend the hours required to establish support for my dependent survivors rather than to invest them in a range of more enjoyable activities. It leads me, at age forty-five, to begin to put forward the enormous amounts of time, energy, and thought needed to try to break life-destroying addictions rather than to continue to suffer them, cover them up, and hope for the best. The prospect of death influences our range of options, and in later years it closes down increasing numbers of them.

Second, observation and realism teach that the end that the prospect of death is a prospect of is often a very negative thing. I refer here to the process of dying, not to whatever state, if any, follows it. Irving Howe wrote of the death of Tolstoy's Ivan Ilych that his "end . . . is pretty much the end of all men: torment, confusion, panic, regret, and finally a span of unbroken pain."[73] Perhaps a few of us will escape the end's being this way, but, again, observation and realism suggest that most of us will not. I have no compunction about saying that I fear the process of dying. Why should I not fear such a thing? The deaths I have observed have met

Howe's description, if they were not instantaneous; and in some cases they have been horrendous.

Third, the mortality that structures my life as a human being presents me with an end that I will experience or suffer by myself, despite whatever efforts at comfort may be made by medical people and, perhaps, by loved ones. The glib saying here is actually deeply profound: no one can die my death but me—the obverse of the usually energizing notion that no one can live my life but me. There is an impending isolation accompanying the prospect of death that is daunting, and this is so even if it is also so, as is emphasized in some forms of existentialism, that our lives in general are lived in isolation. One may hope, at the end, for long periods of unconsciousness.

Fourth, if one remains conscious, then another feature in this small phenomenology of mortality may come into play for some of us. Tolstoy's story is moving because he has Ivan Ilych become sharply aware of his mortality as a consequence of illness but well after much of an ordinary life has been lived. As a result, what Ivan suffers as a part of his dying is not merely the mystery of illness, compounded by the sense that many of life's options are now effectively closed, the fear of the ending itself, and the imminent isolation of death; the suffering is also constituted by the sheer pain of the thought that the one life he has been given to live has been wasted. Tolstoy's crushing assessment is that "Ivan Ilych's life had been most simple and most ordinary and therefore most terrible."[74] When Ivan takes stock of his life, he is dismayed and demoralized. As we recognize the character of Ivan's fate, so too may we worry about our own, for it is very common that one lives one's life according to one's lights, one has one's mortality pressed on one by circumstances of some sort (illness, say, or the death of a friend), and one then reviews one's life, only to find it to have been essentially a waste. One has, as it were, lived little or otherwise lived wrong, and now it is too late.

Ivan, of course, does not leave it there. This interpretation of his life's journey is intolerable for him. He fights back. He struggles to say that his life has been good and to show how it has been worthwhile, but there are glimpses along the way that Ivan himself cannot sustain this view; he cannot muster the conviction that such a view requires. In the end he reaches death "only after he abandons his illusions . . . only after he realizes, thereby in a sense forgiving himself, that it does not really matter any more whether his life has been good—[only then] can Ivan Ilych surrender himself."[75]

I will not attempt to extend this phenomenology of mortality, or, more exactly, the phenomenology of the experience of a creature who lives with or under the prospect of death. All sorts of qualifications would have to made in an extension.[76] Enough has been said, however, to suggest how it is that the prospect of death forms a structural feature of our lives, one that calls for a conceptual-cum-normative response. How to think about the fact that our lives will end is a question most of us find we must work out some sort of answer to, in order to lead the lives we have. In what follows I remind us of some very general views people come to in responses to the prospect of death. My interest is not in recommending one of them over the others; it is, rather, in the assumptions about persons that these general views make.

One of these views, dark and invigorating at first, is that we should respond to death with defiance. Camus's existentialism is well known for this prescription.[77] In Camus's hands this prescription is seen as a consequence of what Camus calls a "skeptical metaphysics,"[78] which finds that the human condition is absurd. The general structure of Camus's view seems to be that both ordinary experience and philosophical analysis show that human life itself is meaningless;[79] and if life is meaningless or the human condition absurd, it is natural for us to ask whether we should end it. Camus finds that even though life is meaningless, we should not end it, either by committing physical suicide or by committing philosophical suicide, that is, by disguising the true nature (the absurdity) of the human condition via acceptance of or adherence to a meaning-giving ideology of some sort, such as a religion, a cosmology, or even a generalized political view, for example, liberalism or Marxism. We should instead live so that we persist in lucid awareness of absurdity, that is, we are to go on with our lives but without interpreting them through the adoption of political, moral, religious, or metaphysical glosses on the world or our places within it. Life is meaningless, however, we are enjoined not to end it, but to live honestly regarding it, that is, in constant awareness of its absurd character.[80] To live thus, that is, in obedience to this maxim of persistence in lucidity, is, in part, for Camus to defy death: "it is essential," Camus writes, "to die unreconciled."[81]

I doubt that Camus can get to the lucidity maxim he recommends, with its correlative defiance maxim regarding death in particular, from the skeptical metaphysics he starts with, but that is not my concern here. I am much more interested in the assumptions about persons that Camus makes when he recommends to us that we live in such a way as to keep in mind at every moment, as we act in the world, the absurdity of the human condition. I want to ask: can we live in the world without, in Camus's colorful vocabulary, committing philosophical suicide? This is to ask: can we act in the world without interpreting and conceptualizing what we do—without, for example, meaning something in or by what we do? Is it even logically open to me to live my life (e.g., teach my classes, perform the part in the play I auditioned for, help my grand-daughter learn to read, try to make out what Camus's position could possibly be, or write my book, etc.) without some understanding of what I am doing and some valuing of its point?

Camus's existentialism is and I think means to be an anti-ideology screed. I am sympathetic to this intention, but, upon reflection, I think that Camus, in the development of his view, has carried it too far. It is one thing to find the human condition absurd, if one means by this that certain ultimate why-questions we are able to ask do not permit provable, verifiable, or otherwise conclusive answers.[82] There is much to accept in this claim, but to move directly from that good point about the lack of conclusive answers to ultimate why-questions to the recommendation that we live in such a way as not to interpret our lives is at best a piece of logical silliness.[83] In fact, I cannot engage in an activity in my life (for example, helping my granddaughter learn to read) without reasoning the concrete, that is, understanding what I am doing and taking its point to heart. If I were somehow to refuse to let the latter two conditions be satisfied, as I would be required to do if I were to live Camus's maxims in my life, then whatever it is that I would be doing as I went through certain processes with my granddaughter on my lap, it clearly would not be helping my granddaughter learn to read.

Paradoxically, even Camus's own advice regarding mortality does not meet his general recommendation not to reason the concrete. To defy death is, after all, to value death in a certain way; at a minimum, to hurl defiance at death is to view it (i.e., to understand it and value it) as a negative, threatening thing; in this view, death is something to challenge, to be belligerent toward, to resist with all one's might. To defy death is to live against a certain structural feature of one's life, rather than to live "in lucid awareness" of the "absurdity of the human condition."

Camus's existential nihilism, then, does indeed provide a conceptual-cum-normative response to the prospect of death. It provides us initially with the nihilism, that is, the skeptical metaphysics, and then it couples with this the general lucidity maxim, whereof the defiance maxim is said to be a consequence. The difficulty in the result, however, is that the general maxim is impossible for a human being to obey, and the defiance maxim is, strictly, not itself in line with, or even logically connected to, the general maxim said to imply it. What Camus's view actually recommends, if one takes the text at face value, is a life strategy of conceptual blackout. I am thus inclined to suggest that any judgment Camus would make of one's failure to respond to the prospect of death with defiance would be an instance of objectionable persona moralism. If, for example, we were to "reason the concrete" regarding our mortality, he would charge us with philosophical suicide, which is, for Camus, a form of intellectual dishonesty; but, if my discussion above is right, this charge against us comes from premises that human beings cannot meet. The standard of how a person is to be that he challenges us to aspire to is, in fact, impossible for us. You and I may make different conceptual-cum-normative responses to our mortality; we may at times be confused, uncertain, or self-deceived about the responses we make; we may argue with one another about which response is best; but that we will make some response seems to me to be something that we, given our nature, are stuck with. Camus has given us a view, but it is not a view that we could follow.[84] Granted, many of us do not have the problem of mortality in mind very often; other things have our attention, and our circumstances can, after all, be nonthreatening now and then. When we do face this problem, however, we will interpret and conceptualize in response to it: we will reason the prospect of death in some way. It is our nature to do so. We live our lives by interpreting and conceptualizing—by understanding and valuing in some fashion—what we deal with. People cannot be expected not to obey their nature in this regard.

Views other than Camus's are of course possible and, if the discussion above is correct, necessary. To reason death may be pressed on us by circumstances with more or less urgency. Camus-style conceptual blackout is not possible for us, though our circumstances may allow us or tempt us to ignore the prospect of death for a period of time. It does not follow, however, that other conceptual-cum-normative responses—even if they do not contain the difficulty I find in Camus's view—are thereby free of persona moralism. A common theme of some possible views outside the range of the defiance theme, which Camus interprets in the odd way I have discussed, is the idea of acceptance. Intuitively, this is the theme that death, while perhaps not to be welcomed or invited, is nevertheless to be taken in stride and indeed to be met with serenity and dignity.[85] Of course, the acceptance maxim also comes with background premises and glosses on the human condition. In religious variants on the theme in question, a human death might be viewed as ultimately an act of God or as a form of expression of God's will. (I have even heard it described as a "service to God," though this is a characterization that I do not immediately understand.) It might be viewed as an event in one's life that makes evident one's ultimate powerlessness in God's creation or an event in acquiescence to which one is, or comes to be, in harmony with God's will. Secular interpretations are possible here; such interpretations might involve treatment of nature in special, perhaps quasi-reverential ways and in that fashion make possible an acceptance maxim that also enjoins harmony—in this case harmony with a naturalized transcendent order or with nature as a bearer of intrinsic value.

Do views in this range also invite persona moralism? I think so. If persona moralism has at its heart the normative imposition on another or oneself of a conception of how persons are that the other or one does not or cannot meet, then persona moralism may well be involved in recommended versions of the acceptance maxim. I have in mind people who do not or, more interestingly, cannot think of themselves as part of a larger order, however interpreted. They are people who cannot muster the conviction required to sustain transcendence sensibility. Intellectually, they may acknowledge certain lines of thought suggesting that such conviction allows one to carry the prospect of death more easily, and they may even want such conviction for themselves, but, in a way that may be familiar to some from the stubbornness of long-term depression, despite the intellectual recognition and the wanting, the conviction fails to become a living part of their or one's own makeup. The fact is, such persons cannot have such conviction for themselves, and when this is realized, they may be deeply saddened by this fact about themselves. Their nature is such that, for whatever reason, they cannot avail themselves of a form of comfort or inner peace regarding a structural feature of life that is or can be available to others. To judge such people in a negative way—to hold them to account or think poorly of them for their failure—is, I believe, an instance of objectionable persona moralism. Some people are at hazard in regard to the basic problematic of life in ways that others are not.

On What to Do

Persona moralism, as I have discussed it here, is a sort of stereotyping and judging that we do of others and ourselves via our participation or acquiescence in certain human artifacts that carry assumptions about how persons are. Among these artifacts are the common institutions and practices we live with or under (including legal institutions and moral practices), very general ideologies concerning how to live, and even general views by which we respond to basic structural features of human lives. These are not the only artifacts that carry assumptions about

persons. Moral theories (e.g., utilitarianism, Kantianism, Aristotelian-
ism) and political philosophies (e.g., liberalism, Marxism, contractualism) do so, too, as do the sometimes-popular economics critiques that
rest loosely on them, and to live such views—to think about others or
oneself in line with the images of persons they emphasize and to act
regarding others or oneself from such thoughts—is, I think, to risk
committing persona moralism in the conduct of one's life.

I will close this part of my discussion with some notes about persona
moralism and about problems raised by it.

The first note is that persona moralism seems built into human lives. It
seems inevitable and unavoidable—at any rate, among people who live
with others. You and I will both commit persona moralism and be
victims of others who commit it insofar as our dealings with others
extend to people we do not know well. This simple fact—that many of
the people we deal with are not known well by us—is among the
conditions of the possibility of persona moralism. Insofar as you and I
engage in life with others we do not know well, we will go about thinking
of them in the terms set out by the assumptions about persons made by
the practices and general ideologies we make use of. Life does not permit
us to study each and every individual we deal with. Even those we think
we know well turn out in certain circumstances to be partially closed
books to us.

Second, though, I do not think that the unavoidability of persona
moralism suggests that it has no interest for moral theory. The plurality
of cases attending persona moralism gives it the same richness for moral-
theoretical reflection as other unavoidable practices (e.g., promising) in
our lives together. (1) In the discussion above I had in mind mainly cases
in which we commit persona moralism and in which it is wrong to do so.
These are cases in which the imposition on others of assumptions about
persons seems unfair to them, because they cannot meet the terms of
such assumptions. There are cases, then, of objectionable persona moralism. (2) In other cases, however, it may very well be morally permitted,
justified, or required to commit persona moralism regarding another
person or oneself. Exhortation and encouragement are practices we
engage in that are in some cases subject to positive moral-valuational
modalities (and in other cases subject to negative ones), and they sometimes proceed in a way that involves some people moralizing others or
themselves by reference to conceptions of persons whose terms the latter
do not, but can and should, meet, or at least aspire to. Persona moralism
can be right in some cases. (3) In still other cases the deliberate committing of persona moralism can be a useful, perhaps temporary, part of a

strategy for helping an individual recover a basic human good, for example, health or a measure of sanity. In recovery from alcoholism, catastrophic illness, or life-threatening depression—in these and other forms of individual suffering, healing may be contributed to through effective uses of conceptions of persons that, in the nature of the case, are not known to apply to the victims or even to be possible for them. When concern for health or sanity supplants concern for truth, moralizing can indeed be noble, that is, permitted, justified, or required.

The third note is a small reflection on the phenomenon of self-imposed persona moralism, as in the story of Willy Loman. In *Death of a Salesman* it appears that Willy didn't get right who he was. Willy did not—perhaps could not—meet the terms of the image of a person that went with the American Dream that he officially endorsed. One is saddened and perhaps angered by Willy's fate, but it is worth noting that in many cases, if not all, we have at least some choices to make in this matter of the image of a person we take on for ourselves. If the top side of the persona-moralism coin includes the possibility of unfairness between people or between a person and himself or herself, the bottom side features a certain openness or fluidity about how we are that invites or allows us to fashion our own identities. The instances in which persona moralism may be morally objectionable, permitted, justified, required—these seem the surface phenomena that reflect, down deep, the autonomy of persons so cherished by many of our freedom- and choice-loving moral theories and political philosophies. Accordingly, I can imagine cases in which the conception of self one has is by and large a result of the workings of social and political oppression—oppression in which one, after a time, comes simply to acquiesce. The sense of agency—that sense that one has choices regarding who and what one is—is diminished. Perhaps oppression is successful when it imposes a conception of person on one and also brings it about that one's sense of choice in the matter is completely lost.

The last note is that even if this is so—that persona moralism has a positive side, insofar as it reflects an autonomy that we think morally important—the fact that it can be objectionable raises questions about how we are to think and act in everyday life. How are we to respond to the fact that in our lives with others and with ourselves we are vulnerable to the unfairness lurking in objectionable persona moralism? Its unavoidability in our lives means that even the morally best of us, the most conscientious and careful among us, will commit persona moralism in such a way as to treat others or ourselves unfairly and, correspondingly, that even the morally best of us will be victimized by persona moralism committed by others and be perhaps helpless witnesses to others committing persona moralism on themselves. To invoke again the theme of the first part of the discussion of this book, our review or survey of our lives will at some point reveal instances in which we treated others or ourselves on terms unfair to them or ourselves, in which we were victims ourselves of unfair treatment by others, or in which we stood by—perhaps were forced to stand by—as others victimized themselves. In that way our pasts will come to seem problematic to us, and we will be vulnerable to certain forms of moral pain. Wrongdoing, victimization, helpless witnessing—all these will be parts of our histories, even when, in the fortunate histories, little or no malice can be found in them.

Chapter 3

Problematic Agency

Fools and young people talk about everything being possible for a human being. But that is a great mistake.

Kierkegaard, *Fear and Trembling*

Art., 8th. If any member shall become decidedly immoral he shall be expelled from the Association.

Oberlin College Alumni Association, Original Constitution (1839)

[T]he metaphorical images of man that we have inherited . . . are now secularized in a modern language of agency that fits with the demands of an economic system and with a social system that rewards extreme exercises of self-reliance. The demands of the metaphor of self-mastery are cruel.

Michael Ignatieff, "Modern Dying"

[Human consciousness is] not normally transparent glass through which [one] views the world, but a cloud of more or less fantastic reverie designed to protect the psyche from pain.

Iris Murdoch, *The Sovereignty of Good*

Persona Moralism: Innocent, Vicious, In-Between

In the discussion above I wrote of persona moralism with cases in mind mainly in which persons unwittingly stereotype and judge others or themselves. These are cases, by and large, of innocent persona moralism. Vicious persona moralism occurs when those who impose a certain conception of persons on others or themselves realize that the others or themselves cannot meet the terms of the conception thus imposed, yet they persist in treating their victims on those terms. Vicious persona moralism seems a form of cruelty. What motivates it could be whatever it is that motivates cruelty. It is like persisting in making demands of someone known to be unable to respond to them.[1]

There are cases between innocent and vicious persona moralism, and the complexity of the cases in the middle area is what I wish to explore now. The question before us is a special-interest instance of the broad question: how are we to understand people, including ourselves, who do not do what they should do (e.g., what they ought to do, or what it would be good for them to do)? If one's philosophical interests went to the "should" here, then one might approach the broad question with these particular questions in mind: how are we to understand people who do not do what we think they should do? Or what they think they should do? Or what objectively they should do, apart from what *we* or *they* think? I do not wish to discuss here, however, the objectivity of morality, or even the different possible perspectives on values. The middle-area cases I have in mind have a certain structure to them that is familiar from experience: one commits innocent persona moralism on *J*, then is confronted by the fact that *J* does not do what he or she should do, then is given to understand that perhaps *J* cannot do what he or she should do, and then finds the "cannot" hypothesis difficult to believe. In such circumstances one may, in fact, persist in imposing on *J* the conception of persons one is operating with. My attention, then, in the discussion that follows, is not directed to the objectivity or perspectival aspects of the "should" in these cases (supposing that there is a reasonable justificatory case for the "should"); it goes instead to the character of the "cannot" in them. Even more specifically, it goes to those cases in which the "cannot" is linked to what I called earlier "unmanageable internal factors" (see the last section in chapter 1 above). These are not situations, then, in which *J* cannot do the "should" because he or she was tied down by ropes, and we had not noticed and which we had difficulty believing when told. In the cases I have in mind *J* is indeed tied down, but by factors that are not so external as ropes.

Why is it that when in these cases we find it hard to believe that *J* is tied down by internal ropes, we respond by persisting in imposing on *J* a conception of persons that denies that *J* is thus tied down? It is as if we reason in some sort of "myself-the-model" fashion: "I can do *x*, *so* you can do *x*, *for* (in general) persons can do *x*." We know perfectly well that in many cases such a form of reasoning will not do. If I can jump ten feet high, it does not follow either that persons in general can do so or that you can do so, but my experience suggests that when alleged unmanageable internal factors are involved in the explanation of *J*'s not being able to do *x*, we do—often—think in this myself-the-model way. If doing *x* is what should be done, and *I* can do *x*, then *you* can do *x*, and, in general, persons can do *x*.

Doubtless there are a number of factors involved in the explanation of our use of this strange but common form of reasoning. I claim no special insight into what goes on in the minds of real people in real life. My guess is that a part of the explanation in some or many cases might be that we operate uncritically with a certain conception of how persons are in our dealings with others, and this conception makes persons out to be not really tied down by what I called unmanageable internal factors. I call this view of or about persons the conception of the in-control agent.

The In-Control Agent

The conception of persons I wish to characterize is a popular or received one. Its main ingredients are uncontroversial, but the interpretation of these might vary among those concerned with understanding them. For me, some remarks of John Stuart Mill in *On Liberty*[2] provide as good a lead-in as any to a sketch of the familiar conception of the in-control agent. Early in his defense of a large personal sphere of liberty for individuals in society, Mill concerns himself with the question: to whom does his liberalism apply? What must people be like for a freedom-loving nonpaternalist society to work? His answer, in effect, is that liberalism is not for children or people who are unable to think for themselves; rather, it is "meant to apply only to human beings in the maturity of their faculties."[3] This interesting phrase is not completely specified in Mill's essay, but, for present purposes (involving, again, not Mill scholarship but rather an understanding of a received conception of persons in a society that takes freedom seriously), the interesting phrase may be interpreted in this way. It treats the ordinary person in a freedom-loving society as a competent individual whose moral personality includes those capacities for rationality, sensibility, and judgment that allow him or her to formulate and pursue self-realizationist projects, give appropriate attention to the interests and needs of others in doing so, and rise to what morality demands, for example, duty or obligation, when in the particular circumstances of life this makes itself known.[4] To say that the competent individual is mature in respect to these faculties is to say that he or she possesses that measure of control over mind, body, and feeling—that efficacy of will—that enables the capacities in question to be exercised in the world, and not merely to be formally present in his or her self but never manifested in action.

I suspect that something like this conception of persons, suggested by Mill's remarks,[5] gets regular use in our dealings with people in everyday life. It is probably the conception of persons assumed by our thinking about what it is for a society to take freedom seriously, and it is certainly the standard default position for us in our everyday dealings with those we do not know well. There are many implications of each main general element in the conception; thus, to say that competent individuals are rational or have the capacity for rationality is to say at least that they are sane in certain fundamental ways, and thus in touch with reality more or less as it actually is,[6] capable of understanding and taking seriously the consequences of what they do, relevantly ordered and coherent in their thoughts, and perhaps even relatively insightful in their judgments as well. For Mill in particular, the competent individual is capable of independent thought and thus able to work out for himself or herself what his or her real interests are, understand what they indicate about how he or she ought to live, and, in general, size up and assess options or alternatives before him or her. To speak of the sensibility of the competent individual is—for Mill in particular[7]—to speak of a structure of sentiments—affective dimensions of personality—that give him or her degrees of sensitivity (varying from person to person) to his or her own welfare or well-being and to the welfare or well-being of others. I do not attempt to interpret the general elements involved in this view of how persons are any further; indeed, it occurs to me that in its use as a standing presumption in our dealings with others, the conception is probably not much more specific or precise in its details than I have been here. This view of persons is, nevertheless, very familiar and, for many of us, quite definitional in our outlook on life. That it can be an especially demanding conception of persons may perhaps be ameliorated or obscured for some of us by its familiarity, for others of us by a combination of its familiarity and fortunate personal circumstances (circumstances in which, say, we need not deal often with people who do not meet its terms), and for still others of us by its familiarity plus the fact that it has features in common with conceptions of persons we use in certain other areas of our lives, for example, economics, politics, or competitive team sports. My reading suggests that even the classical literature of ethical theory (e.g., the texts of Aristotle, Kant, and Mill) standardly presumes about persons that they are the way the model of the in-control agent portrays them, perhaps especially in regard to their powers of under-

standing and acting on certain kinds of reasons.[8] In his introduction to
Earthbound,[9] Tom Regan writes that:

> Moral agents are those who can bring impartial reasons (i.e., reasons that
> respect the requirements of impartiality) to bear on deciding how they
> ought to act. They are thus conceived to be both rational and autonomous.
> Individuals who lack the ability to understand or act on the basis of
> impartial reasons (e.g., young children) fail to qualify as moral agents. They
> cannot meaningfully be said to have obligations to do, or to refrain from
> doing, what is morally right or wrong. Only moral agents can have this
> status, and moral principles can apply only to the determination of how
> moral agents should behave. *Normal adult human beings are the paradigma-
> tic instance of moral agents.*[10]

Let us remind ourselves of an additional feature of our use of the
conception of the in-control agent. If normal adult human beings are
thought of in this in-control fashion, how do we respond to them when
they do not do what they should do (what they ought to do or what it
would be good for them to do)? In this familiar view, when this happens
(setting aside accidents and interference by others), those who do not do
what they should do get charged with some form of irresponsibility,
moral criminality, or moral weakness: people are held to account for
refusing or failing to meet the standards, principles, or obligations
applicable in their situation. We find fault with them, and they are
expected either to defend themselves against our charges or, if they
cannot defend themselves, to suffer guilt, shame, or at least remorse and,
in some cases, to endure punishment. Those who do not do what they
should do are thought to refuse or fail to do what they should do, and in
either case they are blameworthy. If they refuse to do what they should
do, they are vicious, malicious, or in some other way evil; if they fail to
do what they should do, they are not themselves what they should be
but, instead, are weak, uncaring, indifferent, cowardly, or some amalgam
of these or other negative characteristics.

Difficulties

Now, there are, of course, immediate difficulties that come to mind as
one reflects on this brief reminder of the familiar conception of the in-
control agent, though this fact by itself need not suggest that this
conception of persons is immediately to be rejected as our standing

presumption in ordinary life regarding how persons are. Some difficulties, after all, might be met, accommodated, or discounted.

The first difficulty is personal, and I can think of circumstances in which I would be embarrassed to admit it. The difficulty is that I do not fit the characterization of the competent individual I have provided, even allowing for varying or different interpretations of its main parts. Evidence from my life, plus testimony from respected others, indicates that I am not very rational at all if, as above, that refers to one's capacity for understanding and taking seriously the consequences of what one does, for being ordered and coherent in one's thoughts, or for being sane (in touch with reality as it more or less actually is) in any steady and reliable way; nor am I much the independent thinker that I imagine Mill has in mind (one who is able to understand and assess one's options); nor do I have the generalized control—the efficacy of will in the many sections and departments of life—that the nonpaternalistic society supposes me to have. This realization that I do not fit our received model of a person is of course interesting to me in the way that news that means to be alarming is interesting. Mill wants to assume of me, as a possible member of a liberal society, that I am a sort of master of my fate. I notice, though, that I am not, in fact, cleanly a master of my fate in the several ways I think he has in mind, and I sometimes wonder whether that is important.

The second immediate difficulty for the idea of the in-control agent is not personal. It concerns external challenges to our mastery of our lives and the impact these external challenges have on us. We are all subject to forces outside our control; in some cases these forces constitute good luck; in other cases they constitute bad luck; in either set of cases they affect our mastery of our fates not only in terms of what in fact we must face and do in life but also in terms of how we are emotionally and spiritually affected by what we face and do in life. The received conception of the in-control agent is curiously blank on these topics.[11]

In the cases that come first to mind the luck is circumstantial. As one example, the lights in the auditorium go out right when I am about to make the main point in my first political speech, and I freeze (while perhaps you in similar circumstances would make a joke and go on). As another example, the car breaks down right when I must pick up my child at school, and I panic (while perhaps you would make the repair or get help and go on). Less commonly noted: we are all to some extent victims of the issues of our times, and we are such victims to varying degrees. The lives of people growing up in Northern Ireland, the Mideast, or even thirtysomething America are loaded with problems—political, social, moral, economic, educational—and many of these problems come at people from the outside but then end up living rent-free in their minds (absorbing time, energy, and resources and intruding elements into personal identity) whether or not their minds want them to be there. ("Unchosen issues" are a large part of the stuff of life for real people, but the forms of victimization that go with them are too little discussed in moral theory.)

In some cases circumstantial luck feels internal somehow—one does not experience it as coming from outside—and the opportunities for confusion about one's predicament are many. (1) When parents offer parenting to youngsters who refuse it, the confusion and emotional devastation can be as extreme as any faced by human beings: the mix of other-directed and self-directed ascriptions of fault may be bewildering—in some cases impossible to sort, in other cases simply personally terrifying and, indeed, too much to handle. (2) When one is targeted for condemnation or degradation by a messy but forceful ideology of the day (e.g., popular feminism, traditional sexism), then one's life may very well be torn up by an externality in a way that overwhelms the maturity of one's faculties; the result can be emotional insecurity and loss of confidence extreme enough to deflect one from pursuing important self-realizationist projects or even from developing self-realizationist aspirations for oneself. (3) When we suffer low blows that are close to the soul, for example, when our cherished personal relationships are destroyed through betrayal, lack of commitment, or simple misunderstanding, we endure a challenge that again is experienced as mixed in its sources (as between the other and oneself) and whose aftermath may be enormously costly in emotional pain and in losses in time and energy. I do not know anyone who has been free of them.

Third, do the difficulties mentioned so far lead us to reject the conception of the in-control agent as a general idea of how persons are that is serviceable in a broad way in ordinary life? Well, the fact that I do not fit this conception very well is not of wide interest, and its proponent might allow the stray exception. Too, the general fact that our fate-mastering is vulnerable to the effects of bad and good circumstantial luck is something that any proposed idea of how persons are that means to be serviceable in ordinary life would have to accommodate in some fashion.[12] I worry, however, in this matter of estimating the power of difficulties for the received model, about the further general fact that when our fate-mastering vulnerability is realized—that is, when circumstantial luck hits—our emotional and spiritual well-being may be affected, perhaps deeply. It may indeed, perhaps, be affected so deeply that the makeup of the self, orginally in line, say, with the terms of the model of the in-control agent, is altered in important ways, perhaps irretrievably so. I have in mind, for example, the case of a person who suffers devastating life experiences (perhaps steady abuse and humiliation in adolescence and early adulthood) and is emotionally and spiritually downed by it and stays down (e.g., endures major depression), perhaps for years. This person is now different in constitution (i.e., the makeup of the self) from the person who meets the terms of the model of the in-control agent. In subsequent life with us, he or she may very well behave in ways that are out of line with our expectations, as governed by the conception of the in-control agent, ways that are traceable to this altered self-constitution. He or she may be in the grips of unmanageable internal factors that he, she, or we may not fully understand.

We recognize from our own experience plus our understanding of others' experience that not all our disasters in life, after all, originate from outside. Some, perhaps many, of us suffer constitution-affecting luck that places us outside the mainstream model of the in-control agent to some degree or other, for one period of time or other, and we do what we can to accommodate such a fact about ourselves if we are aware of it. In a catalog of the sorts of luck that we as human beings are vulnerable to, Thomas Nagel noted that we suffer or enjoy luck in the kinds of persons we are, and he noted too that being a person of this or that kind is "not just a question of what [we] deliberately do, but of [our] inclinations, capacities, and temperament."[13] What is meant here by saying that inclination, capacity, and temperament are matters of luck is that the makeup of my self may not be the same as the makeup of your self or that of the in-control agent. What is meant here by saying that these elements of the self are constitutional is that they are the "built-ins" of my nature.[14] As such, they are, if taken seriously, considered to be logically prior to the power of my will as expressed in my choices. These luck factors—inclination, capacity, temperament—form, in a phrase I borrow from Harry G. Frankfurt, "necessities of the will."[15]

The idea of constitutional luck, especially bad constitutional luck, when thus construed, can seem a specter of sorts, for it is the idea that my nature has within it certain givens and that these givens—whatever the explanation of their being within my nature—are not subject to manipulation or control via an exercise of will on my part. In this account, the kind of person I am is not located logically posterior to my capacity to choose. I may indeed be a competent individual, of course, in some or many different ways, but no longer would this mean that I am the architect of my nature, fully in control of the details of its makeup and of the actions that flow from it. The idea that there are givens forming necessities of the will need not reach all of my nature or even a large part of it. I may indeed be in control, in principle, of many of the properties or attributes of my persona, but, in the constitutional-luck view in question, there is an important part of me, of my inclinations, capacities, and temperament, that is out of reach of my powers of choice. Given self-deception or lack of self-knowledge, I may even perplex or baffle myself in this connection; I might even find myself fighting myself, struggling for control, in certain departments of life, but constitutional luck may well defeat me in such struggles.

The specter of bad constitutional luck seems to me to bear on how in general we think about ourselves and others. Counter to the familiar model of the in-control agent, the idea of how persons are suggested by these few points about constitutional luck supposes that people are not necessarily competent individuals in the various areas of their lives. These points urge us to take seriously the variety in the results of "nature's lottery" and "social contingency"[16] in the makeup of persons that is at the heart of the idea of constitutional luck. This variety suggests a view of persons as different from one another, such that what you can be or do, perhaps easily, may be for me difficult or impossible, and what I can be or do, perhaps easily, may be for you difficult or impossible. It recognizes that, deep down, people may be stuck with elements of personality or character (Nagel's "inclinations, capacities, and temperament") that they cannot budge—in some cases despite their very best efforts to do so. Alternatively put, it recognizes that people may be powerless over certain aspects of or elements in their nature, and it recognizes further that these aspects or elements may be different from person to person. These recognitions of how persons are, in turn, surely bear on how we should operate our practices of holding to account (e.g., blaming, accusing, criticizing) and, indeed, our practices of praising, respecting, and admiring; but while these recognitions bear on these different practices, they make it very difficult to see how those practices should operate.

Vulnerabilities

There is great variety among the things people can be stuck with (different people, different vulnerabilities), and I do not know of any helpful way of organizing them. I discuss here a small number of cases not from a standpoint of technical expertise but only from the standpoint of one who knows the vulnerabilities involved from experience or who is well-acquainted with them in others whom one cares about. Cases, in fact, flood the mind, though that is not to say that any given case is easily understood or would be similarly dealt with by any participant in our common moral form of life.

In some cases the thing a person is stuck with is familiar or within a certain range of conditions that our experience has informed us of, and acknowledgement of the situation faced by a person with such a condition is relatively easy for most of us. Most teachers have had experience with students who are not merely shy but are in fact constitutionally shy. These are students for whom the report in class or even participation in discussion is not just difficult, that is, something to be overcome with time and patience and repeated effort; it is instead a practical impossibility, something whose forced overcoming may produce physiological trauma.

Constitutional shyness is an interesting vulnerability to think about when one attempts to reflect on the adequacy of the model of the in-control agent. Ordinary shyness is, after all, not strange or foreign to our experience of ourselves and others,[17] and many of us have some sense that shyness can be or become deeply entrenched in a person and then be long lasting and generally stultifying in its effects on his or her life. Ordinary shyness, though, is perhaps so common that the seriousness of deep constitutional shyness for its victim is not fully realized. For this victim the experience of shyness, that is, the anxiety felt when he or she is under real or imagined scrutiny, is so extreme that terror floods the mind, and the reaction words associated with helplessness, namely, "panic" and "trauma," are apt. One is rather literally out of control. This is not the nervousness faced by the shy in-control agent when he or she must make a public speech. It is an experience of a different order: in it one may indeed become "completely paralyzed by anxiety";[18] and, since to be vulnerable to such experiences may be an enduring condition,[19] one's life may become a scramble filled with evasion and avoidance of the scrutiny that many of us simply take in stride. Even though ordinary shyness, even when extreme, is not unfamiliar, constitutional shyness presents participants in our common moral life with difficulties. For example, it arouses mixed responses among us regarding its causation (underlying trauma? emotional weakness? heredity?) and thus regarding both how it should be dealt with by its victims and how far the behavior of victims should be tolerated by others.[20] Also, there is a major epistemological problem: in any given case it is very difficult to identify whether the victim is shy or constitutionally shy, presuming that the latter category is allowed.

Even if ordinary shyness is familiar, however, and the recognition or imaginability of constitutional shyness is available, we may in other cases have some trouble understanding how another person can genuinely be stuck with a certain element in his or her nature. In this second range of cases, especially if there are serious life consequences at stake, our readiness to acknowledge that the other person may be stuck with a certain factor as constitutional may be in question. Such is often the fate of alcoholics even given certain alleged changes in public opinion in the last fifty years. If a person is what in Alcoholics Anonymous is called a "real alcoholic," as opposed to a "problem drinker" or "heavy drinker," then this person is stuck with something in his or her makeup—whether by "nature's lottery" or "social contingency" does not matter here—that you may not be stuck with and that you may have difficulty recognizing that he or she can really be stuck with.

For example, my friend is as smart a person as I know, and within his professional workplace (commercial art) his talent, skill, judgment, discipline, and willpower are the envy of his colleagues; yet he has been through eighteen treatment centers in as many parts of the country and, in fact, cannot stay sober for more than six months at a time despite sincere and strenuous efforts[21] to sustain sobriety. As near as I can tell, and without taking a stand here about the nature or causes of alcoholism, it is simply true to say that my friend is stuck with a factor in his makeup over which his control is nil or controversial and from which he may one day very well die. To say to such a person "just say no" or its intellectually more sophisticated equivalents is worse than foolish. Apart from whatever may be the latest news from medicine or science about how alcoholism is to be understood, it is plain that some people suffer a life-destroying vulnerability regarding alcohol that others do not.[22]

Regarding the third set of cases, perhaps public opinion is opening a little to the idea that a person can genuinely be stuck with alcoholism[23] and, hence, be unable, consistently and over time, to control himself or herself once alcohol has been ingested.[24] In this instance there is perhaps growing recognition of the differential character of constitutional luck, but in still other cases some of us may have serious difficulties in seeing the troubling factor in the other person's makeup as something he or she can really be stuck with—especially, again, when there are large life consequences at stake.

I think in this connection of a response to the Hedda Nussbaum case, which received so much attention in 1988. The columnist Ellen Goodman wrote the following in December of that year.

> Now the attention is focused on Hedda Nussbaum, this woman whose punching-bag face and battered psyche have been reconstructed into some semblance of normality. . . . Her lover [Joel Steinberg] is the one on trial for the murder of their adopted daughter, Lisa. But public attitudes toward Joel Steinberg have become uncomplicated. . . . It is Nussbaum who has become the morbid target of public fascination.
>
> How did this woman descend to the point where she was unable to defend herself and then—even more terrifying—where she was unable to defend her child? In the days before Lisa's death, Hedda Nussbaum testified that Steinberg threw the girl down repeatedly. "What did you do?" the assistant district attorney asked. "Nothing," she said. "Why not?" he asked. "I'm not really sure," she said.

Goodman titled her column: "Why Didn't She Just Get Out of There?"[25] but she responded to Hedda Nussbaum's inaction in these words:

> This is a woman who oh-so-gradually lost control of her life, until she no longer had the free will to dial 911 while her daughter was dying in her arms. She was subtly and overtly, emotionally and physically, isolated and then destroyed. . . . If Nussbaum is to be believed, Joel Steinberg isolated [her] and cowed her into obedience.[26]

Of course, in some cases involving large life consequences, when individuals are said to be powerless in certain ways, we might suspect some sort of conceptual con job. Somehow the "background stories"[27] meant to make sense of the powerlessness become less easy to recognize and acknowledge. Can we believe that a man who sexually molests a child might be a victim of his nature in the way a constitutionally shy student is a victim of his or her nature?[28] Can we believe that a person who is a compulsive gambler might be a victim in the way in which a person is a victim who is trapped in depression as a result of chemical imbalances known to exist in his or her physiological makeup?[29] It may appear that we are being overloaded with new ways in which persons can be victims. I have read recently not only of post-traumatic stress disorder, but also of battered-woman syndrome, rape-trauma syndrome, child-abuse syndrome, postabortion syndrome, oppression-artifact disorder, victimization disorder, and something called action-addict syndrome, wherein the victim "actually craves dangerous, thrilling situations that psychologically create a parallel state to [some] original trauma."[30] Perhaps it is morally right to say that one must try to play well the cards life deals one. We have always known, of course, that some people are dealt lousy cards (even John Stuart Mill suffered years of depression[31]). At this time, however, we seem to be asked to acknowledge that the deck of lousy cards people can be dealt is larger—indeed, much larger—than we thought. Perhaps some or many things we once thought of as weaknesses to be overcome or psychological blows to be moved past are actually lousy cards people are dealt, by nature or social contingency, and the people stuck with them cannot be expected, through normal means, anyway, to move past them.

I make no effort here to enumerate comprehensively the lousy cards.[32] Some of the lousy cards would be familiar to ordinary experience (stuttering, problems with weight, kleptomania, and perhaps even certain of the obsessive-compulsive disorders); others would be less familiar, and, accordingly, the claims that they are lousy cards, that is, forms of constitutional bad luck, would be found suspect by some or many of us. In this latter category, sex addiction comes to mind,[33] as does factitious disorder (Munchhausen syndrome), whose victims manifest it by continually visiting doctors and seeking entry to hospitals (faking illness, as some call it).[34] Somatization disorder features pain "amplified . . . by psychological mechanisms" and leaves the victim suffering depression and anxiety as well as pain, all of which are unrelated to ascertainable physical ailments.[35] Related to my earlier discussion of the problem of living with one's past, one can suffer tyrannization by one's past, that is, the overwhelming presence of the past in one's life, in a way that diminishes or eliminates one's capacity to move forward in one's life.[36] Further examples of factors viewed by some as elements of constitutional bad luck are professorial melancholy,[37] urgency addiction, and, indeed, maleness, the suffering of which has drawn so many to a men's movement.

In the former category, the melancholy called depression is familiar to ordinary experience. The long-recognized constitutional sort is now called major depression. William Styron tries to capture the "most famous and sinister hallmarks" of his depression (his "illness") in the words "confusion, failure of mental focus and lapse of memory"; he added that his "entire mind would be dominated by anarchic disconnections" and that he endured "something that resembled bifurcation of mood: lucidity of sorts in the early hours of the day, gathering murk in the afternoon and evening."[38] In an essay-review titled "The Inconsolable," Helen Vendler describes depression in the literary figures Randall Jarrell, John Berryman, and Robert Lowell in vocabulary that is less lay-clinical: the negative interiority of depression is characterized as being an "inner grave" and also as involving "nameless yearning," "emptiness," "sadness," and—perhaps most on the mark—"desolate vacancy." For a close friend of mine—a colleague in another field—recurrent depression is personified in a terrifying way: a calm reasonable voice insists repeatedly that (1) he will never feel better, (2) while he is considered a caring person, no one desires or loves him, and (3) the only one who could love him would be a necrophiliac. My friend regards his depression as "pure evil."[39]

To close this section, I should mention that, of course, not all the cards we are dealt are lousy. Some people seem to enjoy a native courage, compassion, and humility that enables them never to be brutalized or even made bitter by life's batterings. They possess, constitutionally, an inner strength that gives them unusual stamina and endurance.[40] Earlier, in note 15 of this chapter, I mentioned a possible positive necessity of the will whereby, if one has it, one may be protected from being taken in by "radical disturbances of judgment";[41] but some cards we are dealt are perhaps mixed—lousy in some ways, positive in others. Michael Ignatieff wrote of Simone Weil, in a worried celebration of her independence of mind, that

> she systematically refused to accept who she was. This insistent quarrel with every inherited feature of her fate—her class, her sex, her Jewishness—kept her wading waist-deep against the current of existence. Such a life left her friends divided between admiration for her courage and alarm at her self-destructiveness.[42]

And one can appreciate, in this matter of mixed cards, the charm of John Updike's hollow self-deprecation:

> So wrapped up in my skin . . . I have, it might be, too little concern to spare for the homeless . . . the unfortunate who figure so largely in the inner passions of smooth-pelted liberals like my first wife. *I* am unfortunate, is my prime thought. . . .[43]

Observations, Issues

Suppose, then, that we are not the uniformly rational, sane, mature, in-control agents assumed by the received conception of persons. Suppose, indeed, that we are creatures who are susceptible to various sorts of circumstantial and constitutional luck, some of it positive relative to the practices that structure our common life, but, too, some of it negative relative to them. In the latter case our different fates—the different sorts of constitutional bad luck we end up with as the results of nature's lottery and social contingency—will work against our being able to meet the terms of the model of the in-control agent in a steady and reliable fashion. What follows from this point? Are we simply to reject the received model of the in-control agent as a general presumption for our dealings with people in ordinary life? If so, what is our replacement general presumption to be? Are we, instead, to retain the received conception but modify or qualify it in some way? If so, what are the modifications or qualifications, and how are they derived, organized, and ordered? Is it possible that our different constitutional fates are so various that, strictly, no general presumption about persons—even one with numerous internal qualifications—is reliable in respect to its fairness to the people we deal with? If so, is the ideal of fairness in one's dealings with others itself ultimately an impossibility?

These are large questions. I end this part of my discussion with some observations and issues, presented with these questions in mind.

First, I notice that I am not the only one worried about the possibility that people may be stuck with factors in their makeup that others have difficulty recognizing as such. In a recent issue of a respected mental health newsletter for the general reader, I find these words:

> retardation . . . usually cannot be treated, although the right kinds of support and education help to improve the lives of the retarded. Many mental health professionals think that something similar is true of personality disorders. Personality is too pervasive and ingrained to change very much. It is also usually ego syntonic, that is, felt by the patient as natural and right, as the essence of what he or she is, rather than as a set of troubling symptoms. Patients may regard attempts to change it as brainwashing or punishment.[44]

Perhaps, then, the mental-health professionals, or some of them, also recognize that persons may be stuck with personality factors that others cannot insist that they change. If these factors make the individuals who have them behave in ways that are out of line with what we expect of the rational, sane, controlled individual, then the stage is set for tragedy, or at least confusion, in our collective life.

Second, I should note that I hold no particular view about the causation of the elements of personality, temperament, or character. Perhaps there are genetic stories to be told in some cases, social-conditioning stories in other cases, and even abuse stories (as in the victimization of Hedda Nussbaum) in still other cases. Some cases may involve more than one of these types of stories. There is much we do not know about how people come to be the ways they are. My point is that however they come to be the ways they are, they may not be able to help being those ways or to move past them, at least not by the normal means we are familiar with (means enlisting accusation, blame, and exhortation) when we follow the received model of persons as rational, sane, in-control agents.[45] I see no a priori reason to suppose either that only genetic factors ("nature's lottery") can explain constitutional luck or that "social contingency" (in the form, say, of abuse, deep social conditioning, or sharp traumatic experiences) cannot be fully effective in impacting personality or temperament.

Third, there are, lurking in this problematic posed by the specter of bad constitutional luck, two different conceptions of the individual agent, conceptions that may be expressed in terms of will and luck, and the choice between them depending (apart from antecedent ideological or philosophical commitments) on one's understanding of the vulnerability or fragility of agency. In one conception—a conception tending to be suspicious of constitutional-luck claims—will is prior to the factors of luck; the latter may be heavy in their influence, but in principle they may be overcome. It thus makes sense for us to hold people to account, and logically people can be urged to control their actions and even change themselves.[46] In the other conception (one that finds the idea of constitutional luck intelligible and takes it seriously), some luck factors may be prior to the will, in the sense that they structure it (they are built into it), rather than influence it. These are true givens for a person. It also may not even make sense, in cases in which a person's behavior is governed by such givens, to urge, cajole, or entreat him or her to exercise the will in an effort to control his or her actions or change his or her self. This second conception does not teach that the human will is fully subscribed by luck factors; it is not a conception that finds persons determined in some wholesale way; it does, though, find that they cannot but be what they are or act as they do in certain respects, that is, in certain activities or aspects of their lives, even as they are fully autonomous in some or many other sections of their lives. It is as if they are selectively determined by factors so powerful in them (as the results, again, of nature's lottery or social contingency) as to *constitute* or *structure* the will itself. This conception recognizes also that a person may be the way he or she is despite wishes and aspirations to the contrary and despite time- and energy-consuming activities directed to change.

Fourth, I have no desire to exaggerate. Even if one favors this second conception, as I do, it remains that not everyone who has a problem is stuck with bad constitutional luck, and even when one is, there are sometimes effective strategies to get around one's bad luck. I am not proposing that all shy people are or should be treated as constitutionally shy, that all drunks are or should be considered to be real alcoholics, that all existential nihilists are or should be seen as suffering major depression, or that all those who procrastinate, lack discipline, or exhibit paranoia are or should be viewed as constitutionally so; indeed, even those who are constitutionally this or that may not in fact remain that way forever. Change can occur. There are cases in which one's depression simply lifts, for example, one's phobia weakens, or one's absorption in one's own past diminishes. The shy person goes public. The hopeless alcoholic falls into AA and, somehow, this time sustains his or her recovery. The victim of abuse becomes a strong, resourceful, clear-headed community leader. That change occurs in some cases seems plain. How all this works is unclear, but that we can in general expect or demand morally, as per the first conception, that people overcome, recover, resist, and do right—as if they were dealing with weaknesses, or the stress that we expect the ordinary in-control person to bear—no longer seems right to me.

The fifth note is a small elaboration of the points above. In the second conception, a person who was, say, a victim of abuse in early and middle childhood might now not only suffer anger, fear, resentment, self-pity, or some combination of these but in fact be stuck with this cluster of negative emotions. The result may be a steady-state mass of bad feeling laced with depression, brooding despair, and generalized apprehension (paranoia), the whole mass quite paralyzing to thought and action. I am well aware that this mass of feeling—this form of emotional sensibility—may indeed be, as the mental-health professions might say, ego syntonic, and thus be temperament-defining to as well as of the individual.

My thought is that one's will can come to be structured by such feeling and that, in effect, one can be powerless over it. In the great meaning-of-life essays collected in *The Will to Believe*, William James's view sometimes appears to be that many of us, beneath the layers of surface opinion and ideology, are of optimistic natural temperament, and this view helps support James's well-known appeals to the legitimacy of "passional nature" in serious life decisions when rationality is inconclusive. There are points, however, at which even James seems to allow that a person's natural temperament might instead be pessimistic (in the manner given in the previous paragraph) and thus carry with it the bleak moral psychology of what were for James the negativities of atheism, subjectivism, materialism, relativism, and nihilism.[47] My own background and experience, much direct experience with alcoholics and adult children of alcoholics, and the absence of convincing a priori argument to the contrary lead me to think that there certainly is something like pessimistic natural temperament, and not only for victims of abuse. When one's temperament is constituted in the way James calls pessimistic, then that temperament is not present to one's will as an item to be challenged and overcome; it is instead in one's will, and it structures one's moral-emotional psychology ab initio.

Are there people whose shyness is constitutional? In the view I am exploring, "yes" is a possible answer, and it is cruel to insist with such a person that he or she overcome shyness. Are the people who get called alcoholics really only problem drinkers or, perhaps, what Fingarette calls heavy drinkers, or are they indeed what AA calls "real alcoholics," that is, people who cannot drink safely, consistently, and over time, no matter how hard they try to control themselves? In the view I am exploring, there are real alcoholics, and the worst thing one can do for them or to them is to try to teach them to drink safely (whatever that could mean). In a similar way, and in the face of the distress the question arouses, one may ask: are there victims of abuse whose constitutional luck is such that they cannot rise to resist their fate when they are encouraged, cajoled, and exhorted to do so by those who wish them well? I think the answer must be "yes" in the view I am exploring, and, again, it would be a form of cruelty to such people to demand of them or urge on them forms of resistance that their nature precludes. In the view I have in mind, the possibility is that the person who is stuck with the mass of feeling including anger, fear, resentment, and so forth that I mentioned, that is, the person for whom such a state is both systemic and ego syntonic, is not a person who can respond to the energizing, morale-lifting strategies of common sense, religion, or front-line psychology—strategies that have indeed been helpful and even inspiring to those not constituted in the same way. The predicament of the person whose natural temperament is deep pessimism is of a different order. In this case the abuse has penetrated more deeply.

The sixth note concerns the troubling question about whether persons can change. I find that the notion that persons cannot change meets with considerable resistance. Our popular culture sometimes seems to teach us that you can be whatever you want to be, though actual formulations of this energizing, open-ended dictum (e.g., in advertisements) sometimes enjoin us only to be what we can be, a totally different idea consistent with the claim that persons cannot change. I have been told that professional therapists have a vested (i.e., economic) interest in the notion that persons can change, but, whatever the belief in the popular culture or among therapists, my point here is the modest one that the claim that persons can change cannot be read off the facts and, to that extent, the claim is a priori. In the language of my earlier sections, the claim is neither an inductive generalization over persons as social and historical particulars nor a conceptual truth about persons so considered. When it is used in our dealings with others and ourselves—often with the best of wishes for them or ourselves—it is an assumption about persons functioning normatively in those dealings, for example, as a part of an argument whereby one person urges or exhorts another to do something about his or her difficulties in life, namely, change the self. Of course, exactly the same things can be said about the claim that people cannot change, were this claim in general form somehow to be substituted for its positive general counterpart. In contrast to both general claims, one person may in fact have x as a part but not a constitutional part of her makeup (personality, temperament, character) and thus be able to take up a project involving exercises of will (e.g., resolutions, disciplined exercises, self-directed harangues) targeting change in or of x directly, but another person may in fact have x as a constitutional part of his makeup and, as a result, not be able to implement such a will-based project of change at all. The facts per se favor neither general claim. The view I favor is an antigeneralization claim. It teaches that some people are stuck with things that other people are not. As a guide for our dealings with others and ourselves, of course, this anti-generalization claim is frustrating, for it complicates life—indeed, perhaps too much so, as I will explore later.

In connection with the view I favor, I notice in the literature of moral theory the appearance of a thesis about the self that is at least consistent with the antigeneralization view and may in fact give it a certain sort of plausibility. I will, following the discussion of Owen Flanagan in *Varieties of Moral Personality*,[48] refer to this as the modularity thesis about the self. Flanagan asks: "Do we believe that a good person is one whose moral understanding and theoretical convictions and commitments govern his powerful inclinations and urges across *all* the domains to which they are applicable?"[49] He answers in the following way:

Moral psychology may be less unified than we typically think, and this not merely because of imperfections in our educational practices but rather because our moral dispositions and abilities are of many different types, with different learning histories, different relations to temperament and rationality, and different susceptibilities to different kinds of external forces.[50]

In this account the self is no unity or univocal competence but, instead, a set, or, indeed, a cluster, of elements (dispositions, competencies, abilities, susceptibilities) the precise ingredients of which may very well be different from person to person. It may even be that some persons lack certain elements in their makeup that are commonly found in others or thought in some general way to be desirable in the makeup of the moral agent, or perhaps they have these elements but in a stunted, diminished, or exaggerated fashion. This allows Flanagan to make the following point, which seems to me to fit well with the "stuckness" thoughts (different people, different vulnerabilities) that I have been elaborating.

> [M]oral gappiness . . . everywhere abounds. Some people are extremely just but imperceptive and uncaring. Others are extremely caring to loved ones but have a parochial view of what justice demands. There are the just intemperates and the immoderately courageous. There are the just cowards and the benevolent but spineless, and so on. You name it, we have them. . . . There are persons with extraordinary self-knowledge who are slow on the interpersonal pick-up. And there are subtle interpretors of the minds of others who, for want of sensitivity or interest, or because of certain defense mechanisms, systematically miss seeing themselves clearly.[51]

The modularity thesis is attractive since in its portrayal of the self as "gappy": (1) it allows intelligibility to the possibility of differential constitutional luck among persons; (2) it goes against a unity model of the self, such as that of the in-control agent (now seen as simplistic); and (3) it lends support to the antigeneralization claim (that some people are stuck with things other people are not) and, hence, loosens the grip on us of the idea that we must choose between the simple generalizations about people either that they can or that they cannot change.[52]

Seventh, if the self is modular and, hence, possibly gappy in real people, then constitutional luck may render a person stuck in a way that goes against his or her being able to change through exercise of the will. The modularity idea, on the level of the metaphysics of the self, allows it to be possible that certain difficulties people have with themselves in the conduct of life are something other than weaknesses to be overcome. As Flanagan suggested regarding persons who are constitutionally shy: "there is no learning theory for such persons in the domain of gregariousness. They are destined to remain gappy in this area."[53] Of course, the words used to make these points—Flanagan's "gappiness," my "stuckness," Frankfurt's "outlaw forces"[54]—are merely suggestive in the manner of metaphors. We may still ask: what is it to be stuck or gappy or to have one's will be subject to outlaw forces? The modular thesis by itself does not provide an account of stuckness, either regarding the phenomenology of its experience for the individual or its causation or even when the application of the notion of stuckness is and is not appropriate. In this seventh note (and in the next section), let me say something about these difficult subjects.

In the first place, stuckness, on the part of the person who suffers it, may or may not be recognized or understood. The victim may be as baffled about it (also, in some cases pained by it, in other cases amused or amazed by it) as the observer operating in the terms of the model of the in-control agent. A recent discussion points out, for example, that

> kleptomania is an irresistible impulse to steal objects of no use or monetary value to the person who steals them. . . . People suffering from kleptomania are often plagued by anxiety or depression and may also suffer from other conditions, such as personality and eating disorders. The causes of kleptomania are unknown. . . . people with kleptomania usually do not seek treatment, because they are ashamed of their behavior or need the habit so much that they are unwilling to stop.[55]

In another discussion, obsessive-compulsive disorder is described in this way:

> People with obsessive-compulsive disorder recognize their obsessions or compulsions as getting in the way of what they want to do. They commonly describe a recurrent behavior or thought as "dumb," "foolish," or "point-less." They view themselves, accurately, as unwilling victims of one of their own mental processes. They typically lose 2–3 hours out of each day complying with demands that they know come from within themselves but still perceive as foreign to their own intentions. People who are severely affected may be virtually unable to do anything else with their lives. . . . *Compulsions* are repeated acts. . . . *Obsessions* are intrusive, disturbing beliefs. . . . The unifying theme in both obsessions and compulsions seems to be an inability to feel *certain* about actions or objects that are associated with some degree of risk or fear. An affected person may lock the door at night, *and fully remember locking it*, yet need to go back time and again to verify that the door is indeed locked. Somehow, the memory of what has happened does not get linked to the belief that it really and truly did happen.[56]

The strain of such disorders for the victim, in the form of the pressure of an awareness of in some ways not making sense, is brought out by these descriptions. It is brought out even more forcefully in some remarks of Frankfurt about outlaw forces, for in the grips of such forces "energies tending toward action inconsistent with [one's] intention remain untamed and undispersed, however decisively the person believes his mind has been made up." One may endorse or identify with "certain elements which are then authoritative for the self," but "this authority may be resisted and even defeated by outlaw forces—desires or motives by which the person does not want to be effectively moved, but which are too strong and insistent to be constrained."[57] One ends up a "helpless bystander to the forces that move [one]."[58]

A second point concerns variety in the makeup of the self. If some or many of us suffer outlaw forces or gappiness, we may inquire into the inner nature of the elements in the self. Here the stuckness I have in mind leads me to recognize diversity of elements and to be very open-minded about how it is that a person can be stuck. If the self is made up in part of powers, dispositions, or competencies, elements such as these are logically vulnerable to being (via nature's lottery or social contingency) blocked, or diminished totally or to one degree or other, or exaggerated to some, perhaps great, extent; insofar as such elements are discrete, one or more of them may be missing in a self; insofar as such elements connect somehow with one another, self-element compromises may be effected,[59] and the resulting powers, dispositions, or competencies may in turn become blocked, diminished, or exaggerated.

A third point is that to speak of gaps, stucknesses, or outlaw forces is not necessarily to speak of just those disorders that send their victims to counseling and therapy. There are lots of features of the ordinary person's morality-relevant psychology that may meet the description "constitutional" but that form no difficulty for the person in the conduct of life, perhaps because no challenge to the person's conduct of life has arisen relative to these elements (as a matter of circumstantial good luck) or because the constitutional features are favorable relative to the persona moralisms the person lives with in his or her commerce with others and to the participation in the practices that structure their common life. If shyness is so deep and severe as to constitute *J* agoraphobic, the constitutional-luck result in this case will almost certainly make for difficulty in *J*'s life in a society of the sort we know. If shyness is modest and limited and constitutes *S* "reserved" in personality or temperament, similar difficulty will not be *S*'s lot, and, in fact, *S* might be the object of respect and appreciation for being the way he or she is. If *H* is quick to find the ridiculous in the things that happen, her wit and insight might be admired. If she insists, however, on finding the ridiculous in the assassination of the president, perhaps she will be thought vicious by some, troubled by others. Examples need not be multiplied. If the self is modular in the way being considered here, there is in that metaphysical fact by itself no reason to suppose that the elements of the self by virtue of which persons may be stuck or gappy or suffer outlaw forces are conceptually all of a piece or psychologically all of the kind psychiatrists or psychologists would classify as disorders.[60]

Finally, let me offer a small speculation, with the aid of some philosophical vocabulary, about the logic of the claims we make, and in some cases find controversial, about persons facing difficulties in the conduct of their lives of the sort under consideration. (1) At one level, armed with the model of the rational, sane, in-control agent, we might see *J* as having a problem with shyness (alcohol, depression), and we might judge—correctly, in this case, as it happens—that *J* ought to take a hand with her life and overcome her problem. Here the overcoming injunction has the ring of duty to it, and the judgment we make—demanding action on the part of *J*—is appropriate relative to what *J* can do relative to her problem. (2) At a second level, *S*'s problem with shyness (alcohol, depression) is different in character, and the appropriate judgment for us and *S* to make, apart from whether in fact it is the judgment we actually make, is that *S*'s taking a hand with his life so as to overcome the problem would be supererogation. The interesting feature of this judgment is that it grants a measure of control to *S* regarding his problem, but it stops short of demanding that *S* overcome his problem via an exercise of will. This judgment grants in its way that for *S* as we know him this problem with shyness (alcohol, depression) might be too hard for him. If *S* does overcome, we will be prepared to admire and congratulate him, but we do not, along the way, expect *S* to overcome, as we do when overcoming is a person's duty. (3) At the third level, we can imagine the case in which we make still another sort of judgment about a person's difficulty. In this case we allow that *T*'s taking a hand with his life to overcome the difficulty would be an impossibility. Accordingly, we now see *T* as without control, and we make no demands on him to change, and we do not think in supererogation terms of the possibility of overcoming.[61] Perhaps our attitudes involve regret rather than blame, and end, in time, in sadness.

In general, I think the proponent of the model of the in-control agent would recognize judgments of sorts (1) and (2) but not (3), regarding persons facing difficulties in the conduct of their lives as the result of the impact of luck on them. This preserves the model's approach to agency as unitary, and keeps the results of luck located logically posterior to the will. Judgments of sort (2) might be the model's limit on acknowledgment of the seriousness of the influence of such factors on the will. The view I favor would recognize judgments of all three sorts. It grants that in some cases the luck factors penetrate the will to the core. The will is structurally altered, not just challenged. Certain forms of action then become practical impossibilities or practical necessities for the person.

On What to Think about Persons

What, then, is the best general conception to have of the individual? Differential constitutional luck, taken seriously, is trouble for moral theory, for it challenges smoothed-out general conceptions of persons that treat the self as unitary. How is one to view and deal with people who do not do what they ought to do or what it would be good for them to do? If constitutional luck is taken seriously, it is difficult to know what to say—in advance of detailed knowledge of the social and historical particularity of individuals—about when the person-to-person moral practices of accusation, generosity, blame, tolerance, compassion, praise, and so on are appropriate.

I see no easy way through the complexity to a view about what would be the best general working conception of the individual for the purposes of everyday life. I find it difficult, of course, to give up the conception of the ordinary adult individual as a rational, sane, autonomous agent, more or less in command of his or her faculties as a presumption for conduct; but I am moved by the specter of constitutional luck to become wary of that familiar presumption. It is too easily used—by me on others and by me on myself. It may be that there are background stories behind the behavior of others and myself that should affect the expectations I have of them or myself, the demands I make of them or myself, and the advice I offer them or myself. People are, in part, anyway, their histories, and these histories may contain genetic, social-conditioning, and even abuse factors of which I know little or nothing or, in my own case, about which I deceive myself or suffer misunderstanding.

If one believes in the reality of differential constitutional luck, is there a normative message regarding how one should live or, at any rate, how one should think about others and oneself in the conduct of one's life? (The working out of this message is one of the main tasks of this book.) My first thought about this message, when I take the specter of constitutional luck seriously, is a gentle one: it is that while we still must make our moral judgments about what goes on in the world, we could be easier on the people around us. We could move less quickly to judgment. In a small reading and meditation book I use, the following words appear and seem in line with the gentleness idea:

> Try never to judge. . . . Each mind is so different, actuated by such different motives, controlled by such different circumstances, influenced by such different sufferings, you cannot know all the influences that have gone to make up a personality.[62]

Also on the side of gentleness, Bill Wilson, the cofounder of AA, wrote in his powerful commentary on the Twelve Steps: "Finally, we begin to see that all people, including ourselves, are to some extent emotionally ill as well as frequently wrong, and then we approach true tolerance and see what real love for our fellows actually means."[63]

My second thought, however, adds worry and caution, for even as we take constitutional luck seriously, cases come immediately to mind in which gentleness, compassion, and generosity would not, in life in the real world, be advised, or the stereotypical actions of gentleness, compassion, and generosity might not, at any rate, be safe. Lynne McFall, in her novel *The One True Story of the World*,[64] has her main character, Jesse, reflect on her dealings with people she had known in these words: "Everyone's life was the scene of some terrible accident. And if you didn't know what that accident was, you were just looking for trouble without being able to see it coming." As a result of constitutional luck, the lives of many people may be, in effect, scenes of terrible accidents. The lives of others may be, of course, scenes of fortunate accidents. For still others, perhaps most of us, our lives are scenes involving accidents of both sorts to one degree or other; but whatever the mix of kinds of accidents, it remains that the people who suffer them can be dangerous. In some cases, a person's fate at the hands of constitutional luck may involve the dominance of depression, addiction, or disorder, and our hearts go out to such a person and we want to encourage recovery. In other cases, a person's fate at the hands of constitutional luck may be marked by the dominance of anger, viciousness, or, indeed, very powerful ego, and self-protection requires, in our lives with such a person, something other than the actions that usually go with gentleness, compassion, and generosity. If we are victims of constitutional luck, it does not follow that we are helpless, unthreatening, or eager to change.

The specter of constitutional luck arouses different reactions in our public discussion. Some find it something to ridicule and propose that we not cater to those who do not do what they should do by regarding them as victims. Charles Krauthammer worries about "psychiatry's role in undermining the law."[65] George F. Will finds that our "social atmosphere is heavily dosed" with "assumptions" that people are "creatures of accidents, formed by impersonal forces" and objects to our "delicately sensitive" response, which he labels "the reflexive rhetoric of perfunctory compassion."[66] Another commentator, of course, might bemoan our lack of compassion in his or her ruminations on issues that have the specter of constitutional luck behind them. Mike Royko finds that too many of us have an attitude that "brings back memories of the famous Daniel Moynihan phrase: benign neglect. Live and let live. Or live and let die." He adds: "Well, maybe that's a subtle form of war."[67] Still another commentator might seek a middle position, as if the issue is to get between viewing persons as victims or in-control agents. Richard Cohen writes: "it's important that we all be held responsible for our actions and not create a society of victims. But it's important, too, that we strike some sort of balance."[68]

Some might find my discussion above a tedious elaboration of nonsense—at best, a sort of philosophical pop psychology, and about as intellectually reputable—and resolve to defend the model of the in-control agent as the best general working conception of how persons are for ordinary life. One might argue, for example, (1) that to reject the familiar model is to discourage people's honest efforts to change (if they need to change) and to let them settle too soon for being what they are; (2) that in any case the received model is true enough often enough of the people we deal with in ordinary life; and (3) that for the few for whom negative or positive constitutional-luck factors need to be taken into account, we can in any case, if somehow fairness requires it, work up a theory of exceptions or exemptions to tack on to the received model of the in-control agent.

My thoughts about such defenses are probably predictable from the discussion above. If the point in (1) is that it is risky or dangerous to let go of the model of the in-control agent, my response is that simply to keep it is to continue the cruelty of holding some people to account in ways their nature precludes. If there is a danger in rejecting the familiar model, there is a danger in retaining it. I do not see that this worry about consequences settles the issue one way or the other. Regarding (2)—the notion that the received model is true enough often enough—I have empirical doubts. For whatever it may be worth, I find that the model of the in-control agent is often wrong. Even if it were wrong only some-times, that is not itself positive reason for retaining it as a general presumption about how people are for use in ordinary life. If the model of the in-control agent treats the self as unitary, but in fact the self is modular, then even if the received model often works, it is mistaken about how persons are, and one might suppose that that would be reason enough to search for a more adequate understanding of persons.

The last point, (3), concerning the possibility of supplementing the received model with a theory of exceptions and exemptions, seems to me interesting but at worst conceptually self-defeating and at best both difficult to implement and possibly morally harsh in practice. Suppose you have not come forward to make a public protest when morality requires it of someone in your circumstances, and we are given to understand that this is so because you are shy. Now, how is the model of the in-control agent to decide whether this consideration about you exempts you or makes you an exception to the imperatives of moral responsibility for in-control agents in this case? On the one hand, if the proponent of the model saves the exemptions or exceptions for those who are constitutionally shy, then the possibility is granted that the self is not unitary in the manner supposed by the model, and the question about whether we should treat the model as our working presumption about people becomes serious. In effect, the view of the self in the theory of exceptions or exemptions is in conflict with the view of the self in the model itself. On the other hand, if the in-control-agent model does not recognize the stuckness, gappiness, or outlaw forces that are the residue of the different sorts of constitutional luck, then it must have means by which to figure out whether your shyness is merely a difficulty, such that you should overcome it and rise to the imperatives of morality in this case, or, instead, a deep difficulty for you, such that your overcoming it must be regarded as an act of supererogation and, hence, cannot be morally required of you. How this figuring out is to get done is unclear. This is also true, of course, if one grants structural impacts on the will resulting from the forms of constitutional luck. I also suspect, however, that an approach to the figuring-out task in particular cases that assumes a priori that people's difficulties are never constitutional in their depth stacks the deck against people somehow. I suspect that, in practice, few difficulties would be viewed as deep, and that generosity in the form of the suspension of moral demands when overcoming would be acknowl-edged to be supererogatory would be rare. When holding people to account is the rule and the possibility of unmanageable internal factors is excluded a priori, even the gentleness that is linked to the recognition of supererogation would atrophy.

I thus find these defenses of the received model of the in-control agent inconclusive. It does not follow that I see no problems with the general view that acknowledges the reality of structural impacts on the will resulting from luck. There are different sorts of problems. In the first place, this view, in practice, must recognize that there is a practical epistemological problem of figuring out in particular cases whether people's difficulties are to be regarded merely as difficulties (and, hence, overcoming may be required), deep difficulties (and, hence, overcoming is supererogatory), or constitutional vulnerabilities, that is, difficulties rooted in structural blockages (e.g., stuckness, gappiness, outlaw forces) in the will (and, hence, overcoming is not possible). The view that the self is modular and the further view that the modules may be fixed as a result of background luck stories of one sort or other do not themselves yield practical rules for classifying particular cases. Even though I believe we make in ordinary life the distinctions that this general view recognizes, how we do so I am not able to express in formulas.[69] It seems plain that the soundness of our judgments in this connection has to do with how well we know the person we judge, and this notion of knowing a person well indeed covers many things, for example, length of time, depth of acquaintance, the nature of our own experience, our open-mindedness to difference, and so on. On the whole, it seems that one knows very few people well. This is probably not surprising in circumstances in which the model of the in-control agent prevails, for in those circumstances one typically hides, disguises, or denies those vulnerabilities, if one is aware of them, whereby one is out of line with the received model.

In the second place, there remains a practical problem about how ready we need to be in real life with our acknowledgments that the problems people have are grounded in constitutional vulnerabilities. Even if some people have a problem with gambling or alcohol such that with them we face people suffering constitutional fates different from our own, it does not follow that we must regard the next person we meet with gambling or alcohol problems as constitutionally stuck with the relevant vulnerabilities. Negotiating life with others is not that easy—the next person may be faking. In the view in question, people are different, and some are constitutionally different from others; but it does not follow that if one person is constitutionally a certain way—for example, shy at a certain level—and thus has life difficulties of kind S, then anyone who has life difficulties of kind S is constitutionally shy at that or any level. This general view does not teach us to be uncritical or gullible in how we read the behavior and understand the makeup of the people we deal with, including ourselves.

Finally, this general view faces the major problem of how to formulate it as a general presumption about how persons are for use in the conduct of life. If selves are modular and the deep givens of selves may differ from person to person, then what operational view of persons is appropriate in everyday life? Suppose I resolve to govern my treatment of others and myself without the simplism that others and I are uniformly in-control agents (although some may be that way to some extent in some stretches of experience). The modular view (different persons, different vulnerabilities) is not an alternative or replacement simplism. If anything, it is a warning against simplisms in the matter of our treatment of persons and ourselves. The only general maxim the view suggests for ordinary life is one enjoining us to know well those we deal with; but, of course, while this is recognizable and perhaps familiar as moral advice (the stuff of platitudes), it takes little reflection on the busy lives of real people to realize that it is unworkable as a general maxim for conduct: in fact, we cannot know well all or even many of the people we must deal with not because we are evil or weak but merely because we are epistemologically finite; there are too many such people, too little time available to master the details of lives and selves, and too much else to do. Given the modular understanding of persons suggested above, what is morally required of us in ordinary life is a practical, if not logical, impossibility.

Chapter 4

On Living with Others

It sometimes happens that in the most searching self-examination we can find nothing except the moral ground of duty which could have been powerful enough to move us to this or that good action and to such great sacrifice. But from this we cannot by any means conclude with certainty that a secret impulse of self-love, falsely appearing as the idea of duty, was not actually the true determining cause of the will. For we like to flatter ourselves with a pretended noble motive, while in fact even the strictest examination can never lead us entirely behind the secret incentives. . . .

Kant, *Foundations of the Metaphysics of Morals*

For all liberal societies are premised on a contractual understanding of the social order, which requires that the parties to the contract be understood as rational, in control of their passions, and responsible for the consequences of what they do. These are often stern requirements. To adhere to them, we expect people to rise above external temptation and internal weakness of will. Is it fair to have such expectations of the very poor, whose conditions of life seem so far removed from the traditions of Protestant rectitude out of which contractual liberalism grew?

Alan Wolfe, "The New American Dilemma"

Human beings are never quite alike. . . .

Twelve Steps and Twelve Traditions

The Moral Problem of Personal Justice

The point touched on just above at the end of the previous chapter leaves us with a large practical problem within our moral life. Gather together the following themes from the discussion I have offered so far: (1) the

99

perspective on persons that regards them as social and historical particulars, (2) the conception of the self as modular, and (3) the view that
persons can, in different respects and to different degrees, be stuck or
gappy or subject to outlaw forces regarding some elements of personality
and temperament. These themes are suggestive regarding how we should
think about the persons, including ourselves, we deal with in ordinary
life. Insofar as these themes emphasize the individuality of persons and
also the differences among them (some of which may be constitutional),
they bear on our conceptions of justice and fairness as these conceptions
structure our thoughts concerning the morality of our treatment of
persons. By "treatment" here I mean to include our general attitudes
toward others and ourselves, as well as our overt behavior toward them.
The discussion that follows concerns chiefly what conception should
inform those general attitudes.

The practical problem is this: these themes emphasizing individuality
and difference suggest that morally we must know well those we deal
with in ordinary life, but if, as I suggested at the end of chapter 3, this is
a practical impossibility for epistemologically finite people, many of
whom lead busy lives, then we must ask: given persons as they are—
particular, different, finite—what general attitudes toward others and
ourselves should we have? In shorter form: what should be our conception of person-to-person fairness? I call this the moral problem of
personal justice. It seems to be a very important normative issue for individuals.

The discussion above emphasizes that others may be different from me
in important ways and that they may be stuck with certain of their
differences from me in ways or to degrees that I may not understand
from experience. Whatever general attitude I have toward persons must
rest on a conception of personal justice that allows for such possibilities.
It must allow, for example, for the possibility that J is constitutionally
shy, that S is alcoholic, that T is self-centered (constitutionally so and to
a degree that makes T very irritating to deal with in ordinary life), and
that H is prone to periods of a sort of despair that is just short of what a
trained clinician would label major depression. Not only must my general
attitudes make allowances for these possibilities, they must also allow for
the variety of self-referential stances my colleagues in life adopt toward
their own makeups. Perhaps D realizes that she is alcoholic or prone to
despair or both and perhaps, as a consequence, she has adopted certain
strategies meant to help people like her negotiate life.[1] Alternatively,
perhaps D has been offered such strategies or had them urged on her by
friends but she decided to refuse them or she attempted to follow them

only to discover that she was unable to do so with conviction. In still another alternative, perhaps *D* realizes such facts about herself but covers them up, knowing she is doing so, and, as it happens at this time in her life, succeeding in doing so with others. In yet another alternative, she might deny these facts about herself, that is, suppress them, not fully aware she is doing so and only half-succeeding in keeping others from noticing them. Finally, she might simply not realize these facts about herself and thus live her life (quite used to how she is) bereft of compensating strategies, doing the best she can. This variety of self-referential postures could be elaborated and expanded—many nuances and layers are possible—though I will not do so here. It is enough to see that when the variety of self-referential postures is piled on the initial considerations about what our general attitude must allow, namely, particularity and difference, the moral problem of personal justice becomes complicated and formidable.

In what follows I offer some remarks about person-to-person fairness. I do not pretend that what I say provides a solution to the problem of personal justice. I simply try to get as far as I can toward the development of an account of a usable conception of personal justice. Some philosophical literature seems to suggest that the key notions to be understood in developing a normative account of our attitudes in our life with others are those of tolerance and generosity. What follows might be thought of as an effort to understand how the positive other-regarding attitudes of tolerance and generosity are to be understood when one approaches them with the themes in mind that I explored earlier—the themes emphasizing the individuality of and differences among persons considered as social and historical particulars.

I begin with discussion in the following three sections of recent views I have found helpful regarding the ideas of tolerance and generosity.

Justice Individualized

When John Rawls's *A Theory of Justice* appeared in 1971,[2] it provided a perspective on social justice that has since dominated discussion in political philosophy, moral theory, and philosophy of law. Some philosophers viewed Rawls's theory as essentially correct and proceeded to apply it to issues not directly addressed in the book itself. Others found Rawls's view to be importantly mistaken, for example, in its Kantian underpinnings, in its claims about which principles are the principles of justice, or in the extent to which it actually presupposes the form of liberalism it aims to justify. Still others found Rawls's view to be on the right track but to need qualifications, refinements, less reliance on the contractualist apparatus, or an alternative strategy of argument. Whatever the degree of agreement or disagreement, the focus was on the Rawlsian theory, and, in effect, the Rawlsian way of construing what, in general, justice is came to set the terms of the contemporary discussion.

Let us notice first how justice is thought of in the mainstream contemporary discussion, that is, the discussion for which the Rawlsian view set the terms. Here a philosophical theory of justice is supposed to have at its center a substantive conception of justice, which is construed as a set of principles that applies to what Rawls calls the basic structure of society. In short, justice is viewed as a property of institutions and practices—or, at any rate, those main, important, central institutions and practices that provide the choice-affecting framework for individual lives.[3] What justice so conceived does is constrain[4] the operations of the institutions and practices that make up society's basic structure, and in that way the society that is just or aspires to be just has or comes to have a certain direction, form, or shape to it. It has, according to Rawls, for example, a "tendency to equality."[5] The central tasks of a philosophical theory of justice are thus (1) to formulate the principles in the set of principles constituting the theory's conception of justice, (2) to show how they are ordered or arranged relative to each other, and then (3) to show what justification for them is available.

After nearly a decade of discussion devoted to a philosophical agenda concerning justice set by Rawls's book, materials began to appear that tended to dispute that agenda at a deep level. One discussion that does this and seems helpful to me in the matter of how person-to-person fairness is to be understood is that of J. R. Lucas in *On Justice*.[6] Let me list some points of contrast between Rawls's approach to justice, and that of Lucas.

In the first place, the Rawlsian-centered discussion takes the subject of justice (i.e., what the conception of justice is to apply to) to be, again, the basic structure of society[7]; but for Lucas the subject of justice (what justice applies to) is more nearly the individual case. In general, according to Lucas, justice has to do with deciding something about how an individual is to be treated, and, in particular, it is that way of deciding something about how a person is to be treated that is such that that person can then identify with the decision because all the relevant factors in his or her case have been taken into consideration. While the mainstream discussion is dominated by a concern for basic-structure justice, Lucas's account emphasizes individual-case justice: "Justice demands not merely that we treat like cases alike, but equally important, that we treat different cases differently."[8] In elaboration:

> Equal treatment is often unfair . . . because it fails to do justice to the individual's case. It is not enough that [the individual] should be treated the same as other people similarly situated: it is also required that proper account should be taken of the difference between cases, and that all, and not merely some, of the relevant factors should be taken into consideration in determining what treatment should be accorded to the individual in question. Else his individuality is being denied. He is being treated merely as one of a lump, not in the full particularity of his own case. Only if his treatment is differentiated in the light of the features of his case, can he feel that the decision is one he could himself identify with, since only then is there no relevant factor which has not been taken into consideration, and which, had it been taken into consideration might have had a bearing on the result.[9]

In the second place, the Rawlsian-centered discussion takes the justice that applies to the subject of justice (the basic structure of society) to be, again, a conception of justice, that is, a set of principles that philosophy is to identify, order, and justify[10]; but for Lucas the justice that applies to the subject of justice (the individual case) is not anything very like a set of principles at all; it is instead something much more procedural and attitudinal and like a state of mind. While indeed we may speak of laws, individual decisions, or general economic arrangements as just or unjust, these are for Lucas derivative uses of the notion of justice. They are uses that derive "from the man in a just frame of mind and the laws he would enact, the decisions he would take, the economic arrangements he would approve of and the particular payments he would make. Justinian and Aquinas were right in characterizing justice as a certain state of mind."[11]

What state of mind is justice? For Lucas it is that state of mind in which we are prepared to treat different cases differently and to treat the individual "as tenderly as possible," yet in which we are prepared as well "to take a tough line" when "sufficiently compelling reasons" obtain (e.g., when favorable treatment would yield unfairness to others).[12] In this account, those theorists who construe justice as a set of principles that philosophy can undertake to formulate, order, and justify through argument make a serious mistake. In their effort to fix justice in the form of a static set of principles for "the assignment of benefits, responsibilities and burdens," they fail to see that justice is instead an attitudinal "dynamic equilibrium under tension," whereby we struggle to be not only "impartial as between all parties" but also "impartially partial to all parties."[13]

This last point leads to the third and perhaps most striking contrast of those I list here. In the mainstream discussion, again, the conception of justice that philosophy seeks is thought of as substantive; that is, the principles that make up the conception are to have content enough to be able to set social directions for change, provide bases for moral criticism of institutions and practices, and guide efforts at social reform. The conception provides this content not only by specifying an interpretation for the principles associated with the values that constitute justice (e.g., liberty, equality, and fraternity[14]) but also by ordering those principles in a certain way, that is, weighting them so that one may tell which is prior to or more important than others.[15] The very idea of a conception of justice at work in the mainstream discussion construes justice as internally systematic. When a conception of justice (a set of principles) interprets values and puts them together in a certain order, that is, when justice is rendered internally systematic, it is then substantive, for it then provides guidance by selecting between courses of action.

As I read Lucas's account, though, the justice he has in mind is in an important sense non-systematic. Our struggle to be impartial but also impartially partial is in fact conducted without the benefit of an independently ascertained set of ordered principles. There is nothing prior to the individual case except the state of mind I described above. We are to look sympathetically for relevant factors in the individual case, and then we are to take account of them; but we do not have such factors interpreted or ordered in any special way before we peer into this individual case—and, indeed, to the pressing question of how relevant factors (e.g., needs, status, merit, entitlement, deeds, agreements) are to be ranked, Lucas replies that "there is . . . no single over-all answer":

> Different distinctions need to be drawn in different associations, and with regard to the different benefits to be distributed or burdens to be imposed. *All we can argue in general* is that while justice requires us to treat like cases alike, it requires us also to frame our rules so as to take account of relevant differences, and to respond to them accordingly.[16]

Lucas acknowledges that "we find it difficult to be content with such untidiness" and that "we yearn for a unified over-all system of justice, which shall determine what each of us is worth and give him then his due,"[17] but there is nevertheless an important purpose to his insistence on the nonsystematic character of justice. It is that the individuality of the actual persons caught up in individual cases is to be respected even by the theory of justice itself. The critical point is that when philosophers seek to develop a systematic conception of justice, they circumscribe justice.[18] A heavily egalitarian conception of justice, for example, "abridges reason, and therefore justice itself, but also the range of concern."[19] It narrows the variety of relevant factors and makes important aspects of individual cases unimportant and sometimes even inadmissible. For Lucas, this is perhaps the most serious fault in the approach to justice that prevails in the mainstream discussion. He holds that the idea of justice is not internally systematic in the way assumed by the mainstream discussion.

This leads on, naturally enough, to a fourth point of contrast between Lucas's approach to justice and that of the mainstream discussion. It concerns why justice is important. If the question of importance is put to Rawls, I take it that he answers that the importance of justice (basic-structure justice) is that through the principles that make up the conception of justice each member of society is given "an inviolability . . . that even the welfare of society as a whole cannot override."[20] Now, there are different interpretations of this famous doctrine of Rawls's, and with some of them Lucas may very well agree; nevertheless, Lucas's main answer to the question of why justice is important runs in another direction. At the very end of his book Lucas writes:

> Justice by itself . . . does not make a man happy or fulfilled, and is no guarantee of salvation in this world or the next. . . . Nevertheless, it is not to be despised. It may not be everything, but it is something. It is a virtue, an important virtue, one of the cardinal virtues, for it is *the bond of peace*, which enables the individual to identify with society, and brethren to dwell together in society.[21]

Early in the book, how justice provides "the bond of peace" is spelled out in this interesting fashion:

> I can be happy to be one of We, if We are just, because then We will treat Me as well as reasonably possible; and We will be happy to have Me as one of Us, because We know that I, being just, will see things from Our point of view, and will not exclude wider considerations from My assessment of the situation, and will not construe everything in terms of My own exclusive self-interest. I can be sure that We will do well by Me, and We can count on My behaving as a member of the community should. There is . . . no dissension, in the just society. . . . And so you and I and all of us can live together in harmony and peace, each easily identifying with everyone else,

because we all recognize the individuality of each, and respect his interests, and will cherish his interests as he would himself.[22]

With the hope that the above remarks convey something of the character of the individualizing of justice in Lucas's view, let me next point to a certain question that is raised but not addressed by his theory of justice. According to Lucas, justice is a state of mind in which we are to make decisions about the treatment of individuals with which they could (or should if they are reasonable) identify, and it thus enables us to live together in peace; however, justice is also, Lucas's account suggests, nonsystematic—and, hence, nonsubstantive in the manner I sketched above. A question thus arises. It is a question about how far we want—or need—justice to be substantive. From another angle, it is a question about how far or to what extent we may expect a philosophical account of justice to be able to be detailed in its claims about the guidance that justice provides for our decision making in real cases.

If, as Lucas says, "circumstances alter cases, and . . . we fail to do justice unless we recognize that fact, and take into account all the relevant factors in each individual case,"[23] then, clearly, what we need to know in order to do justice is how this taking into account of relevant factors is to proceed. An account of this, I think, is what we would ask a philosophical theory of justice to provide. It is not enough, however, to satisfy this need to learn that justice is a state of mind in which to approach decision making in individual cases, nor does it satisfy this need to list procedural directives (what Lucas calls "rules of natural justice," such as "no man is to be judge in his own case" or "hear all sides of an issue"), as Lucas himself acknowledges.[24] What is needed to make guidance available is the substance of ordered principles, that is, the sort of content that is sought after by the participants in the Rawlsian-centered discussion who attempt to develop and justify a conception of justice that interprets and orders values and that thus, among other things, ranks what Lucas calls "relevant factors." It is substance of this sort that Lucas claims is unavailable or, more exactly, that he claims it would be wrong to establish independently of individual cases, for to do so would be to circumscribe justice. The cost we incur if we follow Lucas here is that the theory of justice at a certain point (just beyond the list of procedural rules of natural justice) is empty. It says nothing in advance of individual cases about how values are to be interpreted and ordered or about which relevant factors are more important than others.

This seems to be a troubling result. I do not know how to show that Lucas is mistaken on the point, but I observe that he does not himself argue for his claim that justice is nonsystematic in the way I have reported. His claim, again, is that substantive conceptions of justice circumscribe justice, but my thought is that this claim only assumes that justice is nonsystematic and does not argue that it is. Of course, those on the other side, who develop and attempt to justify a certain substantive conception, first assume that the contents of justice may somehow be ascertained and do not argue that this is so.

On the one hand, we may want—in fact, need—the guidance of a substantive conception of justice in practice, but it does not follow from this that there is such a thing as the correct substantive conception. On the other hand, a given theorist's conception of justice may indeed circumscribe justice, but it does not follow from this that there is no such thing as the correct substantive conception of justice. Lucas's discussion presses on us a deep initial question about how justice is to be thought of: is justice to be construed as of the nature of an independently ascertainable position on the interpretation and ordering of selected values for the basic structure of society, or is it to be construed as of the nature of a state of mind in which we arrive at decisions only as a result of judgment and wisdom in individual cases. What I want to be so is for justice to be individualized in the manner suggested by Lucas's account, but that individualized justice be substantive in a way that philosophy can help reveal.

A Note on the Subject of Justice

Before proceeding with an effort to make individualized justice substantive, it might be worth noting one other feature of the issue between Rawls and Lucas. According to the discussion above, Rawls treats the subject of justice as the basic structure of society, while Lucas treats the subject of justice as the individual case. Lucas's theory, as I interpret it, individualizes justice, and I find myself interested in this approach since it appears to fit with my earlier resolve to discuss our moral life in a way that keeps in mind the social and historical particularity of persons and, hence, emphasizes the individuality of and differences among persons as we know them in ordinary life.

Rawlsian theory is, of course, not unaware of the idea of individual case justice. At one point in *A Theory of Justice*, Rawls writes in the following way about the difference between "principles for institutions" and "principles for individuals":

[T]he principles of natural duty and obligation that apply to individuals . . . would be chosen in the original position. They are an essential part of a conception of right: they define our institutional ties and how we become bound to one another. The conception of justice as fairness is incomplete until these principles have been accounted for. . . . Now the choice of principles for individuals is greatly simplified by the fact that the principles for institutions have already been adopted. The feasible alternatives are straightway narrowed down to those that constitute a coherent conception of duty and obligation when taken together with the two principles of justice. . . . Taking any natural duty by itself, the reasons favoring its adoption are fairly obvious. At least it is evident why these duties are preferable to no similar requirements at all. Although their definition and systematic arrangement is untidy, there is little question that they would be acknowledged. The real difficulty lies in their more detailed specification and with questions of priority: how are these duties to be balanced when they come into conflict, either with each other or with obligations, and with the good that can be achieved by supererogatory actions? There are no obvious rules for settling these questions. . . . I do not know how this problem is to be settled, or even whether a systematic solution formulating useful and practicable rules is possible. It would seem that the theory for the basic structure is actually simpler. Since we are dealing with a comprehensive scheme of general rules, we can rely on certain procedures of aggregation to cancel out the significance of the complicating elements of particular situations once we take the larger long-term view.[25]

These remarks suggest, then, that for Rawls principles for institutions come before principles for individuals. This is to say that basic-structure justice is prior to individual-case justice.[26] Lucas, of course, wants to place individual-case justice before basic-structure justice. That, at any rate, seems the force of his criticism that the mainstream (Rawlsian) discussion of justice circumscribes justice and treats derivative uses of the notion of justice (those concerning laws, general economic arrangements, etc.) as primary. This issue between Rawls and Lucas seems to be the question, "Which comes first: individual-case justice or basic-structure justice?"

Curiously, while there is a difference between Rawls and Lucas over which comes first, they both appear to agree that individual-case justice, when considered in itself and in isolation from other things, is nonsystematic, that is, not substantive. Lucas responds to this logical fact by saying, in effect, "that's a hard fact, but so be it." Rawls, though, responds to this fact by, in effect, finding in it a reason for placing basic-structure justice before individual-case justice. When we do this, we then are able to tidy up the messy, nonsystematic fact and, again, "cancel out the significance of the complicating elements of particular situations."[27] For Rawls, then, we render workable the issues of individual duty by approaching them with a worked-out conception of justice for the basic structure of society. Lucas, of course, finds this tidying-up process objectionable: it is a way of circumscribing individual-case justice, that is, a way of disguising or ignoring possibly relevant particularities in individual cases or of marking as relevant certain particularities in them that need not or should not be so considered.

In this account the issue between Rawls and Lucas is philosophically deep. The leading "which comes first" question about the subject of justice cannot be answered quickly or briefly. There seem to be different visions of justice at stake: one occupied with the problem of a design for the framework of institutions and practices within which individuals lead lives, the other occupied with the character of the individual's state of mind in dealing with others, and perhaps himself or herself, in the conduct of life. The Rawlsian move is to undertake to solve the design problem first, suggesting that this will give us what we need to solve the person-to-person problem. Lucas warns that to make that move is to circumscribe justice and thus to lose sight of relevant particularities in our dealings with others and ourselves.

My concern here is not to resolve the "which comes first" issue between Rawls and Lucas. I do not see how to do that without moving to extended discussion in the theory of justice. My interest is in the problem of personal justice that I indicated earlier, and hence my attention goes to the point of agreement in the views of Rawls and Lucas, namely, that justice individualized by itself is not systematic or substantive. I still want to know what person-to-person fairness requires of me as I deal with the persons around me, especially given my emphases in the earlier discussion on individuality and difference. After all, my earlier discussion suggests to me that there is unfairness in the common assumption that persons are in-control agents. This makes me suspicious of the Rawlsian move, whereby justice for individuals is viewed as posterior to justice for institutions, for two reasons. First, it would tempt us to approach individual cases with the conceptions of persons associated with just institutions already in mind, and this, my earlier discussion warns, risks committing possibly unjustified persona moralism in individual cases. Second, it seems incredible to me to suppose that I must work out a solution to the problem of justice for the basic structure of society as a condition of having an account of what person-to-person fairness requires of me in ordinary life, that is, that my understanding of what morality requires of me in my treatment of others and myself must wait on my understanding of what morality requires of the structure of society. Also, I do not wish to join Rawls and Lucas in supposing that personal justice in itself is nonsystematic or not substantive, for this seems to be to suppose that the idea of person-to-person fairness has little or no content of its own, and this does not seem right to me.

One other comment here. The Rawlsian theory of justice not only recommends a conception of justice for the basic structure of society; it also recommends a way of theorizing about (i.e., locating) the substance of the idea of justice when the subject of justice is considered to be the basic structure of society. One distinctive part of the proposed way of theorizing involves our thinking about principles for the subject of justice from the perspective of parties to an original position, that is, from the perspective of a specially credentialed choosing position for moral principles—a position whose features, as Rawls develops them, provide a heuristic interpretation of the moral idea of impartiality or disinterestedness. The principles that are the products of this original-position thinking are to be compared to the principles that stand behind the considered judgments we make in the context of specific moral issues, and then all elements in this elaborate construction are qualified or manipulated, if necessary, to achieve a coherence among them that Rawls calls "reflective equilibrium." Can this distinctive approach be brought to bear on what I call the moral problem of personal justice? That is, can we develop a substantive conception of justice giving content to the notion of person-to-person fairness by use of Rawlsian reflective-equilibrium reflection?

This is an intriguing possibility. In the next section I explore a view that may be interpreted as taking such a suggestion seriously, but here I note three things. First, nowhere in *A Theory of Justice*[28] is there discussion of the issues of problematic agency that I emphasized in my earlier discussion. Second, if parties to the original position are to be aware of such issues—in particular, of the difficulties for thought and action arising from the facts of differential constitutional luck among real people, including the unmanageable internal factors I pointed to with terms such as "gappiness," "stuckness," and "outlaw forces"—I cannot tell from Rawls's text how they think about them or whether they find them necessary to take into account in their deliberations about the substance of justice for the basic structure of society. Third, I am left with the worry that the general proposal that we make use of original-position thinking and reflective-equilibrium reflection in our attempts to locate the content of major moral ideas may not settle anything regarding the substance of the idea of person-to-person fairness. Whether the

Rawlsian strategy for moral theorizing would be fruitful regarding a conception of personal justice remains to be discovered.

Toleration without Equal Liberties

Historically, a source of views concerning tolerance and in some cases generosity has been liberalism. In this section I examine a recent study of liberalism by a sympathetic critic, a critic who wishes to enable liberalism to overcome certain problems in its formulation. Vinit Haksar, in *Equality, Liberty, and Perfectionism*,[29] makes clear his respect for the liberal tradition, or that part of it that he calls "the liberal-egalitarian philosophy" or "egalitarianism with liberal implications," even as he is a critic of the versions of liberalism of, among others, John Stuart Mill, John Rawls, and Ronald Dworkin. The liberal tradition that Haksar respects yet wants to improve is the tradition in which equality and liberty are considered cardinal values for the political order. Its main figures address the questions of how equality and liberty are to be understood, how they are related, and, above all, how they can be effectively implemented in the life of society so as to allow for diversity of individual answers to the central personal question of how one is to live a human life.

In fact, it is definitional of the liberalism Haksar discusses that it endorses toleration of a great diversity of individual answers to that question. Equality and liberty may be cardinal values for liberalism, but the flourishing of individuality is its point. The theoretical interest of Haksar's work is that if he is right, a philosophically adequate liberal egalitarianism requires conceptual elements of a kind that main figures in the liberal tradition often wish to reject in the name of a toleration that prizes individuality. Haksar calls these required elements "perfectionist considerations." His thesis is that a defensible liberalism will contain equality, liberty, and perfectionism, but this does not mean that liberalism should be rebuilt as a cluster of three distinct and separable values or doctrines. The theme is rather that perfectionism is not only to be added to the liberal's doctrines of equality and liberty but is also to be found in those doctrines themselves.

In general, I find that Haksar makes two kinds of points about how a defensible liberalism requires perfectionism. (1) In some cases his claim is that perfectionism is involved in the foundations of familiar liberal doctrines, such as those of equality and liberty, and here his aim is not to dispute the substance of liberal doctrines but to show the inadequacy of rationales for them that attempt to do without perfectionist considerations. (2) In other cases Haksar's quarrel seems more directly with the substance of liberalism itself. If, for example, liberalism is famous for its view that the good state avoids interfering, through laws and policies, with the efforts of individuals to answer for themselves that central personal question of how to live a human life, we nevertheless find Haksar arguing that an adequate theory of the good state must contain perfectionism about forms of life. That is, the good state must take a stand on what count as superior and inferior forms of life for human beings. In the end Haksar proposes toleration without equal liberties as the policy best suited to the form-of-life perfectionism of the good state.

I return to this second subject below, since I think those sympathetic to the liberal tradition will find this part of Haksar's critique controversial and also because it seems relevant to my inquiry into the possibility of a substantive conception of person-to-person fairness for individuals concerned about their treatment of others and themselves. First, however, I must say what I can about what Haksar means by "perfectionism" and thereby give some idea of the character of his toleration prescription for the good state.

Suppose we are liberals in the sense that we have such "egalitarian moral beliefs" as that (1) there are certain basic rights (e.g., the right to life, the right to respect and consideration) held equally by all human beings and (2) this equality in basic rights does not extend to animals, that is, that animal interests, ceteris paribus, count for less than the interests of human beings. Haksar's view is that insofar as our egalitarianism can be supported, then it has presuppositions that do the following several jobs: (a) they specify something, some common property, that persons have but animals do not; (b) they maintain that this something "constitutes a ground for giving greater weight to those who possess it"[30] over those who do not; and (c) in the event that this something is "found in different degrees among human beings," they argue for neglecting such differences. In general terms, the presupposed views and judgments that do job (a) are metaphysical, those that do job (b) are perfectionist, and those that do job (c) are pragmatic.

In connection with (a), Haksar argues that the metaphysics that best fits our egalitarian beliefs treats persons as persistent entities that have a certain potential, namely, the potential "to acquire certain capacities such as the ability to use language, self-consciousness, autonomy, the ability to form life-plans and to carry them out with zest, capacity for moral sentiments, capacity for sense of justice."[31] In short, persons have "the potential to lead a significant life . . . which [they] can develop while retaining [their] identity."[32] Even if some animals have part of this potential at a rudimentary level, "we could make the cut-off point sufficiently high so that all human beings, except for congenital idiots, possess the relevant potential, whereas all non-human animals fall below the cut-off point."[33]

In connection with (b), Haksar argues that our egalitarian beliefs commit us to the perfectionist judgment that human beings "have more intrinsic worth than animals."[34] Alternatively expressed: "there is something rather wonderful about human beings who possess certain capacities . . . or the potential for them."[35] Persons are, then, ends in themselves in this perfectionist sense, that is, they have, via this potential, an intrinsic worth whereby there is something wonderful about them. Haksar makes the further interesting point that our beliefs make most sense under the "doctrine of the transitivity of ends," according to which "if an individual is an end in itself during any part of its life-span, then it is an end in itself throughout its life-span," so that "once you are a member of the egalitarian club . . . you cannot be expelled from it."[36] He adds (though with little supporting discussion) that insofar as their wonderful potential gives persons a superior status over animals, then "it seems reasonable to insist that human beings have a duty to lead a significant life."[37]

In connection with (c), Haksar argues that if this wonderful-making potential is found in different degrees among persons, we can make a "pragmatic case"[38] for neglecting such differences and treating persons as if they have "equal intrinsic worth"; for "if we said that people with greater worth should get greater facilities, this will lead to considerable quarrels among individuals as to who are the superior ones," and in any case the "differences of intrinsic worth among human beings" are not well-marked, and this too raises criteriological and other sorts of quarrels that are worth avoiding.[39]

When we string all this together, then, as Haksar sees the situation, our egalitarianism has extensive metaphysical-cum-perfectionist-cum-pragmatic presuppositions,[40] but it is mainly the perfectionism to which Haksar wishes to draw our attention. Haksar nowhere gives a systematic analysis of the idea of perfectionism for its own sake, but I gather from what he says that when perfectionism is presupposed by our beliefs or our beliefs involve "an appeal to perfectionist considerations," he means that in the background of those beliefs there are, somewhere, judgments of intrinsic worth ("a kind of absolute worth"[41]) that are controversial and that cannot be proved.[42] According to Haksar, such perfectionist considerations are not only present in the background but, in fact, must be present there for liberal beliefs to have substance. He argues, for example, that since "there is no right . . . to liberty as such, but only the right to specific liberties that are essential for our well-being and our dignity and self-respect, or that are essential for the workings of representative democracy,"[43] an adequate political philosophy must incorporate perfectionist judgments involving these latter notions to give content to its system of rights.

At this point Haksar develops the controversial view mentioned above, for if egalitarianism presupposes perfectionism, then "it is difficult to see what is wrong with giving some forms of life . . . lower status than other forms of life."[44] Here we appear to challenge liberalism's traditional theme of openness to diversity among individuals, for the claim now is that we are not to treat the various forms of life that are not obviously anti-social as on a par with one another, for "to give equal status to all forms of life is to refuse to learn from experience that some forms of life are *prima facie* more suited to human beings, including children."[45] We must, in fact, "help individuals to try to avoid the inferior forms of life and encourage them to go in for one of the non-inferior forms of life," and the good state does this best by putting in place "a system of unequal liberties where the inferior forms of life are given lower status than in a system of equal liberties."[46]

Of course, the society that follows Haksar's recommended policy of "toleration without equal liberties" is tolerant in certain ways. It does not, for example, punish those "who practice degrading forms of life in private,"[47] and it does not condemn the practitioners themselves as inferior, only their forms of life.[48] The perfectionism involved in viewing some persons as intrinsically inferior to others is incompatible with egalitarianism, Haksar claims, "and would lead to intolerance and sacrifice of the interests of the inferior for the sake of the superior."[49] His policy even allows people "full liberty to discuss and criticize and try to change the ranking between different forms of life," a permission that may countenance disobedience "in extreme situations" as a means of "altering the majority's moral perceptions."[50] All this said, however, it remains that Haksar's recommended state is one that takes a stand on what forms of life are and are not in line with human dignity, well-being, and self-development. It officially and publicly, albeit gently, endorses certain forms of life and not others. In the end the person who follows an inferior form of life will get a worse deal under Haksar's policy than the person who adopts a better form of life; but this, he insists, is not ultimately incompatible with "the fundamental equality of respect owed to all human beings."[51]

I do not myself have much trouble with the general direction of certain of Haksar's claims about the makeup of liberalism, for example, that liberal egalitarianism presupposes perfectionism in some sense, and that perfectionism of some sort is needed to derive a liberal society from egalitarian premises. In the remarks that follow I limit my attention to Haksar's form-of-life perfectionism and his associated policy of toleration without equal liberties, for these seem both controversial relative to received opinion about what the liberal tradition represents and germane to my effort to understand person-to-person fairness. When I consider Haksar's view on its own terms, and independently for the most part of my special interest in how life with others is to be conducted when differential constitutional luck among persons as social and historical particulars is emphasized, I have three concerns.

The First Concern

The first concern begins with the observation that Haksar's form-of-life perfectionism is empty in many ways, despite its aim of providing appropriate substance for liberalism. Whether it is thought of as for the state or for individuals, it raises natural questions about content and administration, but does little to answer them. Suppose we distance ourselves from the liberal tradition and Haksar's question about how far a state's taking a stand on forms of life is compatible with it, and just ask whether Haksar's form-of-life perfectionism is itself attractive. Consider this question from the standpoint of the individual ideologically uncommitted prospective citizen of Haksar's recommended state. What do we prospective citizens need to know to figure out whether to accept Haksar's form-of-life perfectionism? At a minimum we need to know (1) what, in general, a form of life is. Beyond that we certainly need to know, at least roughly, (2) what the superior and inferior forms of life are that are prescribed by the state or generally endorsed by most of those individuals in the state who think of themselves as members of it. Surely, if we have our own thoughts about what forms of life are superior and inferior and are at all worried, as we should be, about how far our views fit with the views of the state or of most individuals who think of themselves as members of the state, we need to know (3) how, in rough outline anyway, the state goes about discouraging and encouraging forms of life. Curiously, Haksar offers little discussion of these topics, and what there is is rather nonspecific and noncommittal.

For example, Haksar does not provide an analysis or general account of what a form of life is, and I doubt that this much-used notion has a standard interpretation even within today's philosophical circles. I cannot tell, for example, whether Haksar regards a form of life as a many-yeared thing, a short-term thing, a thing that dominates one's life (affecting, say, one's personal identity for practical purposes), a thing that occupies a subordinate, perhaps negligible, position in one's plan of life, and so on. Perhaps forms of life are or can be any of these things, but in that case what is not a form of life and hence outside the perfectionist purview of the state or of most of those who view themselves as members of the state? Haksar, of course, gives some examples of forms of life, but even so what is provided is unhelpful. Included among the inferior forms of life are bestiality, eating one's own excrement, nudism, and smoking cigarettes; among the superior ones are the life of contemplation and heterosexuality.[52] Among the ones whose status Haksar seems to treat as controversial are individual versus communal families. (A varied group of examples indeed. What could it mean to say that eating one's own excrement and communal families are both forms of life?) In general, Haksar's account limps along with a miscellany of examples of things some people do or might do, some of which I suppose he thinks most of his readers will view as more or less obviously inferior, others more or less obviously superior. In fact, very few examples of superior, or at least noninferior, things persons do or might do are given. This, I suppose, is itself liberal if it is meant to suggest that the good state, or most people in it, allows lots of things persons do or might do to count as noninferior.[53] It is unhelpful, however, if we wish, either for philosophical reasons or for the practical reasons of prospective citizens, to learn what forms of life are really or at least politically in line with the human dignity, well-being, and self-development Haksar so often speaks of. It is also worth noting that Haksar steers clear of the difficult problem of ranking different forms of life located on the same side of the distinction between inferior and noninferior forms of life. If, say, the life of contemplation, the life of social service, and the life of honest material accumulation are all noninferior, is the first nevertheless better than the others? Haksar appears to hold that the state is not to take a stand on the hierarchy, if there is one, within the category of the noninferior,[54] but why, in principle, the state should take a stand on forms of life and then stop short in this way is unclear. Finally, it is not clear what taking a stand on forms of life amounts to. If the state does not punish those who practice the inferior forms of life in private, what does it do to give lower status to those forms of life? What rules and regulations does it promulgate, and how does it enforce them? What encouragement programs does it conduct? Is attendance required? What discouragement policies does it implement? Do they make people feel bad about themselves? Do they commit unjustified persona moralism, that is, impose conceptions of persons on people who cannot meet their terms? Do they make it too hard for practitioners of inferior forms of life to keep alive their sense of being of equal intrinsic worth with everyone else?

My point, of course, is not merely that these natural questions are not answered. It is rather that in the absence of answers to them, we prospective citizens are in no position to determine whether Haksar's form-of-life perfectionism is itself even initially attractive; and if we draw a blank on this topic, I do not see that we prospective citizens can make much at all of Haksar's proposal that the state or individuals within the state should follow the doctrine of toleration without equal liberties, for this is an area in which, for ideologically uncommitted prospective citizens, the burden of proof, or even of initial attractiveness, is carried by a policy proposal's contents and associated administrative apparatus. Is it wrong somehow to judge what Haksar says in this area from the standpoint of the uncommitted prospective citizens? I do not see that it should be.

The Second Concern

Perhaps Haksar would respond that the particulars of a state's form-of-life perfectionism are not for him to establish. They are to be established through discussion, debate, protest, and, in extreme situations, disobedience by the citizens of a given society. He might say that even if his proposal seems empty from the standpoint of the uncommitted prospective citizen, his main point in any case is that a good society is one that takes a stand on what superior and inferior forms of life are.[55] The good state is one that has views about what constitutes human dignity, well-being, and self-development, and, whatever the content of those views and whatever the apparatus needed to administer and implement them, the good state does not give all not obviously antisocial forms of life equal status.

My trouble here begins with puzzlement about what Haksar is ascribing to his liberal opposition. Haksar writes as if his policy of toleration without equal liberties is to be preferred to some other liberal theorist's policy of giving all not obviously antisocial forms of life equal status, but what is this equal-status policy? Is it the positive indiscriminate policy according to which all not obviously antisocial forms of life are encouraged and facilitated, including, for example, bestiality, the life of contemplation, and eating one's own excrement? If so, the opposition policy is silly on its face, and I cannot think of any liberal thinker who recommends it. If, however, the opposition policy is really the nonpolicy whereby the state simply takes no position on any of the many not obviously antisocial forms of life, then we are not considering a policy of liberalism at all, but rather some kind of hands-off libertarianism, which Haksar and the liberal theorists he criticizes jointly reject.

What, then, is the policy that Haksar's policy is supposed to oppose and be preferable to? I cannot offer a detailed policy statement in terms of programs, rules, and enforcement measures in answer to this question, but I do have certain unoriginal thoughts about what the liberal wishes to achieve in this area. The liberal's wish to avoid perfectionism, as Haksar puts it in the matter of the state's role regarding forms of life is grounded not so much in a worry that perfectionism is somehow incompatible with egalitarianism or some other key liberal doctrine as it is in a perfectly natural worry about the tendency to close-mindedness in human beings. This moral-psychological worry need not (though for some theorists it may) reflect any dark or low opinion of human nature. It may simply recognize that people—especially those busy with things other than their society's degree of receptivity to new or different ways of life—tend to become comfortable with the ways of life they are familiar with, to think of them as natural, and to block out thoughts of alternatives. They may consequently find alternative ways of life strange and even unnatural and in encounters with them be inclined to react with disapproval of some sort. One might elaborate on this familiar fact at length, though I will not do so here. Let it suffice to say that liberalism wishes to resist such tendencies and to foster open-mindedness in the citizens of the good state. Haksar grants that the risk of people becoming "smug, dogmatic, and bigoted" provides a case for "tolerating inferior forms of life," but he insists that this does not show that such forms of life "should be given equal status to the ordinary ways of life."[56] We may agree with this if it means that neither the silly positive indiscriminate policy mentioned above nor the hands-off libertarian policy will necessarily work against close-mindedness and for open-mindedness, but I do not see how Haksar's policy of toleration without equal liberties, even when its gentleness is emphasized, is helpful relative to that end either. Since I find the liberal's concern with fostering open-mindedness admirable (let different forms of life be innocent until proven guilty), I am inclined to table, if not reject, Haksar's policy recommendation and to explore other possibilities. Even if form-of-life perfectionism is in principle compatible with other liberal doctrines, we might still be ill-advised to adopt the policy of toleration without equal liberties, for such a policy, assuming that it has some content in the form of programs, rules, and enforcement measures, might, in practice, work gently against and not for the strengthening of the capacity for open-mindedness, weak at best, in the citizenry of the good state.

The Third Concern

Haksar might of course reply that under the scheme he has in mind it is quite possible to argue "that some of the unconventional forms of life that are given inferior status . . . should have equal status with the conventional forms of life."[57] Homosexuality, he imagines, might be an example of an unconventional form of life that some would argue should be upgraded to equal status with heterosexuality, but his view is that "the case for upgrading" is "not an automatic one but has to be made by appealing to perfectionist considerations," such as, for example, whether homosexuality "is as fulfilling and worthwhile as heterosexuality."[58]

This point about the possibility of upgrading forms of life brings me to my last concern. It is directed toward the question of how far Haksar's view allows such upgrading to take place and extends to the question of how far policy recommendations for the good state—or, indeed, entire moral codes—may be justified and defended.

Haksar makes clear that he is a reflective-equilibrium theorist in much of his work. This means that he proceeds by matching and mutually adjusting "our moral and other principles with our moral beliefs and intuitions until we get a harmonious fit."[59] He uses this approach "to construct an egalitarian theory which harmonizes better with our egalitarian intuitions *in general*, than alternative egalitarian theories do."[60] Now, as I follow Haksar's methodological remarks, his reflective-equilibrium approach aims at getting us to see the background and implications of our moral beliefs. The importance of understanding these things is that they can help us "give a ruling on controversial cases" and also acquaint us with the foundations of our beliefs so that we might then "compare the pros and cons of the egalitarian moral code with those of non-egalitarian moral codes" and thus not "blindly make a choice just on the basis of which one we happen to like and commend for general acceptance."[61]

Haksar's reflective-equilibrium approach[62] thus provides a sort of prolegomenon to justification. It gets us to see what our view is in some depth, but it does not itself afford a justification for our view, that is, a reason for choosing our view over some other view.[63] The justification for our view, which involves examining foundations for soundness and comparing pros and cons of competing views, seems to be a further task that is beyond the reach of the tasks covered by Haksar's reflective-equilibrium approach. My problem is that I do not see, in Haksar's view, how this further task is to proceed or, indeed, that it can proceed, for it has been Haksar's main point throughout the discussion that the perfectionism he finds in the liberal code is, as I reported above, a matter of controversial judgments of intrinsic worth that cannot be proved. If perfectionism is of this character, however, then it is unclear what we can do after we have used Haksar's reflective-equilibrium approach to discern the perfectionism in competing codes, other than blindly choose among them. I do not think this is what Haksar intends. I think he holds that some further task of justification is available to us as we attempt to work out what finally shall be our moral code; but what this further task is or could be is unclear. In the absence of the further justification, our state's or our personal stand remains a batch of controversial, not-to-be proved judgments of the intrinsic value of some forms of life. If there can be no further justification, we can only hope that the measures that implement our state's or our own stand will operate very gently indeed, for we have nothing beyond our perfectionist judgments to offer those to whom we give the worse deal, other than the lame assurance that we have given them that respect and consideration owed equally to all.

Personal Fairness

What, then, should be the content of our conception of person-to-person fairness? Even though I have not canvassed the views present in the literature on tolerance, I think it is already clear enough from the earlier discussion plus the discussion above that a practical dilemma is generated by reflection on what I call the problem of personal justice. I said above that I was attracted to Lucas's view of justice individualized but troubled by his view that justice individualized is nonsystematic. I noticed that Rawls, too, apart from his view that a conception of justice for the basic structure of society can be substantive, that is, systematic, appears to hold that individual-case justice in the form of principles for individuals, considered in itself and in isolation from other things, is nonsystematic, so that providing substance for personal justice is best achieved by placing the conception of justice for the basic structure of society logically first and then filling out the content of individual duties from that base. I wondered whether there could be a substantive conception of personal justice, that is, person-to-person fairness, independently of a prior account of justice for the basic structure of society. I thought Haksar's form-of-life perfectionism might provide a workable conception of personal justice, even though Haksar proposes it as set of policies for the state, but I found difficulties in this conception, as reported in the discussion toward the end of the previous section.

In general, responding to the problem of personal justice finds us caught between these alternatives. On the one side, if one proposes to respond to the problem by working out a conception of personal justice that is substantive, that is, systematic and thus containing ordered principles, one ends up risking failing to take into account the special features of individual cases. As Lucas suggests, one ends up circumscribing justice in individual cases via the use of the general principles making up one's substantive conception, for these principles have a way of deciding in advance what are relevant and irrelevant features of cases. In individual cases these advance decisions do not always seem right: features blocked out by them sometimes seem morally relevant after all; features interpreted as decisive by them sometimes seem morally beside the point. In short, if one adopts substance, one risks not giving adequate attention to particularity.

On the other side, if one proposes to respond to the problem of personal justice by resolving not to make advance commitments to principles that, in effect, render certain features in individual cases relevant and other features irrelevant, then one seems importantly left without guidance in individual cases. Even if one accompanies one's resolution not to make advance commitments with a further resolution to be tolerant, kind, gentle yet firm, generous, or appreciative toward others as the facts demand, it is unclear, in the absence of advance commitments to principles, what one's further resolution teaches in this or that individual case. In short, if one resolves to attend to particularity, one risks the confusion or even paralysis of the absence of substance. Paradoxically, as one keeps an open mind in individual cases, one ends up unprincipled regarding how to act.

How is one to respond to this dilemma? Philosophers might see in it familiar issues involving the general and the particular. Here, however, I have in mind the practical concerns that I sketched at the beginning of this discussion of the problem of personal justice. After all, my life in the world is and cannot avoid being a life with others to some extent. How am I to think of and treat the people around me? What is to be my general approach to them, especially when I recognize the impossibility of my knowing well all or even many of those I must deal with?

My first thought is that here again our form of moral life presents us with a no-win situation. If I work up a conception of person-to-person fairness to use in my dealings with others, a conception involving my having commitments to certain principles, then I may circumscribe justice in a way that involves unfairness in individual cases, and I will be vulnerable to the moral pain of guilt. If, however, I keep myself open to the particulars of individual cases, I will be left at a loss in some and perhaps many cases regarding what I ought to do, and I will be vulnerable to the pain of indecision and perhaps as well to the pain that goes with a sense of having failed to act when one should. Must I just live with this problem and chalk it up to the nature of the human condition—or, at any rate, the human condition for the one who takes seriously the challenge of moral responsibility? Is it a problem regarding which moral philosophy can provide no preferred solution? Of course, even if I believe one or both of these things and thus step back from the problem—that is, recognize the issue but do not resolve it because it is not resolvable—I am at best left theoretically pure but practically stranded. After all, even those who wish to be philosophically honest must act in the world and thus with others, and for life with others we need some working conception of how people are.

My second thought is a sort of wonder. There is a risk of unfairness in my adopting a conception of personal justice involving advance commitments to principles defining relevance and irrelevance for individual cases, but there is a risk of emptiness or indecision if I do not bring such commitments to individual cases. What happens if I avoid both these alternatives but stay with the general view of persons as, in the language used earlier, different, modular, and finite, including all that these elements of the general view imply? Is there content in this general view of persons that is at least helpful regarding dealing with others, even if it does not have the power of normative principles defining relevance and irrelevance?

If my general view of persons is that they are, typically, in-control agents, then I am equipped with a basis or ground for certain expectations in my dealings with them. I can, by and large, expect them to be able to keep their promises, to drink in moderation, to speak out when principle demands, and so on. When they do not do these things, I am prepared to accuse and blame to the point, at any rate, at which mitigating factors become apparent or considerations invoked to show that the presumption of in-control agency was incorrect become convincing. My earlier discussion, however, emphasized the modularity of and differences among persons and suggested that the assumption of in-control agency is often an instance of persona moralism. In Lucas's vocabulary, to make this assumption a main element in one's general approach to others is to risk circumscribing justice on the level of the individual case. Suppose, then,

I replace my general in-control-agency thinking about persons with general modularity-and-difference thinking about them. What happens?

Well, the world I live in changes in certain ways.

First, among those I know well, I am aware of some who not only can but will keep their promises, drink in moderation, and speak out when principle demands; I am aware of others who can but might or might not keep their promises, drink in moderation, or speak out when principle demands; I am aware of still others who pretty much cannot do one or more of these things. Of those I do not know well but with whom I must deal, I can have no general expectations that go in any of these directions. I must live with others without the support for my expectations provided by the simplism that persons are, by and large, in-control agents.

Second, if *J* does something one ought not to do (insult my guest, say) or fails to do what one ought to do (e.g., protest an injustice), I cannot accuse and blame until *J*'s action or omission is explained. I must, assuming I am interested in what happened or have a stake in it, seek to understand first, that is, before even considering whether accusation and blame are in order. It may of course turn out that accusation and blame are in order, but, in this world of modular and differential people, no immediate or even weak entitlement to accusation and blame is made possible by these facts (the wrong action or omission in which I am interested or have a stake). The usual practice of judgment—sometimes a rush to judgment—is not the common practice in response to such facts.

Third, if *S* makes a mistake in judgment, or is untactful in a social situation, or is slow in seeing the point of an argument, or procrastinates in getting the job done, I am not thereby entitled to criticize *S*, for, given the makeup of *S*'s modular, constitutionally different self, *S* may have done the best he or she could in the matter in question. Perhaps, in the world of modular and differential people, such mistakes, tactlessness, slowness, and delays are treated as simply occurrences rather than as indicators of fault.

Fourth, if *T* is in a negative mood or responds defiantly and unhelpfully to whatever I say, and this bothers or irritates me, I may not thereby be entitled to find fault, get angry, or become impatient with *T*, for perhaps *T* here reflects or manifests constitutional factors in his or her makeup. In a world of modular and differential people I may more often find the grounds of my discontents in myself than in others, raising, indeed, some issues about the nature of my own constitutional makeup.

Fifth, in a world of modular and differential people, the familiar moral assessments I make of the rightness or goodness of others' actions are not somehow canceled or disallowed, but the characteristic responses to them found in the world of in-control agents—namely, accusation and blame for the negative assessments, approval or even praise for the positive ones—are no longer the first or immediate responses. In fact, in the world of modular and differential people our responses to such assessments are governed by the imperative to know well the people one deals with.[64] If in the circumstances of ordinary life I cannot meet this latter imperative in some or many cases (e.g., time does not permit the inquiry involved), then in those cases I must restrict my assessments to evaluations of outcomes and suspend judgment about the people I deal with.

Given this handful of reflections on life in a world of modular and differential people, we may ask again whether the general view of persons as modular, different, and finite provides content that is helpful regarding our practical task of living with others. There is such content, even though it is not of the sort we associate with the normative power of principles to define what are to count as relevant and irrelevant features in individual cases. The content seems to me more proceduralist than relevance defining. In contrast to relevance-defining principles (familiar examples of which instruct me never to allow race, gender, or sexual preference to figure in moral decision making in individual cases), the view emphasizing modularity and difference enjoins us to know well those with whom we deal and thus to cultivate in ourselves, insofar as we aspire to moral responsibility, a willingness to try to understand their individuality or, at any rate, those elements in it relevant to the concerns that bring us into contact[65]; with those we cannot know well it urges us not to make generalizations or assumptions about capacities and dispositions and not immediately to demand change when behavior and attitudes are not in line with the expectations generated by the model of the in-control agent.[66] The content here is not entirely given in a series of "nots," in my view. On the positive side, the modularity and difference view teaches us to open ourselves to the people we deal with and to be alert to differences among them. I suspect that it may not be easy to follow these positive instructions; perhaps there are some among us who would do well with them and others who would not or could not, even when their efforts are full and sincere.

It needs to be said, too, that the injunction to approach life with others on modularity and difference terms does not reduce to a simple injunction to love others or to show them compassion or even to appreciate them. Human diversity can in some cases be something to celebrate, but in other cases it is dangerous or tragic. "Be careful" is as much a maxim for life with modular and different others as "be kind" or "be generous." The tolerance that involves putting up with others even as one is angry with them also has a place in life with such others, for, as was explained earlier (in the last two sections of chapter 3), the world of modular and different people is not a world in which everyone is determined and no one has will. The world of modular and different people is a world in which in-control agency and constitutional fixes are mixed in people such that, again, the people one deals with are different from one another in different ways, and some of these differences they can do something about and others they cannot.

Is modular and differential thinking about persons practical? Can we live with others on the terms it offers? I think so. An approach to others emphasizing modularity and difference seems to me in fact to fit persons as social and historical particulars better than an approach to them as in-control agents. Of course, as I have suggested, the former approach may not be easy to live, perhaps especially not if one has spent years of one's life with others construing people as in-control agents. The difficulty is not just in making the change in general views operative in one's attitudes and behavior; it is also in trying to meet one's now very important duty to know well or attempt to know well the others with whom one lives. Given the familiar difficulties of limits on time, obstacles to communication (including recalcitrance and self-deception), expanding sets of obligations, and so on, it is probably right to suppose that the duty in question would not be met often or fully. Difficulty per se is not, however, a denial that a duty exists or a reason not to take a duty seriously.

Finally, we may ask: what is the status of the idea of justice individualized that takes seriously the notion that people are modular and constitutionally different relative to the idea of basic-structure justice? Does personal justice thus construed somehow supplant or replace the Rawlsian-mainstream concern for basic-structure justice? This seems to me a question that is raised by the discussion above, but it is certainly not answered by it directly or by implication. My main concern here has been to make the problem of personal justice come alive and to suggest the importance to this problem of the conception of persons as modular and constitutionally different. One might hope that basic-structure justice and personal justice are two different things, such that one might attempt to develop a view about one without risk of conflict with different views of the other. Perhaps, however, this is not so. The issue raised by the discussion above in this connection seems to me to be this: does justice for the basic structure of society carry with it a conception of persons as, for example, in-control agents, that conflicts with the view of persons as modular and constitutionally different that I have said is important to personal justice? Again, this important and difficult question is not treated in the discussion above. To answer it would require working out a conception of basic-structure justice, and this I have not attempted. If basic-structure justice could not make do with persons as modular and constitutionally different and required of persons some more uniform nature, then we would face a tension between major moral ideas and perhaps suffer confusion in our lives with others.

Chapter 5

On Recovery and Self-Protection

In infinite resignation there is peace and repose and consolation. . . .
Kierkegaard, Fear and Trembling

A mind imbued with the absurd merely judges that . . .consequences must be considered calmly.
Camus, The Myth of Sisyphus

My *life* consists in my being content to accept many things.
Wittgenstein, On Certainty

The transition from tenseness, self-responsibility, and worry, to equanimity, receptivity, and peace, is the most wonderful of all those shiftings of inner equilibrium, those changes of the personal centre of energy. . . . and the chief wonder of it is that it so often comes about, not by doing, but by simply relaxing and throwing the burden down.
William James, The Varieties of Religious Experience

The Going-On Problem

In the discussion above I said what I could about living with others, given certain themes of the earlier discussion, namely, the perspective on persons that regards them as social and historical particulars, the conception of the self as modular, and the view that persons can, in different respects and to different degrees, be stuck, gappy, or subject to outlaw forces regarding some elements of personality and temperament. Toward the end of the discussion above, I suggested something of the proceduralist content of these themes for the other-regarding problem of personal justice. Now, with the same themes in mind, I turn to the self-regarding side of the coin: the problem of living with oneself.

It might seem that if the themes I mentioned have a way of enjoining us, in the task of fairness to others, to know a person well, then the self-regarding issue could be thought to be easier than the other-regarding issue, for it might seem that knowing oneself well, as enjoined by the task of fairness to oneself, is not so difficult as knowing another well. I suspect, however, that the notion that self-knowledge is somehow easier than other-knowledge is mistaken. It is indeed hard to know another person well, and in any case it is a practical impossibility for most of us to know well all or even many of those with whom we deal; but it is also hard to know oneself well, and there are reasons for this that have to do with, among other things, our vulnerability to self-deception, our capacity for denial, and our tendencies to what earlier I called self-imposed persona moralism. There is in fact a social dimension to knowing oneself.[1] One's knowledge of oneself is mediated, if not determined, by ideologies, others' opinions, family traditions, and much else. One's view of oneself may seem, to sensibility, factual in character and a result of discovery; but one's view of oneself is also normative and a product of decision, at least in part. Accordingly, one can be mistaken in the more nearly factual sections of one's view of oneself but also unwise in the normative section of it that is a product of decision.

Let me narrow the subject of this discussion somewhat, for living with oneself is too broad a title for what is on my mind in what follows. When we think of the problem of living with oneself, perhaps our thoughts go first to cases of people coping with their awareness of their own disease, their bitterness over victimization,[2] their sense of loss from a family tragedy,[3] their anger at the cruel fate of a parent suffering dementia in a nursing home, their sensitivity to a loaded social label (e.g., born illegitimate), or, indeed, the headiness of their success. While the cases I have in mind, however, share with these the presentation of a challenge of going on from what one experiences as a distinctive low or high point in one's life, they have additional features that these living-with problems do not. In the cases I have in mind the distinctive point in one's life from which one must go on is indeed low, and it is so by virtue of being moral-emotionally painful and at the same time to some degree cognitively opaque. The low point has embedded in it what the individual suffering it views as wrongdoing of some sort—wrongdoing, at any rate, for which he or she seems accountable; and why this is so, that is, why this wrongdoing is embedded in the individual's life, is difficult for him or her to understand.

It is important both to recognize the moral-emotional pain involved in these cases and to highlight the latter first-person understanding difficulty embedded in the low point suffered in them. The identity of this pain may be unclear to the individual suffering it, even as its severity is uncontroversial. It may simply be an ache, and to the sufferer the philosophical characterizations of the different phenomenologies of guilt, shame, regret, remorse, and the other negative moral emotions may indeed seem abstract, remote, and unhelpful relative to the relief of the suffering.[4] The first-person understanding difficulty may be as pronounced in the individual's suffering as the negative moral-emotional ache. It is essentially the difficulty of understanding how it is that one did a certain wrong thing or failed to do a certain right thing, when it is plausible to suppose that one knew better. Put another way, it is the difficulty of understanding those negatively moralized low points in one's life at or in which one's agency fails or goes out of control gratuitously, that is, for no reason recognized as legitimate by moral common sense or ordinary views of how persons are. In these cases, then, when a low point in one's life is morally negative, and accountability for it is painful to bear, and in any case the existence of the low point is not understood by one, then the living-with problem seems different from what it is in those cases in which one must live with, say, one's sensitivity to being illegitimate, one's awareness of one's cancer, one's devastation over the loss of a child, or the flush of one's success. In the cases I have in mind, one turns out not to have been what one was supposed to be or meant to be, and one finds oneself at once pained and baffled by this fact about one's life. The fact, experienced as thus interpreted, has a tendency to run one into self-reproach. In these cases, when the philosophical observer lifts the particularized agent into view, the usual features of in-control agency targeted by received ethical theories, for example, rationality and capacity for utilitarian calculation, are obfuscated or smothered in emotional pain and confusion. This individual is, to one degree or other, absorbed by negative evaluations of past actions and flooded by regret or remorse and by despair and uncertainty over his or her future.

The latter three of the four cases sketched in chapter 1 are all of the sort I wish to focus on here. They are cases in which one has difficulty living with one's past, and, in effect, going on from a low point in which the presence in one's history of one's own wrongdoing is baffling in the way just indicated. In this later part of my discussion, then, I revisit this subject.

What, then, can be said philosophically about how a conscientious, responsible person enduring a living-with problem of the sort thus characterized is to go on? I am aware of course of some difficulties in the way of treating living-with problems of this sort philosophically. One wonders whether there is or can be a going-on strategy for dealing with such problems that is objective in any important sense, or at least generally recommendable, for even if a given strategy seems worthy of general recommendation, the themes I bring to this discussion suggest that there may be different sorts of obstacles to acceptance of such a recommended strategy in different cases. In one sort of case, a person's condition, that is, the makeup of the self, may be such that he or she could adopt the strategy by a relatively easy exercise of will; in another sort of case, such adoption, were it to occur, would be a feat of supererogation; in still another sort of case—so we are warned, in a world of modular and differential selves—the person to whom the strategy is recommended is not able to adopt it at all, which is not to say that there is no relevant strategy available that might help him or her go on. To recognize, however, that there are different sorts of persons and, hence, prospective complications for the acceptance of proposed strategies is not necessarily to suggest that the working out of strategies for helping people go on from living-with problems in their lives of the sort I have sketched is a hopeless or nonsensical project. Something can be helpful without being so for anyone or everyone who needs help.

Another aspect of my subject requires comment. What I wish to explore here is not so much the development or even the application of an ethical theory as it is the development of a how-to-live strategy for real people (modular and differential selves) enduring or suffering a living-with problem of the general kind I sketched. In the context of theory, the activity of working out a view has a certain timelessness to it. The development of an adequate form of utilitarianism, for example, is a philosophical activity that is participated in by real-life proponents of utilitarianism, such as Bentham, Mill, Sidgwick, and Russell Hardin, and also by real-life critics of utilitarianism, such as Kant, John Rawls, and Bernard Williams; but one's location in time or history does not seem to matter much to the conversation that goes into the development of utilitarianism, and, in fact, a proponent of utilitarianism who comes to be well known (e.g., John Stuart Mill) might not be uniformly the most helpful contributor to the development of utilitarianism.[5] In the development of Kantianism, real-life proponents include Kant and John Rawls, and critics include Bernard Williams, Aristotle, and Michael Stocker; but some of the most difficult contributions to their conversation are those given in the writings of Kant. However exactly the timelessness aspect of the development of ethical theory is to be understood, the problem of developing a how-to-live strategy that I take up here is different in its orientation. The development of an adequate ethical theory is governed by concerns for truth, coherence, and, to some extent, feasibility. The development of an adequate how-to-live strategy—a strategy relevant to this individual, this social and historical particular—is guided by concerns for the health, energy, and functioning of this individual.[6] The point of the development of an ethical theory is understanding of our form of moral life.[7] In the end the theory's achievement is given in statements of principles internally ordered in certain ways, accompanied by explanations as needed for exceptions, exemptions, and special provisos, the whole glossed by accounts, explanatory and (to whatever extent is possible) justificatory, of the theory's basic premises. The point of the development of a how-to-live strategy, regarding cases of the sort I have in mind, is not, however, understanding of this order. It is, instead, the recovery of agency, or what I have called going on in life. If enduring a low point is a sort of living death for the sufferer, what the how-to-live strategy means to offer is a way of returning to life. What this recovery is of (viz., "agency") is then lots of things, including a sense of oneself as intact in a way that allows responsible forward-looking action, plus a measure of self-worth, and perhaps even the capacity to find in oneself interests and enthusiasms with enough strength to give meaningfulness to certain of one's activities.[8] This difference in orientation may be important to philosophical assessment of, respectively, a proposed ethical theory or recovery strategy, for perhaps the latter, but not the former, can tolerate conceptual elements whose interpretations may, within limits, be left to individuals or be able to tolerate beliefs in support of which reason is inconclusive,[9] as long as the strategy reaches effectively to the return to life of the individual.

On the Ideas of Recovery and Self-Protection

What is a recovery strategy or recovery program? Even though main ethical theories—for example, those of Aristotle, Kant, or the utilitarian tradition—do not treat the idea of recovery programs or directly suggest content for one, the philosophical literature is not completely empty on the subject. At any rate some materials come to mind that are usually counted as a part of philosophical literature, for example, the writings of Epictetus in *The Enchiridion*,[10] Camus in *The Myth of Sisyphus*, and William James in *The Will to Believe* and *The Varieties of Religious Experience*. In this discussion, however, I will have in mind and focus on some materials that are not usually considered a part of philosophical literature, even though they speak very directly to the going-on problem in cases of the sort I wish to emphasize. I refer here to the discussion given in *Alcoholics Anonymous*[11] and, in more detail, *Twelve Steps and Twelve Traditions*,[12] for both of which the principal author is the cofounder of AA, Bill Wilson.[13]

In the next sections I discuss the AA recovery program in some detail. Here, though, I wish to speak more generally about the recovery and self-protection the AA program means to provide.

In general form, a recovery program instructs the victim of the moralized despair I sketched above in three main maneuvers, the overall point of which is a sort of reorientation of the victim's basic attitudes toward his or her own life. The recovery program might be thus thought of as basic attitude heuristics. As such, the program supposes that one can detach from one's own basic attitudes, review them for wisdom, and implement alternatives to them. Of course, the conception of the self as modular and different that I have invoked in the discussion above appears to suggest that this detaching, reviewing, and implementing might be possible for some people, difficult for others, and impossible for still others. Of the writings I mentioned above, the AA program clearly acknowledges the latter impossibility; James's discussion comes close to acknowledging it; the treatments of Epictetus and Camus are not explicit on the point and perhaps for that reason seem to me not to recognize it.

A recovery program will have a four-part logic to it.

First, it will recognize, and to some extent help the sufferer characterize, his or her baseline moralized despair. This is both the point of departure for the strategy, that is, a reason for a strategy to be attempted, and the test of the strategy, in the sense that the amelioration of the despair is what following the strategy is supposed to achieve.

Second, the program will offer an interpretation of what it is to detach from one's life, that is, gain a measure of relief from the pain of the moralized despair. In one way or another a recovery program will provide a victim with a means of standing back from his or her interpretations of his or her past and current life, loaded as they are with negative moral emotion. Something of this sort is necessary if indeed proposals for going on are to be actionable.

A third element in a recovery program will be the stuff of a generalized understanding of the nature and makeup of the human condition one is enduring. Philosophers might be inclined to view this part of the program as metaphysics of a sort, and as philosophers they might find the materials in this area typically underwritten, unrigorous, less than clear, and so forth.[14] Here it is important to remember the purposes of the recovery program and to consider from that angle whether the human-condition understanding is sufficient.

The final element in the program will be normative and might be expressed in practice in a small or large number of maxims. Here the program says, in effect, against the background of the three elements outlined above: "Try this: (a) . . . , (b) . . . , (c) . . . ." That is, given its reading of the moralized despair, its detachment strategy, and its generalized understanding of the human condition, the program recommends to the victim how to live. Such a normative account may contain prescriptions of different sorts: some very concrete (suggested ways of taking inventory of oneself, bits of writing to do, people to place in certain positions in one's life, warnings about specific threats to well-being), others very general or abstract (slogans, forms of guidance) that without context may seem platitudinous or banal but that in context may seem insightful, helpful, and even profound.

Perhaps it would be helpful to see a recovery program as a strategy for a person enduring a certain sort of difficulty to move toward a reconciliation or accommodation with the contents or his or her life.[15] What the strategy helps one do is put together one's own autonomy, that is, capacity for choice, with the givens of one's physical, emotional, and mental being and the contingencies that come to one from the outside (the external luck factors discussed earlier) to secure a spiritual condition more adequate to the task of life. There are of course many sorts of accommodations, insofar as there are many ways of putting together such items that will withstand the tests of consistency. For most recovery programs, however, and certainly for my thoughts in this discussion, the aim is not simply or only consistency. (One can be consistent, yet quite miserable.) What one seeks—perhaps especially in cases of the sort I have mainly in mind—is a reconciliation with the circumstances and contents of one's life that carries with it a measure of serenity.

About the AA Program

The AA program, as an example of a program of recovery and self-protection, was of course developed with the victim of alcoholism in mind, but there is no special logical reason to confine this program to those seeking to recover from alcoholism; in fact, a wide variety of people have adapted or tried to adapt the AA program to their living-with issues and sought its support for their efforts to go on from low points in their lives, whatever the causation of those low points.[16] One of my reasons for giving attention to the AA program here is that it addresses directly the sort of living-with problem I sketched above, and it does so in a full and detailed way; but, again, recovering alcoholics are hardly the only people who face living-with problems of that kind.

A further introductory point is that the AA program, as a program of recovery and self-protection, has no logical connection to the idea that alcoholism is a disease. There has been much discussion of this latter idea, and participants in the discussion have included medical doctors, psychologists and psychiatrists, those who do counseling and therapy for recovering alcoholics, and professionals of many other kinds, even philosophers.[17] Too, discussion of the idea occurs in AA, and sometimes at AA meetings references are made by victims to alcoholism as a disease.[18] From the angle of an interest in recovery from alcoholism, however, the controversy over whether alcoholism is a disease need not be entered. The AA program, as I discuss it here, would not have to change its makeup or character however that controversy is resolved. Whether alcoholism is best understood as a disease (in any sense interesting to medicine), addiction, allergy, way of life, moral weakness, or simply condition would not change or alter the AA program of recovery and self-protection.[19] All that is needed for the AA program to be considered as a candidate proposal regarding how one might go on with one's life is that one's life fit the criteria I have listed above: one suffers a negatively moralized low point, shot through with seeming accountability and cognitive opacity; and one is stuck with this life condition and finds it intolerable—it constitutes a bottom, as AA says, below which one knows not. Whether the heavy drinking connected with one's being in this state is glossed in the terms of disease, addiction, weakness, and so on, does not matter to recovery and self-protection. What matters is that the negative force of this state is sufficient for the victim to suffer that combination of helplessness, frustration, and sheer pain that renders the state intolerable for him or her.[20] (For some heavy drinkers, as AA recognizes, the point at which the state is intolerable is never reached.) AA doctrine does not logically require that alcoholism be a disease; it holds only that one must hit bottom for one's interest in the AA recovery program to be deep enough to motivate one to take the program seriously.[21] For the purposes of this discussion of recovery and self-protection, I will set aside the controversy over whether alcoholism is a disease.

When a suffering alcoholic—again, call him Severance[22]—hits bottom, either naturally or through a created crisis (what in treatment circles is called an intervention), then Severance is in pain. The literature of AA suggests that this pain has physical, emotional, and spiritual dimensions, and it is the forcefulness of the pain in these different dimensions that forms the bottom from which Severance seeks recovery and against which he seeks protection. Since there are three dimensions in this account, and pain may be suffered in these dimensions in different degrees of intensity by different persons, there can be no standard characterization of the bottom the alcoholic suffers. The "leads" (life histories) one hears at AA meetings may fit the general dimensional categories but be very different in details and emphases. Perhaps the best that can be said in general is that the bottom is a self-perceived low point in one's life, with physical, emotional, and spiritual dimensions, perhaps including material losses (e.g., employment difficulties, relationship difficulties, losses of home, family, or friends). Let us suppose, then, that in Severance's case in particular the pain in the physical dimension is many things, but, typically, it is a localized steady burning in the center of the body, combined with experiences of blackout (some of them very prolonged), nausea, and heavy fatigue. Severance finds that the only thing that cuts this pain is more alcohol, and reliance on alcohol is thus embedded in his life routine, not for fun now, obviously, but simply for survival, as he might say, that is, for getting through days and nights chopped into two-hour intervals. At some point after recovery begins (when clarity and reflection become possible) the pain in the emotional dimension may seem aptly expressed in the moral-emotional vocabulary of guilt, shame, remorse, and regret; but in the bottom itself—that self-perceived low point that Severance endures for weeks and months—it is experienced mainly as overwhelming turmoil, bewilderment, and confusion. Severance is, in first-person sensibility, lost to himself even as he struggles with successes and failures to maintain appearances, keep his job, and face his family.[23] The pain in the spiritual dimension feels to Severance, an intellectual, like the combination of extreme disappointment, disillusionment, bitterness, and anger that he supposes goes with the realization that life is meaningless. Interests and enthusiasms are nonexistent or seem silly; nothing matters; the idea of suicide dominates his thoughts. Severance is alternately lethargic and jittery; he feels somehow trapped in his life; there seems no way out.[24]

The net result of all this is a lengthy low point in Severance's life. The characterization of its phenomenology requires not the terminology of disease or genetics, but in due time (after recovery begins) such heavy moral-psychological words as isolation, despair, worthlessness, and the classic triad anger, resentment, and fear, as well as the negative staples of guilt, shame, regret, and remorse. This is the condition Severance is in and from which the AA program proposes the possibility of relief.[25] I must comment that in Severance the recovery program faces a major challenge. What is needed here is no simple heart-to-heart talk or half-hour arm-around-the-shoulder morale boost. Whatever the medical facts in Severance's case, he is systemically down in a way that has physical, emotional, and spiritual aspects to it. AA recognizes what friends, family, and well-wishers may not be able to recognize, that recovery in such a case is not simple, quick, or easy; it even recognizes that it may not be possible.[26] How, then, does one take Severance from his pain and confusion—his particular instantiation of living death—to human functionality? How might Severance recover agency and, perhaps, a measure of peace of mind as well?

Notice, in this connection, that there is a certain modesty in what AA construes to be the goal of its recovery and self-protection program. If we stop for interpretation of the philosopher's term "agency" here, the perhaps more ordinary word "functionality," or merely the relative term "relief" used above, AA and associated literature are refreshingly concrete and limited. One is not promised success in business, tenure, a terrific sex life, or first place in the marathon. Instead, "all that we hope for is sobriety and regeneration, so that we can live normal respectable lives and can be recognized by others as men and women willing to do unto others as we would be done by."[27] More elaborately, but in the same spirit, AA speaks of the Twelve Promises that the practice of its Twelve Steps helps bring into one's life. The promises, as follows,[28] reflect in their makeup the bottom that recovery is from and something of the richness of what AA sometimes calls "emotional sobriety"[29]; as such they afford an interpretation of agency, functionality, or simply relief that seems appropriate to the positive living of one's life that is the aim of a recovery strategy, especially given the context and clientele at stake,[30] even if they do not offer a solution to the analytic questions about agency that philosophers have asked.

1. We are going to know a new freedom and a new happiness.
2. We will not regret the past nor wish to shut the door on it.
3. We will comprehend the word serenity.
4. We will know peace.
5. No matter how far down the scale we have gone, we will see how our experience can benefit others.
6. That feeling of uselessness and self-pity will disappear.
7. We will lose interest in selfish things and gain interest in our fellows.

8. Self-seeking will slip away.
9. Our whole attitude and outlook on life will change.
10. Fear of people and economic insecurity will leave us.
11. We will intuitively know how to handle situations which used to baffle us.
12. We will suddenly realize that God is doing for us what we could not do for ourselves.

How, again, does Severance recover agency, thus understood? The AA program has many things to offer Severance in this connection. I will sketch some of these below; but first it is worth noting what the AA program per se will not offer Severance. The AA program is not, for example, a treatment center or a hospital, though sometimes bits and pieces of the program are employed in the forms of care offered in such settings. The AA program is not a religion, group therapy, sect, political organization, cult, or some sort of secret society, though I have heard it referred to as one or more of these things, even by otherwise responsible people in public positions who make such damaging references as if they knew whereof they speak. More important, perhaps, the AA program is not diagnostic in its operations, that is, it does not purport to figure out for Severance whether he is alcoholic. All Severance needs to join AA is "a desire to stop drinking,"[31] but AA will not tell Severance that he has that desire or somehow force it on him. How Severance comes to have that desire, if he ever does, may have to do with his personal suffering or with the social, relational, or emotional byproducts of his suffering, such as family troubles, legal hassles, or the pain of remorse, guilt, or shame[32]; but the operations of the AA program are logically posterior to the existence of that desire.

Regarding what the AA program is, the first point to be made is that it is the famous Twelve Steps, but the immediate next point to be made is that it is this plus many other things. I will, of course, give an account of the Twelve-Step Program (in the next section), but the practical importance to recovery and self-protection of the other ingredients of AA membership must first be emphasized. Recovery of agency is not accomplished by cognition alone. The other ingredients include at least the following.

First, there is a calculated social dimension to the AA program. It involves Severance in sharing his "experience, strength, and hope" with those who themselves have suffering in common with him.[33] This seems to me a point of some importance. Those who actually make the effort to practice the AA program (something that is not easy to do) do not have in common an ideology, theology, or politics, nor do they have similar talents, interests, social station, or ethnic background, nor do they necessarily share any of the other differentiating features of human life[34] around which people often group. In fact, it is a principle within AA that its members are anonymous with respect to these trappings of life in the human condition.[35] As a result of this, the AA experience is very leveling for those who take the program seriously.[36] The closeness—the bonding, as some regard it—that can occur among people within AA seems an empathy-cum-loyalty grounded in the common experience of life-threatening pain and supported by the gradual realization that a sort of solidarity can make recovery possible whereas going it alone has failed. Accordingly, AA meetings are daily or near daily for recovering alcoholics, and members are urged to equip themselves with sponsors, take phone numbers of other members, and, in short, connect with those who can from experience understand their suffering and share strategies for responding to threats to sobriety.[37]

Second, alongside the multifaceted social dimension, the AA program carries with it what might be called depressurization techniques. These are of different kinds and are perhaps functionally analogous to the relaxation techniques included in some programs of psychotherapy. Their point is simply to slow down the racing mind and to quiet the emotional agitation characteristic of the person seeking recovery. At AA meetings the typical practice is to begin a meeting with the Serenity Prayer, itself both soothing and emotionally balancing for those who take it seriously.[38] A similar purpose attaches to the famous AA maxims, the ones that so often show up on automobile bumper stickers: "One Day at a Time!" "Easy Does It!" "Keep It Simple!" These propositions, so empty, banal, or platitudinous in themselves, come to be profound when their application is shown in the details of the shared experience, strength, and hope in leads and in discussions at meetings. AA members are also urged to develop for themselves daily practices that help calm the soul. These might involve readings, times for prayer, quiet times at certain points in the day, meditation, or whatever, as long as the practices are made a part of one's daily routine, so as to remind one that one is not reducible to the commotion in one's life.

The AA program, then, will urge on Severance the informal elements I have described above. No one gains the sobriety-cum-serenity Severance seeks just by learning and knowing the Twelve Steps. The AA program surrounds its cognitive center (the Twelve Steps) with daily social activities (Severance's isolation must be overcome) and depressurization strategies usable daily (Severance cannot think clearly or sustain the self-reflection needed for detachment when agitated or consumed by the negativity of his thoughts about his life). For real people suffering the moralized despair I characterized above, there is much more to making recovery and self-protection possible than memorizing some steps, even if they are AA's Twelve Steps.

AA's Twelve Steps

The Twelve Steps provide the AA program with its central intellectual and normative content. Some drunks come into AA and manage to stay sober for awhile on meetings and slogans; they do not "work the steps," as it is put in AA, in any sustained way[39]; but my impression is that recovery and self-protection over the long term are facilitated by steady—indeed, daily—attention to the steps. I find no clarity, however, on success rates among those who attempt AA's Twelve Step Program. It is plain enough that many people with serious drinking problems in fact find their way to sustained sobriety; they work hard at the AA program, and they credit AA and its Twelve-Step Program for their recovery. Others do not have such success; some of those in the former group argue, as might be expected, that the unsuccessful ones did not work the program in a full and serious way. I believe it is enough to merit the attention that I give the Twelve-Step Program here that the former group exists. The steps, without explanation, are as follows:[40]

(1) We admitted we were powerless over alcohol—that our lives had become unmanageable.
(2) Came to believe that a Power greater than ourselves could restore us to sanity.
(3) Made a decision to turn our will and our lives over to the care of God *as we understood Him.*
(4) Made a searching and fearless moral inventory of ourselves.
(5) Admitted to God, to ourselves, and to another human being the exact nature of our wrongs.
(6) Were entirely ready to have God remove all these defects of character.
(7) Humbly asked Him to remove our shortcomings.
(8) Made a list of all persons we had harmed, and became willing to make amends to them all.
(9) Made direct amends to such people wherever possible, except when to do so would injure them or others.

(10) Continued to take personal inventory and when we were wrong promptly admitted it.

(11) Sought through prayer and meditation to improve our conscious contact with God *as we understood Him*, praying only for knowledge of His will for us and the power to carry that out.

(12) Having had a spiritual awakening as the result of these steps we tried to carry this message to alcoholics, and to practice these principles in all our affairs.

It might be useful first to comment in a general way on the contents of the steps, so as to begin to elicit AA's view about what is centrally involved in recovery and self-protection for people suffering the various bottoms of alcoholism.

Step 1 is in effect a surrender of sorts. It is not simply an admission that one has had a tough time in life and that this is somehow connected with drinking. There is a step 0 assumed by AA's Twelve Steps, namely, the bottoming-out process itself.[41] Recovery, then, begins with one's taking a step that represents one to oneself as understanding that one is not able to control one's drinking and that this fact—previously perhaps ignored, tolerated, or ineffectively compensated for—has had devastating results in one's life.[42]

After the negativity of the admission of defeat in step 1, steps 2 and 3 are an immediate turn in a positive, albeit importantly undefined, direction. For the purposes of this discussion, I take seriously AA's distinction between spirituality and religion, and its general insistence that it is "not allied with any sect, denomination, politics, organization or institution,"[43] and its aim to cast its net widely among those suffering alcoholism. Neither step requires one to believe in God in ways involving theological commitments or participation in the practices of an organized religion. Neither step requires any particular interpretation of what in AA is called "higher power." Some very interesting interpretations of "higher power" may be heard at AA meetings—let it never be said that recovering drunks have no imagination or wit; I have not, in twelve years, heard any such interpretation ruled AA-illegal or even criticized. The main point in step 2 for the drunk now admitting that a perhaps many-yeared way of life has failed is, after all, the sheer existence of the prospect of restoration to sanity; the main point in step 3 is the perhaps even surprising existence—surprising to the drunk suffering a bottom—of the possibility of detachment from the dictates of one's own will—the driving power of one's own wants, needs, and, indeed, cravings—in favor of commitment to the imperatives of a more credentialed will.[44] AA realizes what many outside observers apparently do not: that the battles the recovering drunk fights are not those involving the cognitive challenges of an acceptable theology, but, rather, those involving one's own appetites and habits, some of which are as embedded or constitutive as appetites and habits can get. Step 2 puts hope before one; it suggests that the admission of powerlessness in step 1 is not necessarily the end of the matter as far as going on in life is concerned; one is not necessarily trapped forever in the alcoholic way of life. Step 3 reinforces and strengthens for the victim the fundamental notion that his or her way of life involving heavy drinking is not necessarily fixed. The force of the phenomenology of being trapped in one's pain that the bottoming-out drunk experiences should not be underestimated in this dynamic. The idea that one's will and life could be better directed and cared for, that is, that this is even a prospect for one, is in its own way for the suffering bottomed-out drunk a glimpse of the possibility of liberation. The metaphor that occurs to me is that the set of steps 1 through 3 dislodges one from oneself; they loosen the hold on one of a way-of-life that has not worked. Despite the admission of powerlessness in step 1, steps 1 through 3 firmly point the sufferer toward a positive future, and they do so without unfairly burdening the turn toward a positive future with intellectual or theological demands that current confusion or previous thought make impossibilities for some, perhaps many, in any case.

The next major chunk of the Twelve-Step Program is the set of steps 4 though 7. These steps fit together and, if worked steadily over the long term, make possible a recovering drunk's self-confrontation and then, together with step 10, the cultivation of a general daily habit of reflection on his or her motives. It is important to notice that the AA program urges on the recovering drunk not only abstinence and not only basic changes in way of life, but, indeed, a change in the person. My thought is that AA spirituality has less to do with religion or theology and more to do with character than popular outside opinion recognizes.

We should notice some interesting features of the self-confrontation called for in these steps. The AA program is neither simple nor easy in its construal of what it is to know oneself and change oneself. The "searching and fearless" moral inventory of the self in step 4 is not just an attempt to put together the anecdotal story line of one's life, though it may begin that way; AA means it to reach behind the story line to the main dispositions of character and also to include practical judgments of their worth and efficacy. The recommended process for self-inventory guards against self-deception, insofar as this is possible, through the advice of patience and thoroughness (the inventory is to be "searching and fearless"), explicit warnings about self-deception,[45] and the workings of the "confessional" step 5 wherein one is in close contact with a person one trusts about the results of one's self-inventory—a form of contact that extends to the other's views about the accuracy of one's results. AA does not require professional counseling for its members, though it allows it; its membership is open without regard to the sufferer's economic status; its program recognizes the difficulties attending the acquisition of self-knowledge, and it makes do with safeguards that do not cost money. A further interesting feature of this self-confrontational chunk of the program is its skepticism toward any naive pop-psychological maxim to the effect that knowledge is power. The set of steps 4 through 7 does not promise that once one knows oneself, one is thereby enabled to change oneself. AA knows people better than that, and its program does not make demands of its members that will frustrate their sincere efforts to meet them. In step 6 one does what one can to make oneself "entirely ready" to change—but even that does not guarantee that one will change. Step 7 is an appeal beyond oneself in this connection. One's shortcomings are finally not one's own to control through exercises of one's own will. Life and the change in the person that AA urges on one are not that easy. The change in the person AA has in mind is something one can work at to some extent, of course, but finally it is something that happens to one. Recovering alcoholics are often impatient, and they often suffer frustration at the pace of recovery and, indeed, at their own inability to change themselves. Such impatience and frustration must surely be common among people attempting to move on in their lives from moralized low points. The AA program seems fully aware of such tendencies and vulnerabilities in people and makes explicit this awareness in its program at many points. The attention to character, or the program's near-synonym, "spirituality," that AA sees as a condition of the emotional detachment and calm that are conducive to sobriety for the long term is viewed as a practice that is difficult yet necessary to the development of a sober way of life. Steps 4 through 7 structure this practice somewhat, that is, they show one how to attend to character, and in that way they make it possible for one to learn how to confront oneself in a constructive way. My way of expressing the central point of this part of the AA program is this: the recovery of agency requires attention to the makeup of the self—attention protected as far as possible against deception—but it must avoid aggrandizement of the powers of the will. It is perhaps no surprise that discussions of these steps in AA meetings often focus on the notions of humility and honesty.[46]

Steps 8 and 9 concern personal relations.[47] In this part of the AA program one reaches out to others, in particular, those with whom one's relationships have been damaged or destroyed. The two steps divide up the reaching-out in an interesting fashion: the first calls for one merely to list those harmed in the course of one's drinking career and then to become willing to make amends to them all; the second calls for one to make amends, but this call is not without qualifications. AA recognizes many times over[48] that it does not follow from the listing of those harmed and the development of the willingness to make amends that one can or ought to make amends to this or that particular person on one's list. In some cases amends may not be possible (the person harmed has died or left for parts unknown); in other cases making amends may cause injury to others or, in an especially tricky sort of case, to oneself. It is sometimes said that the three-part amends project in AA (listing, willingness, and action) is undertaken for oneself as much as for others, the point being that what is at stake here as elsewhere in the program is the formation of character and way of life conducive to emotional calm and detachment and, hence, sobriety. It is thought that what is so conducive is a character and way of life in which one acknowledges such harm as one does to others and attempts to ameliorate it insofar as circumstances allow, rather than a character and way of life filled with evading, hiding, explaining away, and denying in regard to such harm as one does to others. Such a point may seem platitudinous to many, but when it is directed to people whose previous way of life was typically filled with evading and rationalizing,[49] the change in character and way of life called for may in fact be a formidable challenge.[50] What is at stake are the habits of a lifetime.

Steps 10, 11, and 12 are sometimes referred to as "maintenance steps." It is here that it becomes clear that the Twelve-Step Program is a strategy for recovery and self-protection. In the text of *Alcoholics Anonymous* the promises appear just after the discussion of steps 8 and 9, but one can see that the program dare not stop there. It is one thing to recover but another to stay sober. After all, as the text reminds the recovering drunk, "we deal with alcohol—cunning, baffling, powerful!"[51] As anyone with inside or outside experience of alcoholism knows, relapse is a standing threat. AA is aware of this threat—acutely so—in all aspects of its program. Its doors are of course always open to the one who relapses, or "goes out," as AA jargon has it, but AA also realizes that alcoholism for the real alcoholic can be a life-or-death matter and that, accordingly, relapse can be fatal.[52] How one protects oneself, especially in a drinking culture featuring a powerful association between drinking and good times, has to be a main concern for the AA program. There is no cure for alcoholism,[53] and AA's life of sobriety (life-long abstinence) requires support and nurturance. The AA program is daily or near daily for the recovering drunk with one year of sobriety and also for the recovering drunk with twenty years of sobriety.

The final three steps in the program carve up the task of self-protection in an interesting fashion. In very brief terms, they recommend, in step 10, a sort of daily version of the self-examination involved in steps 4 through 7 plus immediate amends when one does wrong to another; in step 11 continued cultivation of spirituality is proposed, urging on the recovering person the importance of steps 2 and 3 plus prayer and meditation as strategies by which one may calm oneself and also enhance one's spirituality.[54] In step 12 the recovering person is urged to be available to others who are suffering alcoholism[55] and to generalize the various principles involved in the recovery strategy across the many departments of life. In summary here, self-protection turns out, in AA, to involve a concatenation of self-examination and readiness to admit one's wrongdoing, plus the calming to be derived from practices cultivating one's spirituality and the selflessness involved in extending a helping hand to the victim whose pain one recognizes from one's own experience.

Notes

Let me follow this too-brief interpretation of the AA program and AA's Twelve Steps with some notes. In one way or another these notes concern how it is that the program and the steps provide recovery and self-protection for those who take them seriously. It must be said again that not everyone who seeks recovery through AA succeeds, though I do not know that helpful generalizations about those who relapse can be made: the details of the different situations of the different individuals who "go out" may not exhibit illuminating patterns. Still, recovery through AA is a positive result for many drunks, and it seems to me legitimate to ask how and why this is so.

One interesting feature of the Twelve-Step Program is the order of the steps. It is important in this connection to see that the order of the steps is not set by the natural impulses of the bottomed-out drunk in the first days of recovery. When a drunk with a long drinking history bottoms out in the fashion described earlier and then reaches out for help in a way that brings him or her to AA, the typical first thing he or she wants to do is to restore some semblance of decent relationships with others, for example, family members, friends, colleagues at work, and even neighbors—if, of course, any of these others remain in his or her life. The isolation in the suffering of the alcoholic is such that the sufferer conceives of relief, should it be possible, as, or as involving, renewed contact with the human community. Accordingly, the Twelve-Step Program often seems puzzling to the newcomer when it places steps 8 and 9, about making amends, at a relatively late point in the recovery strategy. The newcomer wants badly to set things right with others and only then work on the self and, if time permits, work on God.

The program, however, reverses this order of things. I find this interesting and seek the human wisdom in the reversal. The Twelve-Step Program does indeed propose that the recovering drunk restore his or her relationships with others through amends, but not immediately. The program sees the unwisdom of a newly dry drunk rushing around apologizing to everyone and anyone within moral sight, vulnerable to possibly exaggerated conceptions of his or her past life as well as to rebuke from those unwilling to receive his or her amends or to being taken advantage of by some recipients of amends who recognize in the situation opportunities for exercising a certain control over the one who offers amends. The program realizes that the brand-new recovering drunk is likely to be neither clear about his or her past and present nor strong enough to sustain sobriety in the face of rejection from some among those to whom he or she offers amends,[56] nor able to protect himself or herself from or against the recipient who responds by manipulation.

The program orders the steps in a way that prepares the newcomer for the possibly dangerous task of reaching out to others, and in this way it reflects a certain wisdom about life and people that may facilitate recovery and self-protection. As the point is sometimes made in discussion meetings, AA helps one make peace in three different respects. After the admission of powerlessness in step 1, steps 2 and 3 invite one to make peace with a higher power (even if, as in my interpretation, this is essentially a matter of detaching oneself from one's own will), and steps 4 through 7 invite one to make peace with oneself; only then—now twice protected by detachment from one's own will and, possibly, a connection with a higher power, plus a more adequate self-understanding—may one venture into the risky terrain involving making peace with others, some of whom may be welcoming, others not. The AA program not only divides recovery into discrete parts, thereby providing rather concrete guidance about how to proceed with the problem of returning to life; it also carefully positions the one who works it to reach out to others when the time comes in such a way that unwelcoming, unexpected, or negative responses do not defeat fragile sobriety. This insightful ordering of the Steps helps the chances of recovery. It also makes clear AA's patience with recovery and, hence, its recognition of the difficulty involved in the recovery of agency. AA never rushes anyone. The steps are to be worked, slowly and repeatedly, over one's life, as recovery in effect becomes self-protection.

Not only does the AA program order the steps in a way that facilitates recovery, recognize the difficulty of recovery and self-protection, and manifest its patience with the difficult task, it also persistently reminds those who work the steps that life in AA is more than staying dry and helping others. It warns against the indifference that can accompany the common occurrence of satisfaction with one's new life early in recovery. It turns out that recovering alcoholics, sometimes pleased with their progress and perhaps impatient with the many challenges and tasks involved in AA's recovery program, appear to settle for what Bill Wilson calls "that blissful state . . . known as 'two-stepping,' " wherein one works only step 1 plus the part of step 12 involving carrying the message.[57] (One admits one's powerlessness over alcohol and then turns to missionary work among those still suffering.) The notion that the AA program reduces to keeping dry and carrying the message is referred to as "the 'two step' illusion,"[58] and the recovering drunk is warned against any such reduction. In fact, it seems right to say that for AA the key to a sustained, rich, and even joyful life[59] is alcoholic sobriety, that is, abstinence, backed by emotional sobriety, or a state or condition of calm, of what Bill Wilson describes as "an inner stength and peace that could not be deeply shaken by the shortcomings of others or by any calamity not of [one's] own making," that is much more than what is suggested or achieved by two-stepping. It helps one's chances of recovery and, especially, one's prospects for self-protection to understand that the development of emotional sobriety is not a light, simple, univocal, or easy matter. Recovery and self-protection are serious life tasks for the recovering person, and everything in AA plays up their seriousness and warns against the relegation of these tasks to the sidelines of one's life. My experience indicates that AA has made, or helped make, functional people of, in some cases, "hopeless drunks," and I appreciate its view that this does not occur on one meeting a month, an occasional chat with a sponsor, and some skimming of the Twelve Steps. What facilitates recovery? Well, a certain seriousness about it and a recognition that it covers many things—simple points, I suppose, but ones the forgetting of which is potentially tragic. The recovery of agency, for one who suffers the sort of low point that AA has in mind, is not part-time work.

Let me add some words here about what is sometimes called—even in AA literature—"the God thing." I have deliberately offered a minimalist interpretation of the program's many references to God and a higher power.[60] This seems to me reasonable, given AA's own distinction between religion and spirituality and its wish, after all, to cast its net widely among suffering alcoholics. Religion is baffling or off-putting to many drunks, and insistence on theological commitments more likely to generate anger or to be frightening than inviting. I need to add here, though, so that my own higher-power minimalism is not distorting in the opposite direction, that AA is accommodating and even welcoming to those who are sympathetic to religion. The recovery of agency involves, for many, a rediscovery of religious sensibility from earlier years, and AA welcomes such a thing as long as it does not carry with it an intolerance that impugns the terms of recovery of other members of AA. It remains that what is at stake for AA is recovery from alcoholism and, while some or many individuals in the fellowship might be pleased that one has "found religion" in the course of one's quest for sobriety, one is not urged to preach one's religion at meetings. The situation here seems to me to fit the view William James offers in *The Will to Believe*: the agency celebrated in James's famous essays is of the sort that constitutes life worth living and is explicitly not a matter of dogma or definition. Neither William James nor AA begrudge one's going beyond life-energizing agency to religious or theological doctrine, but they both hold that the former does not require the latter to be effective and also that the latter must not declare anathema alternative doctrines.[61]

It seems natural to follow the note above, concerning AA's openness to all (sympathetic to religion or not), with some words about the down-to-earth nature of the work done in and through the program. AA does not insist on one's learning or absorbing a theory or religion, such that when that theory or religion is learned or absorbed, one is then cured. It is closer to the mark to notice that through meetings, discussions, and reflections on the Twelve-Step Program AA focuses on breaking some of the many small but crucial connections that typically define the alcoholic way of life for the drunk. These are connections that have somehow, over time, come to be embedded in the drunk's daily life in such a way as to surround his or her use of alcohol with a small protective (at times, defensive) ideology of sorts. For example, the small ideology might closely associate alcohol and good times, so that it gradually comes to be difficult for the victim to understand how an occasion or event could promise enjoyment, relaxation, or celebration if it involved no alcohol. The ideology also treats alcohol as something that supports one in life, so that with it one will perform well in social situations or even at work. The view of alcohol as helpmate or friend is especially stubborn in the drunk's way of life and one the breaking down of which is a main target in AA meetings. The funniest—yet most serious—account I know of these connections that the recovering drunk must break is the one that reminds him or her that the AA promises, meant to come true after a certain amount of effort with the Twelve Steps, were in his or her earlier drinking life thought to be the promises of alcohol.

Perhaps this is not the place, however, to detail these on-the-ground AA activities further. It is enough for this note to point out that the program focuses on breaking the many connections that define and structure an alcoholic way of life, and it focuses on breaking these connections rather than losing itself and those it attempts to help in elaborations of explanations, general theories, or current medical research regarding alcoholism. AA offers a recovery program and does not pretend to be a learned society. Accordingly, in its work it attends to the needs of its members, as these are evident in the rough-and-tumble of the task of returning to life.

I should note, too, AA's way with metaphors, word pictures, and stories. The discourse of AA discussions is neither polite, precise, nor disciplined. In their efforts to share their experience, strength, and hope, people say strange things to one another. Some of these things are exaggerations; others are distortions; still others are less than fully true. Some of them are very funny.[62] I have had atheists speak to me of "acts of the higher power" in their lives, as, for example, when one treats one's good luck as one's having been saved from disaster or folly, and, when pressed, go on to explain that their higher power is their AA group, their cat, or the tree by their garage—very puzzling to the literal, analytic inquirer. I have heard people resolve to reject AA and its activities "because AA makes you believe what is not true," but I have come to see that that rests on a mistake about AA's functions and the nature of its discourse. In line with the discussion above regarding AA and "the God thing," I note here that AA offers no doctrine of a sort that is such that subscribing to it would involve one in risking believing what is not true. The Twelve-Step Program is not so much an ideology as it is a set of topics whose exploration with others, who may hold different views, has a way of helping one stay sober. Why attention to these topics helps keep one sober is not clear[63]; that this is so, though, seems evident. AA, of course, is not cognitively empty, but it is far more cognitively proceduralist than doctrinal in its content. When, before or after a meeting, one AA member talks with another about the latter's problems in his or her work, about the limits on his or her responsibility for children, or about how to bear the death of a parent, the response is not in terms of AA beliefs on these matters. It is, again, a response that runs in the terms of shared experience, plus, in fortunate cases, a good deal of simple, old-fashioned, one-person-to-another-person patience and quiet listening,[64] and such a response is likely to contain in it a morale boost and a reminder that one can deal with life's problems without drinking. The latter reminder might seem unnecessary or insulting to nonalcoholic people ("earth people," as they are called in AA), but it is not so considered among recovering drunks. For these practices—that is, for the discourse of the shared experience, the morale boost, and the priority of sobriety, plus the responses of patience and openness to the troubled person's efforts to articulate his or her experience—the recovering drunk can be grateful, for these contribute more effectively to sustaining sobriety and thus recovery on a daily basis than would the recitation of ideology or the explanation of theory.

Let me place three items together in this last note. First, AA recognizes, with sadness, what seems endorsed by the model of the self invoked earlier in my discussion: there can be the genuinely "hard case," namely, the case of the heavy drinker who cannot overcome his or her drinking problem, even with AA's help. In Bill Wilson's words, this is the case of the one who is "constitutionally incapable of being honest" with himself or herself. Wilson adds that "there are such unfortunates. They are not at fault; they seem to have been born that way."[65] I find these added words both very important regarding the experience of alcoholism and also philosophically interesting in regard to how moral theory is to think about the persons it treats as moral agents. If people are, in the term I used earlier, modular and differential and thus vulnerable to stucknesses, gappiness, and outlaw forces of various sorts, then a general uncritical use of the model of persons as in-control agents is probably detrimental in the long term to the relevance and interest of moral theory.

Second, regarding AA in particular, I think its recovery program has in mind mainly the person whose drinking problem is such that overcoming it is a supererogatory task, relative to that person's constitutional makeup at the time of his or her bottom. The relevant makeup involves constitutional incapacity regarding sustaining control over drinking once started and difficulty—but not constitutional incapacity—regarding being honest. In overview fashion: (1) the AA program can indeed be for the in-control agent whose drinking becomes a problem in his or her life; such a person can benefit from the program through its practices, discourse, and common sense, and, indeed, such a person may not require the program as an extended support system for a lifetime. (2) I think, however, that there are those whose drinking problem presents a supererogatory challenge relative to their constitutional makeup, and for them AA's activities may support the living of life for a lifetime, and, indeed, for them life itself may be in genuine jeopardy if participation in AA diminishes or stops. (3) Too, the hard cases exist—the cases of those Bill Wilson calls "unfortunates." I know people who are hard cases, and perhaps those who read these words will know others. It is possible, regarding the hard case, that life prospects may change for a person, because constitutional makeup can change. Depression, as I said above, can lift, and this can be so in a way that is not related causally to therapy or chemicals; similarly, it seems a fact that the alcohol-entrapment characteristic of alcoholism can lift, or undergo what medical terminology calls remission. It is not only some recovering people in AA who get beyond the drinking problem. Beyond these three sorts of cases I cannot myself go. The modular and differential conceptual picture of how persons are is helpful, but it is not itself a view that yields ways of diagnosing given people or prescriptions for those who are hard cases.

My last point might be considered a point about the ethics of skeptics. My impression is that intellectuals have a difficult time acknowledging the worth of the AA program and, in particular, the notions that for some drinkers the task of overcoming their problem is supererogatory and that for other drinkers the overcoming through exercise of will is impossible. I have come to find these latter notions not hard to acknowledge at all. My wish is that we could relate to one another in such a way that we do not make little or light of the difficulties others have that we do not have ourselves. If a person is seriously entrapped in alcoholism and then finds in AA a way up and out,[66] then we may celebrate the person and express gratitude to AA.

Remarks on Peace of Mind

Let me end this account of the AA program and AA's Twelve Steps by returning briefly to my subject at the beginning of this extended discussion. I worried there that peace of mind is lost to the person whose past is morally problematic. A view I ascribed to Hume and Falk holds that a condition of peace of mind, that is, of being morally at ease with oneself, is one's being able to bear or tolerate a review of one's past. It appears that, for some or many of us, this condition cannot be satisfied, and so, for some or many of us, the personal good of peace of mind seems forfeited or out of reach.

Now, the AA program is of course aware of the problem of peace of mind for its membership. One of the most important parts of the task of recovery is coming to terms with one's own problematic past. I have suggested that in AA one attempts to make peace with a higher power, but also with oneself and others, but, of course, these forms of making peace do not necessarily constitute or yield peace of mind, or, at any rate, the peace of mind that meets the Hume-Falk condition. In fact, if we hold firmly to the Hume-Falk suggestion regarding what peace of mind is or involves, then it seems indeed that a good many—perhaps most—recovering alcoholics will not have or be entitled to peace of mind—something similar might be true for many others as well—for the AA program is characterized by AA as a program of rigorous honesty, and the recovering person is not urged or allowed to ignore, set aside, or revise his or her past.

One wants to ask, then, how AA handles this matter. If Hume-Falk peace of mind is not available to the recovering alcoholic, yet peace of mind is an important personal good, then how does AA respond? Is something else, something similar or analogous to peace of mind, available instead? Or is the recovering alcoholic condemned to a sober life laced with moral-emotional negativity? As I also suggested above, AA may have many ways of breaking down the ideology by which the alcoholic protects and defends, to himself if not to others, his or her drinking,[67] and AA may also have ways of helping the recovering alcoholic manage and contain the anger, fear, and resentment that it considers so threatening to honesty and thus to sobriety. The recovery distance that AA maps out for the recovering drunk to travel via the Twelve Steps is very great. Bill Wilson's words at the beginning of his commentary on step 1 and those at the beginning of his commentary on step 12 are remarkable for the contrast in the state of the soul of the suffering alcoholic and of the recovering alcoholic that they provide. The first words are these:

> No other kind of bankruptcy is like this one. Alcohol, now become the rapacious creditor, bleeds us of all self-sufficiency and all will to resist its demands. Once this stark fact is accepted, our bankruptcy as going human concerns is complete.[68]

The second words are these:

Our Twelfth step . . . says that as a result of practicing all the Steps, we have each found something called a spiritual awakening. To new A.A.'s, this often seems like a very dubious and improbable state of affairs. "What do you mean when you talk about a 'spiritual awakening'?" they ask.

Maybe there are as many definitions of spiritual awakening as there are people who have had them. But certainly each genuine one has something in common with all the others. And these things which they have in common are not too hard to understand. When a man or a woman has a spiritual awakening, the most important meaning of it is that he has now become able to do, feel, and believe that which he could not do before on his unaided stength and resources alone. He has been granted a gift which amounts to a new state of consciousness and being. He has been set on a path which tells him he is really going somewhere, that life is not a dead end, not something to be endured or mastered. In a very real sense he has been transformed, because he has laid hold of a source of strength which, in one way or another, he had hitherto denied himself. He finds himself in possession of a degree of honesty, tolerance, unselfishness, peace of mind, and love of which he had thought himself quite incapable. What he has received is a free gift, and yet usually, at least in some small part, he has made himself ready to receive it.[69]

One cannot but be moved by the recovery-of-agency aspiration expressed here by Bill Wilson, and one might also be struck by the distance of the latter state from the beginning state of alcoholic bankruptcy. Still, all this said, is the peace of mind Bill Wilson enumerates as a part of the spiritual awakening the same as or different from the peace of mind of Hume and Falk?

It must, of course, be different. AA peace of mind is not Hume-Falk peace of mind and cannot be. Nothing in AA practice teaches one to find one's problematic past bearable or tolerable, if that means finding it approvable, not to matter, ignorable, right in the long term, or something of the sort. The interesting thing about AA practice is that it never lets one forget or revise the past, and, in fact, it is rigorous honesty about the past that provides one form of motivation in support of the sobriety of today,[70] so one does not get Hume-Falk peace of mind in AA. One has forfeited that sort of being at ease with oneself. What one does or can get, though, seems to be an important alternative sort of personal good, one with its own logic, structure, and philosophical interest, for, after all, if some or many of us, for whatever reasons, cannot have Hume-Falk peace of mind because our pasts are morally botched, then, if we are to go on, we need something that will enable us to bear that. That is, on the assumption that morality wants to make it possible for the recovering alcoholic to proceed with his or her life, but without ignoring or revising the past, then it must make available to him or her ways of living with the past and, in particular, ways of overcoming the loss or diminishment of agency involved in the recognition and acknowledgement of one's own moral wrongdoing. AA recognizes that there is a moral-psychological reduction of agency involved in the recognition and acknowledgment of one's own moral wrongdoing, perhaps especially so when, as in the cases I have mainly had in mind in this study, the wrongdoing lodged in one's past is such that one's sense of direct connection with it is clouded and dim even as one admits one's responsibility (i.e., the legitimacy of one's being held accountable) for it.

The beauty of AA—perhaps "power" would be the better term—is that it helps one come back from a bottom involving moralized despair and, in particular, from a past whose review one cannot bear. It somehow, through its many practices, steps, patient people, weird and funny stories, and endless bad coffee, gets its people to live with their past. It takes many things, not one thing, to achieve this remarkable result, and the result itself is indeed perhaps best expressed in the string of words Bill Wilson uses toward the end of the passage quoted above. The AA alternative to Hume-Falk peace of mind is a cluster involving, among other things, humility, honesty, tolerance, unselfishness, a certain openness to and patience with others, a certain willingness to help others, and a certain degree of resignation to and thus acceptance of the facts of failure and folly in human beings, including oneself. AA recognizes the complexity and difficulty of the recovery of agency. It will not help one erase or change the past, but it will help one attempt to achieve a sort of inner calm that will allow one to go forward with one's life.

Notes

Preface

1. John Rawls, *A Theory of Justice* (Cambridge, Mass.: Belknap Press of Harvard University Press, 1971).
2. Rawls, 7.
3. Rawls, 512.
4. Norman S. Care, *On Sharing Fate* (Philadelphia: Temple University Press, 1987).

Chapter 1

1. Perhaps this highlighting of "sense of control" puts my account here in line with these remarks of Herbert Morris:

> Guilt, perhaps more than any other concept, serves our need to believe ourselves capable of some effectiveness in the world, a need all the more insistent as conditions of modern life promote feelings of helplessness. Intimately involved as it is with responsibility, guilt testifies to human freedom and agency and, as such, it may serve to counteract one's sense of victimization.

("The Decline of Guilt," *Ethics* 99:1 [October 1988]: 69.)

2. In *The Importance of What We Care About* (Cambridge: Cambridge University Press, 1988), Harry G. Frankfurt writes that "a person's will is that by which he moves himself" (p. 84). The idea of agency I have in mind incorporates the element of will, but it also contains the moral-psychological aspect of sensibility I referred to above. The agency I have in mind is one's capacity to move oneself, as evidenced through the sense one has of being in control of one's life.

3. Immanuel Kant, *Foundations of the Metaphysics of Morals*, trans. and intro. Lewis White Beck (Indianapolis: Bobbs-Merrill, 1959).

4. See Onora O'Neill's discussion of how we are implicated in destitution in the world community in "Lifeboat Earth," *Philosophy and Public Affairs* 4 (Spring 1975), reprinted in Charles R. Beitz, et al., eds., *International Ethics* (Princeton: Princeton University Press, 1985).

5. There are, of course, other cases that might be explored, though I will not do so at this point. I find two essays by Herbert Morris especially helpful: "Shared Guilt," *On Guilt and Innocence* (Berkeley: University of California Press, 1976); and "Nonmoral Guilt," in Ferdinand Schoeman, ed., *Responsibility, Character, and the Emotions* (Cambridge: Cambridge University Press, 1987).

6. L. A. Selby-Bigge, ed., *Hume's Enquiries* (Oxford: Clarendon, 1962), 283.

7. In "Morality, Self, and Others," in Hector-Neri Castañeda and George Nakhnikian, eds., *Morality and the Language of Conduct* (Detroit: Wayne State University Press, 1963), 63–64.

8. John Rawls's characterization of the "deliberative rationality" of those in the original position makes use of this connection of ideas in an interesting way: "it means that the parties cannot agree to a conception of justice if the consequences of applying it may lead to self-reproach should the least happy possibilities be realized. They should strive to be free from such regrets." *A Theory of Justice* (Cambridge, Mass.: The Belknap Press of Harvard University Press, 1971), 427. Cf. p. 176.

9. Thomas Nagel suggests that the world might be not only a "bad place" but "an evil place as well," for even innocent persons can face genuine moral dilemmas involving only "morally abominable courses of action." ("War and Massacre," *Mortal Questions* [Cambridge: Cambridge University Press, 1979], 74.) If there are genuine moral dilemmas, a steady conscientiousness would not necessarily be protection against having the problem of living with one's past.

10. The "memory . . . gnaws constantly at the soul. . . ." In Martin P. Golding, "Forgiveness and Regret," *The Philosophical Forum* 16 (Fall–Winter 1984–85): 124.

11. Cf. Richard Wollheim, *The Thread of Life* (Cambridge, Mass.: Harvard University Press, 1984), 131.

12. Cf. Golding, "Forgiveness and Regret," 127.

13. Here I set aside certain religious beliefs that counsel that our forgiveness of others and ourselves is required by God's forgiveness of all his children.

14. Golding writes:

wrongs having this degree of culpability and enormity may put one permanently in debt to the victim such that the moral amends are unending and resentment is forever justified. As far as the moral regeneration of the wrongdoer is concerned, the process would be a never-ending one and he would not be able to think of himself as having passed the stage of making moral amends; the wrongdoer must constantly regret his wrong both as regards its (im)morality and its other-directedness; the wrong need not, may not, be forgiven.

He adds that "if anything is a wrong of this order it is the German's destruction of the Jews." "Forgiveness and Regret," 135.

15. "Pilot's Nightmare Becomes Reality," in *The (Cleveland) Plain Dealer* (27 October 1987).

16. Cf. Bernard Williams's discussion of a case of a similar kind in "Moral Luck," *Moral Luck* (Cambridge: Cambridge University Press, 1981), 28.

17. Professor Alan Severance is the main figure in the essentially autobiographical novel *Recovery* (New York: Farrar, Straus, and Giroux, 1973) by the poet John Berryman. My sketch has only parts of Berryman's deeply moving story in mind. It is not my purpose to discuss the novel (which is unfinished) as a whole.

18. This is in line with Rawls's remarks about "moral personality" in *A Theory of Justice*.

19. Such families are sometimes called "dysfunctional."

20. I should emphasize, keeping in mind points to be made later, that it is not part of my view that damage to moral personality is necessarily irretrievable.

21. I have in mind here not only Alanon and Alateen, but also the recovery program Adult Children of Alcoholics. A text that has been very important to this latter program's becoming a movement of sorts is Janet Geringer Woititz, *Adult Children of Alcoholics* (Pompano Beach, Fla.: Health Communications, Inc., 1983). Also helpful regarding adult-children issues is Claudia Black, *It Will Never Happen to Me!* (Denver: M.A.C., 1981). For a scholarly study offering a critical appraisal of theory and research in this area, see Kenneth J. Sher, *Children of Alcoholics* (Chicago and London: University of Chicago Press, 1991).

22. Toward the end of Book 2 of *The Confessions*, trans. J. M. Cohen (Harmondsworth, England: Penguin Books, 1954). All the quotations in the following few paragraphs are from pp. 86–89 in this edition. I am directed to this case by some words of Wollheim, *The Thread of Life*, 154: "the powerfully charged memories that absorbed [Rousseau], if we are to believe [his] testimony. . . ."

23. Despite this resolution Rousseau returned to the subject again at the end of his life, in the "Fourth Walk," of *The Reveries of the Solitary Walker*, trans., preface, notes, and interpretive essay, Charles E. Butterworth (New York: Harper Colophon edition, 1982). Apparently, as a form of therapy Rousseau's writing of *Confessions* did not succeed in ridding him of the cruel memory; in *Reveries* he speaks of the "dreadful lie I told in my early youth, the memory of which has troubled me all my life and even comes in my old age to sadden my heart again, already distressed as it is in so many other ways" (pp. 43–44).

24. Wollheim, *The Thread of Life*, chap. 1.

25. The view of self-conception I suggest here is reminiscent of, but is not as extreme as, Jean-Paul Sartre's view of the "image" one creates in acting, in "Existentialism is a Humanism," in Walter Kaufman, ed., *Existentialism from Dostoevsky to Sartre* (New York: Meridian Books, 1956). For Sartre, that image is "an image of man such as [one] believes he ought to be," and it is also thought to be "valid for all and for the entire epoch in which we find ourselves. Our

responsibility . . . concerns mankind as a whole" (pp. 291–92). I do not maintain that the conception of oneself, by which one leads one's life, must be quite that grand.

26. For a full discussion, see David Pears, *Motivated Irrationality* (Oxford: Oxford University Press, 1984).

27. Some blackouts are more complete than others. In other cases one may have a dim recollection of what one did. Here, in Severance's case, no recollection is the most apt description.

28. Joel Feinberg's words come to mind: "insofar as the choices are not voluntary they are just as alien to him as the choices of someone else." "Legal Paternalism," *Rights, Justice, and the Bounds of Liberty* (Princeton: Princeton University Press, 1980), 117.

29. Berryman's *Recovery* is helpful and moving on this matter.

30. Cf. George E. Vaillant, *The Natural History of Alcoholism* (Cambridge, Mass.: Harvard University Press, 1983), 299:

> I believe it is important to explain to patients that their alcoholism, like a disease, has a life of its own and is not a moral or psychological problem. Repeated relapses that injure an alcoholic's loved ones generate enormous guilt and confusion. The ensuing shame further enhances denial. My experience has convinced me that the concept of disease facilitates rather than impedes patients' acceptance of responsibility for their illness and its treatment.

For the view that the disease concept may instead promote "pseudoscientific proselytizing that induces self-deception" (p. 65), see Herbert Fingarette, "Alcoholism and Self-Deception," in Mike W. Martin, ed., *Self-Deception and Self-Understanding* (Lawrence, Kans.: University Press of Kansas, 1985). Professor Fingarette's book, *Heavy Drinking* (Berkeley: University of California Press, 1988), is a sustained critique of the idea that alcoholism is a disease. For brief discussions of the cases for and against the disease concept, see Herbert Fingarette, "We Should Reject the Disease Concept of Alcoholism," *The Harvard Medical School Mental Health Letter* 6:8 (February 1990); and George E. Vaillant, "We Should Retain the Disease Concept of Alcoholism," *The Harvard Medical School Mental Health Letter* 6:9 (March 1990); both of these essays are reprinted in Lester Grinspoon and James B. Bakala, eds., "Alcohol Abuse and Dependence," *The Harvard Medical School Mental Health Review* (President and Fellows of Harvard College, 1990).

31. In chap. 5 below I separate the issue of whether alcoholism is a disease from the issue of how one might recover from alcoholism. Throughout that chapter I discuss the latter issue in some detail.

32. For a study in which it is argued that "a significant class of drunk drivers who cause death does indeed commit, and often get away with, murder," see Bonnie Steinbock, "Drunk Driving," *Philosophy and Public Affairs* 14 (Summer 1985): 278. With the alcoholic in mind, Steinbock comments: "Even if one is not responsible for getting drunk, and if one has had a great deal of advance warning

about what one is likely to do when drunk, then the fact that one was drunk does not lessen one's responsibility at all" (p. 289). It may be that the alcoholic should be held responsible in the way Steinbock has in mind, but her argument for this view seems to rest on the premise that the alcoholic recognizes and acknowledges his or her alcoholism; thus, she writes that

> although the alcoholic has less (or no) control over his drinking than the ordinary social drinker, intoxication is even less of an excuse for him than for the inexperienced inebriate, just because he knows that he will become intoxicated and that he endangers others by driving. If he has the capacity to act rationally when not intoxicated, he is morally required to take steps to ensure that he does not drive after he gets drunk. (p. 290)

Perhaps there are some alcoholics who interpret their condition in the way Steinbock assumes, but my undestanding is that typically the practicing alcoholic does not recognize and acknowledge his or her alcoholism. In fact, one of the most curious and troubling features of alcoholism is that it is a condition whose denial on the part of the victim is a common symptom. Such denial often seems a part of the self-psychology of the victim of the condition. Insofar as this is so, then while Steinbock's normative position whereby alcoholics are to be held responsible for what they do might be acceptable, some other argument would be needed to support it.

33. Cf. Joel Feinberg's remarks about self-government in his discussion of the idea of autonomy, in *Harm to Self* (New York: Oxford University Press, 1986), chap. 18.

34. The following passages, from *Twelve Steps and Twelve Traditions* (New York: Alcoholics Anonymous World Services, Inc., 1952, 1953), which are directed to recovering alcoholics, seem to me helpful on this point:

> We might next ask ourselves what we mean when we say that we "harmed" other people. What kind of "harm" do people do one another, anyway? To define the word "harm" in a practical way, we might call it the result of instincts in collision, which cause physical, mental, emotional, or spiritual damage to people. If our tempers are consistently bad, we arouse anger in others. If we lie or cheat, we deprive others not only of their worldly goods, but of their emotional security and peace of mind. We really issue them an invitation to become contemptuous and vengeful. . . . Such gross misbehavior is not by any means a full catalogue of the harms we do. Let us think of some of the subtler ones which can sometimes be quite as damaging. Suppose that in our family lives we happen to be miserly, irresponsible, callous, or cold. Suppose that we are irritable, critical, impatient, and humorless. Suppose we lavish attention upon one member of the family and neglect the others. What happens when we try to dominate the whole family, either by a rule of iron or by a constant outpouring of minute directions for just how their lives should be lived from hour to hour? What happens when we wallow in depression, self-pity oozing from every pore, and inflict that upon

those about us? Such a roster of harms done others—the kind that make daily living with us as practicing alcoholics difficult and often unbearable—could be extended almost indefinitely. When we take such personality traits as these into shop, office, and the society of our fellows, they can do damage almost as extensive as that we have caused at home. (pp. 80–81)

35. Cf. the next to last paragraph in the discussion of example 2 in "Some Cases" above.

36. Why is other-forgiveness not sufficient for self-forgiveness? After all, if you forgive me, presumably you have some reasons for doing so; and since reasons (on a familiar view) are considerations that a detached or objective person could have or recognize, I could have them, too; but, clearly, our experience is that other-forgiveness is not sufficient for self-forgiveness. Perhaps the first explanation that comes to mind is that the reasons on the basis of which you forgive me may be forward-looking from now, and have little or nothing to do with the substance of what I did, that is, that which makes a forgiveness problem arise in the first place.

37. The AA program does not work for everyone who tries it. This is noted often enough. The more interesting fact is that it is effective for many. Why is this so? This is a difficult question. Even if it is difficult, we may be grateful that the program is effective for many, given the human misery involved in alcoholism, and addictions generally. AA's Twelve-Step Program has been adopted for use in recovery programs for persons with addictions other than alcoholism. Perhaps a part of its effectiveness rests in its ability to help the recovering alcoholic distance himself or herself from his or her life—to "hate the addiction but not the person," as it is sometimes put. More often than not, the alcoholic is bewildered regarding what has happened in his or her life and at a loss regarding what to do with the sense of responsibility he or she has for what has happened. To be able to stand back from one's life to take the measure of the seriousness of one's trouble does not itself eradicate such trouble, but it may facilitate more constructive thought and action relative to it than one managed earlier. At the same time, admitting the past, acknowledging responsibility, and making amends are themselves motivational toward changes (often improvements) in future conduct and in personal frame of mind; and they also tend to increase the alcoholic's chances for reconciliation with family and friends and, thus, for overcoming the feeling of isolation so commonly a feature of the sensibility of those trapped in alcoholism. It is interesting to see similar themes explored (though not with reference to alcoholism) in Robert Merrihew Adams's helpful essay, "Involuntary Sins," *The Philosophical Review*, 94 (January 1985), especially 16.

The following remarks from Vaillant's *Natural History of Alcoholism* seem to me helpful on the effectiveness question. Vaillant argues that treatment "directed toward altering an ingrained habit of maladaptive use of alcohol" (p. 300) should involve four components, namely, "(1) offering the patient a nonchemical substitute dependence for alcohol, (2) reminding him ritually that even one drink can lead to pain and relapse, (3) repairing the social and medical damage that he has experienced, and (4) restoring his self-esteem" (p. 300). He then comments:

Self-help groups, of which Alcoholics Anonymous is one model, offer the simplest way of providing the alcoholic with all four components. . . . First, the continuous hope, the gentle peer support, and the selected exposure to the most stable recoveries provide the alcoholic with a ritualized substitute dependency, and a substitute for lost drinking companions. Second, like the best behavior therapy, AA meetings not only go on daily, especially on weekends and holidays, but also singlemindedly underscore the special ways that alcoholics delude themselves. Thus, in a ritual manner, AA allows the alcoholic, who might unconsciously be driven to relapse, to remain conscious of this danger. Third, belonging to a group of caring individuals who have found solutions to the typical problems that beset the newly sober alcoholic alleviates loneliness. Fourth, the opportunity to identify with helpers who once were equally disabled and the opportunity to help others stay sober enhances self-worth. (p. 301)

38. Cf. Williams, "Moral Luck," 36.

39. Cf. Williams, "Moral Luck."

40. Cf. Aurel Kolnai, *Ethics, Value, and Reality* (Indianapolis: Hackett, 1978), 224.

41. I suppose qualifications are needed here so as to set aside cases in which the person whose moral personality is damaged is a moral monster, but I will not attempt to work out those qualifications here.

42. It may also be the approach of Rawls and Nagel as well. Rawls writes of the "deliberative rationality" of those in the original position that "it means that the parties cannot agree to a conception of justice if the consequences of applying it may lead to self-reproach should the least happy possibilities be realized. They should strive to be free from such regrets" (*A Theory of Justice*, 427. Cf. p. 176.) In a different vocabulary Thomas Nagel appears to endorse this approach and also to indicate some of what can be involved in one's review of past conduct being satisfactory:

We want to be able to understand and accept the way we live from outside, but it may not always follow that we should control our lives from inside by the terms of that external understanding. . . . We should be *able* to view our lives from outside without extreme dissociation or distaste, and the extent to which we should live without *considering* the objective point of view or even any reasons *at all* is itself *determined* largely from that point of view.

"The Limits of Objectivity," in Sterling M. McMurrin, ed., *The Tanner Lectures on Human Values* 1 (Salt Lake City: University of Utah Press; and Cambridge: Cambridge University Press, 1980), 105–6.

43. For a discussion following up a similar concern in another context, see W. H. Walsh, "Pride, Shame, and Responsibility," *The Philosophical Quarterly* 20 (January 1970), especially 4.

44. Kant, *Foundations of the Metaphysics of Morals*, 19.

Chapter 2

1. "Mentally Unstable Walk a Thin Line," *The (Cleveland) Plain Dealer* (27 January 1988).

2. The exasperation and irritation generated by the assumption that "they know better" is evident in the views of many who have troubled themselves to write about people other than themselves. Richard E. Vatz and Lee S. Winberg gave the title "Gamblers Aren't Sick, Just Silly" to their piece criticizing the notion that gambling might be for some a disease or serious compulsion, and they recommended "substantially less sympathy" for the gambler than they found in public opinion. (In *The (Cleveland) Plain Dealer* (5 July 1989). In a "My Turn" column in *Newsweek* (30 September 1991), L. Christopher Awalt, after detailing his own work with the homeless, concluded about one man in particular that "the only person who can be blamed for his failure to get off the streets is the man himself. To argue otherwise is a waste of time and compassion." Then, after raising the possibility that "one case does not a policy make," Awalt proposes that

> whatever policy we decide upon must include some notion of self-reliance and individual responsibility. Simply giving over our parks, our airports and our streets to those who cannot and will not take care of themselves is nothing but a retreat from the problem. . . . [W]ithout requiring some effort and accountability on the part of the homeless for whom . . . programs [of education, counseling, and job-training] are implemented, all these efforts do is break the taxpayer. Unless the homeless are willing to help themselves, there is nothing anyone else can do. Not you. Not me. Not the government. Not anyone.

Awalt's piece is titled "Brother, Don't Spare a Dime."

3. I make an effort not to bring to the discussion a normative account specifying which elements can or cannot be fixed in personality or character. My experience suggests that it is difficult to do this, that is, keep the mind open regarding what can be deep and serious problems for people. Perhaps we have no difficulty understanding that another person might be permanently stuck with the difficulties in living generated by having arthritis, tendinitus, or diabetes. Some of us, though, apparently have great trouble understanding that another lives permanently with the difficulties in living that arise from recurring bouts of depression, impulsive anger, agoraphobia, or body-dysmorphic disorder. For this last problem (imagined ugliness), I find Daniel Goleman's piece to the *New York Times*, "Imagined Ugliness an Illness," in *The (Cleveland) Plain Dealer* (8 October 1991) very helpful. Goleman reports that

> Psychologists studying body image estimate that 2% to 10% of people are so self-conscious about some aspect of their looks that it constricts their life in some way: keeping them from making love or dating, and even

rendering them homebound or suicidal. Many make a fruitless round of cosmetic surgeons, never satisfied.

4. I do not hold the view that moralism per se is bad. In some cases moralizing a person is in the service of exhortation or encouragement, and when the victim meets the terms thus imposed, even he or she grants that a good thing has happened. It may be, too, that moralizing is a necessary part of certain one-to-one relational practices, for example, parenting, mentoring, or friendship. This, however, is not to immunize moralizing in these settings from criticism; parents, children, mentors, those mentored, and friends can all report instances of unjustified moralizing.

5. The judge (Colonel Reid W. Kennedy) in the Calley trial, in Arthur Everett, Kathryn Johnson, Harvey Rosenthal, *Calley* (New York: Dell, 1971), 206–7, quoted in Kurt Baier, "Guilt and Responsibility," in Peter A. French, ed., *Individual and Collective Responsibility: The Massacre at My Lai* (Cambridge, Mass.: Schenkman, 1972), 42.

6. Richard Hammer, *The Court Martial of Lt. Calley* (New York: Coward, McCann and Geoghegan, 1971), 17, quoted in Baier, "Guilt and Responsibility," 37.

7. Baier, "Guilt and Responsibility," 43.

8. Baier, "Guilt and Responsibility," 43.

9. I find Ira S. Steinberg's *Educational Myths and Realities* (Reading, Mass.: Addison-Wesley, 1968) very helpful on this point.

10. The issues here are fascinating and some cases are poignant. When the Internal Revenue Service was criticized for "auditing taxpayers who do file returns" rather than "seeking out those who do not," Commissioner Jerome Kurtz responded: "We will not overreact to the non-filer problem by directing a disproportionate part of our compliance effort against persons the statistics show to be largely poor, undereducated and unskilled." (AP report, "Tax on $100 Billion Illegally Escaping," in *The (Cleveland) Plain Dealer* [17 July 1979].) In connection with the Tax Reform Act of 1986 and its so-called simplified tax return, columnist Thomas J. Brazaitis wrote as follows:

Rep. Donald J. Pease, one of the congressional parents of the [Act] . . . conceded the new federal income tax is not as simple as he had hoped it would be. Pease said fairness is the enemy of simplicity; it is possible to have one or the other, but probably not both. . . . James Childs, an Akron U. law professor and director of the university's tax clinic, said [a team of law students and graduate business students] tested the new Form 1040 and found that it was harder to read than the *Wall Street Journal* or the *New York Times*. . . . 'When you [consider] the general literacy statistics for the population, you find that four out of five blacks, six of 10 Hispanics and over half of the general population cannot read or understand the instructions,' Childs said. ("Pease's Office Door is Open," *The (Cleveland) Plain Dealer* (20 March 1988).)

11. Perhaps the following AP report illustrates the point:

Since last spring, Albert and Helen have lived in a garbage container, a cemetery, a railroad tunnel and a sandbox. Now they are back inside a state mental hospital—another frequent home—awaiting trial for allegedly breaking into a restaurant to steal food. State officials say the system has no place for the couple. . . . They are not mentally ill. They are not dangerous. Yet they refuse to care for themselves in the way society expects. . . . [According to] Anne Vargus, regional administrator of the state Department of Mental Health[,] "Their main problem is that they are poor and uneducated and disorganized rather than mentally ill." . . . David Girard of the state welfare office . . . said: "It's absolutely impossible for them to manage money. If Albert doesn't drink it away, then he gets beat up or just gives it away. What we're talking about here is the dregs of society. Everybody dumps on them." ["Unbathed Couple Baffles Society," *The (Cleveland) Plain Dealer* 24 July 1979].

12. Here I have in mind in particular the work of Laurence Thomas, in, for example, *Living Morally* (Philadelphia: Temple University Press, 1989), especially chaps. 4 and 5.

13. My thanks to David Love for this understanding of what is involved in promising.

14. In "My Lai and Vietnam: The Issues of Responsibility," in Peter A. French, ed., *Individual and Collective Responsibility*, 149.

15. *Foundations of the Metaphysics of Morals*, trans. and intro. Lewis White Beck (Indianapolis: Bobbs-Merrill, 1959).

16. "Law, Morals, and Rescue," in James M. Ratcliffe, ed., *The Good Samaritan and the Law* (New York: Doubleday, 1966); reprinted in Joel Feinberg and Hyman Gross, eds., *Philosophy of Law*, 2d ed., (Belmont, Calif.: Wadsworth, 1980), 426.

17. Lynne McFall's essay, "Integrity," in *Ethics* 98 (October 1987), emphasizes that integrity requires of a person the cultivation of an identity wherein moral values, principles, and commitments are central. In my *On Sharing Fate* (Philadelphia: Temple University Press, 1987), I suggested that integrity includes being "principled and accountable for what one does" and that this involves one in the possession of "personal moral absolutes," including among them "certain things one aspires never to do." (pp. 171–73) I would want my view to be in line with the account McFall gives.

18. Peter McInerney has written in great depth about this form of self-construal. See "Person-Stages and Unity of Consciousness," *American Philosophical Quarterly* 22 (July 1985); and "The Nature of a Person-Stage," *American Philosophical Quarterly* 28 (July 1991).

19. Cambridge, Mass.: The Belknap Press of Harvard University Press, 1971, 422–23 (emphasis mine).

20. Boston: Little, Brown, 1968.

21. Irving Howe speaks of Banfield's "notions about the poor" as "benighted," in "The Right Menace," in *The New Republic* (9 September 1978) 13.

22. Banfield, *The Unheavenly City*, 47.

23. In "Welfare and Freedom," *Ethics* 89 (April 1979): 262.

24. Banfield, *Unheavenly City*, 53, 62.

25. Banfield, *Unheavenly City*, 210–11.

26. Kant, *Foundations of the Metaphysics of Morals*, sec. 2.

27. Rawls sets out the Aristotelian Principle in these words: "other things equal, human beings enjoy the exercise of their realized capacities (their innate or trained abilities), and this enjoyment increases the more the capacity is realized, or the greater its complexity." *A Theory of Justice*, 426.

28. In *Hume's Enquiries*, ed. L. A. Selby-Bigge (Oxford: Clarendon Press, 1962), 282–83.

29. In "Morality and Art," *The Proceedings of the British Academy*, 56 (1970): 15.

30. This demand is, I think, an example of the "natural necessity" discussed in H. L. A. Hart, *The Concept of Law* (London: Oxford University Press [Clarendon], 1961), 189–95.

31. That of Edmund L. Pincoffs in *The Rationale of Legal Punishment* (New York: Humanities Press, 1966). The quoted passages below are from pp. 129–31.

32. I have not reported all the assumptions of fact that Pincoffs sees to be behind the practice of punishment; I have given only some of those that concern how persons are.

33. Pincoffs writes: "it does not pretend to offer a conclusive argument for punishment, whatever that would be. It presents the case for punishment: a case which must be compared with the case which can be made out for available alternative practices." *Rationale*, 133.

34. Pincoffs, *Rationale*, 120.

35. It may be that by designating these propositions "assumptions of fact" Pincoffs has in mind that they are propositions of the sort that H. L. A. Hart construes as expressing "salient facts" about persons that provide reasons why all legal systems have certain features in common. Hart's discussion is in *The Concept of Law* (London: Oxford University Press [Clarendon], 1961) 189–95, but Pincoffs does not refer to *The Concept of Law* in his book.

36. I find it interesting that the features indicated in these claims about how persons are, which Pincoffs finds involved in the justification of legal punishment—or some features very like them—are referred to by Barrington Moore, Jr. as needing to be developed by persons relative to the overcoming of poverty and oppression. Moore writes:

For audacity to occur and become effective—that is, for it to be more than an occasional flare-up of hopeless rage, important changes are necessary in the human character produced by poverty and oppression. Roughly the same changes appear to be necessary (1) for effective political resistance, (2) for adapting to the new discipline of the machine, and (3) for individual efforts to struggle up a rung or two on the social ladder. They amount to a strengthening of the ego at the expense of the id, the taming of natural impulses, and the deferral of present gratifications for the sake of a better future. *Injustice: The Social Bases of Obedience and Revolt* (White Plains, N.Y.: M.E. Sharpe, 1978), 464.

37. My effort here to make and elaborate the distinction is motivated in part by Bernard Williams's critique of the conceptions of the individual involved in the utilitarian and Kantian moral theories in the first essay, "Persons, Character, and Morality," in Williams's *Moral Luck* (Cambridge: Cambrige University Press, 1981). I discuss this critique in a limited way and with different purposes in mind in *On Sharing Fate*, 178–84. Another use is made of the distinction I explore here in *On Sharing Fate*, 126–29.

38. I set aside here the view that persons can become (e.g., be brought to be or be made to be) the same in some way of interest to philosophy, but such a view should not be forgotten. It seems central, for example, to Rousseau's project in *The Social Contract*, especially chaps. 6–9 of Book 1 (*The Social Contract and Discourses*, trans. and intro. G. D. H. Cole [New York: Everyman, 1950], 13–22).

39. I think, though, that neither of the candidates just mentioned could stand as a conceptual truth about persons, that is, as definitional of the idea of person. If we allow words to have their ordinary meanings, there are people who are motivated by something other than what they perceive to be in their own interest, for example, what they perceive to be their community's interest, and others who aspire to something other than a sense of self-respect, for example, a full regard for truth above all else.

40. Thomas Hobbes, *Leviathan*, ed. and intro. Michael Oakeshott (Oxford: Blackwell, 1957), 80–93.

41. John Locke, *The Second Treatise of Government*, in *Locke's Two Treatises of Government*, ed. and intro. Peter Laslett (Cambridge: Cambridge University Press, 1963), 287.

42. Laslett, *Locke's Two Treatises*, 342.

43. In contractualism, the point of providing an account of what persons are by nature is usually to get us to see how a certain form of society is appropriate or legitimate. For historicist critics, contractualism is seen as an attempt to characterize persons independently of society so that we may see what form of society fits persons the best. Historicist critics propose objections of the following sorts. First, the contractualist account of what persons are by nature risks being ideological. Steven Lukes writes:

Seeing real, actual individuals as so many representatives of the genus *man* involved singling out a particular set of characteristics—particular motives, interests, needs, etc.—as distinctively human; and this was, at the same time, a way of seeing society and social relations, in a particular way. But every way of seeing is also a way of not seeing; and in this case a view of man as essentially property-owning or self-interested or "rational" or concerned to maximize his utility amounts to the ideological legitimation of a particular view of society and social relations—and the implicit delegitimation of others. (*Individualism* [Oxford: Blackwell, 1973], 149–50)

Second, the contractualist account of what persons are by nature "directly contradicts all the accumulated lessons of sociology and social anthropology and of social psychology" and "the sociological apperception reveals society as irreducibly constitutive of or built into the individual in crucial and profound ways." (*Individualism*, 151, 150–51) A third critical point is that there simply are no beings, independent of society, to which the contractualist can apply his account. Persons have society in them in such a way that the whole enterprise of determining what persons are independently of society is ill-conceived. As F. H. Bradley put it, the enterprise itself is "a theoretical attempt to isolate what cannot be isolated" ("My Station and its Duties," *Ethical Studies* (Oxford: Clarendon, 1927).

This, I take it, is strong criticism: the contractualist's view of what persons are by nature is said to be slanted (ideological), unsociological, and misconceived. My own critique is not quite so condemnatory: when I suggest that contractualist propositions about persons are normative in character, I allow that there might be reasons supporting their use.

44. The passage is from Jeremy Bentham's *Principles of Morals and Legislation*, 14:28, and is quoted by Pincoffs in *Rationale*, 129. Notice how a general utilitarian premise (the claim in parentheses) informs Bentham's alleged factual claim here.

45. Gregory Zilbourg, *The Psychology of the Criminal Act and Punishment* (New York: Harcourt Brace, 1954), 32. This passage is quoted in Pincoffs in *Rationale*, 129.

46. Pincoffs retains these propositions as true in the face of their controversiality (for he reports the issue between Bentham and Zilbourg) and, more puzzling, even in the face of his own further remarks that "Bentham does not need to claim that everybody calculates. Even if the percentage of people who calculate is relatively small, punishment would so far be worthwhile; for by the threat of punishment crime could be reduced" (*Rationale*, 130). The thrust of what is said in these remarks is clearly against viewing the proposition that persons calculate as a factual generalization about persons as we know them.

47. Cf. Hume's remark that "mixed phenomena can never prove . . . unmixed principles," in *Dialogues Concerning Natural Religion*, part 11 (*Hume: Dialogues Concerning Natural Religion*, ed. with commentary by Nelson Pike [Indianapolis and New York: Bobbs-Merrill, 1970], 104).

48. Here I follow Rawls's conception of "society" in *A Theory of Justice*, 4.

49. I have in mind here the view of Herbert Morris in *On Guilt and Innocence* (Berkeley: University of California Press, 1976), especially as expressed in the essay "Persons and Punishment" (originally in *The Monist* 51 (October 1968)). Morris argues the unpopular view that we have a right to punishment ultimately

grounded in our natural right to be treated as persons; one of his main objectives is to show that any across-the-board replacement of legal punishment with a system of therapy, rehabilitation, and cure is bound to undercut the status of persons as responsible moral agents. Morris's aim, however, is not to undermine efforts to make our actual penal arrangements more humane, nor is it to reject the validity of legal appeals to mental illness; it is rather to show that the general substitution of therapy for punishment presumes a view of persons as victims or mere creatures of their environment rather than as free, rational, autonomous agents capable of recognizing and judging the rights and wrongs of what they do. The widening application in the law of the metaphors of health and sickness may logically be an increasing threat to our conception of ourselves as moral agents engaged in a social life understood as a cooperative venture for mutual gain. For autonomous agents capable of deliberate wrongdoing, punishment may be, on occasion, what is deserved. In this part of his writings, Morris's view reflects the historically important but, until very recently, unfashionable retributivist theory of punishment.

50. Cf., for example, the last few sentences of the second section of Kant's *Foundations of the Metaphysics of Morals*.

51. For a discussion of the implications of this point for the philosophical problem of the justification of punishment in less than just societies, see Jeffrie G. Murphy, "Marxism and Retribution," *Philosophy and Public Affairs* 2 (Spring 1973).

52. For example, Rawls's theory of justice (in *A Theory of Justice*), or Marx's critique of capitalist society from "alienation" (in "Alienated Labour," in *Karl Marx: Early Writings*, trans. and ed. T. B. Bottomore [New York: McGraw-Hill, 1963], 120–34).

53. New York: The Viking Press, 1949.

54. He is also a familiar one. It is common for members of American audiences to see their fathers in Willy. In the play, Linda, Willy's wife, sees him as "a small man" (Act 2, p. 57), but this label is without malice. Willy is one of what lower-middle-class Americans call "the little people." Willy, though, resists this way of thinking of himself. When his son Biff says, "Pop! I'm a dime a dozen, and so are you," Willy shouts back, "I am not a dime a dozen! I am Willy Loman, and you are Biff Loman!" (Act 2, pp. 132–33)

55. Act 1:49.

56. Act 2:86.

57. Act 1:33.

58. Act 1:65 (my emphasis).

59. Act 1:41.

60. Act 2:72.

61. Act 1:36–37.

62. Act 1:78.

63. Act 1:41.

64. Act 2:84.

65. Act 2:81.

66. In the Requiem, Biff remarks of his father: "He had the wrong dreams. All, all wrong. . . . He never knew who he was" (p. 138).

67. Act 2:125–26.

68. Could Willy have disallowed such power to this dream? I do not see that *Death of a Salesman* actually answers this question. My approach in this discussion permits, but does not require, a "no" answer to it.

69. In my earlier discussion of the problem of living with one's past, I suggested that we are similarly vulnerable to our own understandings of our histories. This theme, too, is among Arthur Miller's thoughts about Willy Loman. Miller writes, in reference to his construction of the play: "if I could make [Willy] remember enough he would kill himself . . . the structure of the play was determined by what was needed to draw up his memories like a mass of tangled roots without end or beginning" (In "Introduction to the Collected Plays," *Arthur Miller's Collected Plays* [New York: Viking Press, 1957], 25).

70. I am aware that in certain medical cases, learning or relearning how to perform ordinary bodily functions is required and conceptual preparation is needed. I am helped here by William F. May's discussion of "catastrophic illness" in *The Patient's Ordeal* (Bloomington and Indianapolis: Indiana University Press, 1991). Also, there are psychiatric disorders, including severe forms of phobia, whose treatment may involve the victim in cognitive unlearning and relearning. Phobias are stubborn. Apparently, treatment success rates are not impressive. The literature is immense. Donald W. Goodwin's *Anxiety* (New York: Oxford University Press, 1986) is a useful general discussion. A detailed discussion from the perspective of cognitive therapy is given in Aaron J. Beck and Gary Emery, with Ruth L. Greenberg, *Anxiety Disorders and Phobias* (New York: Basic Books, 1985).

71. The word "work" here is broad in the way Marx's term "labor" is broad (in, e.g., the essay "Alienated Labor"). My *On Sharing Fate* dealt in a limited way with this structural feature of human lives and, in particular, with the Socratic question of "what kind of person I am to be" in connection with the time, energy, and personal resources one invests in career or vocation. I have no theory about sexual union or children, but I suspect that the views we come to in responding to these features of human life (including the views of those who are childless or celibate) typically make certain assumptions about persons and thus are vehicles for persona moralism.

72. I suppose this claim is merely an empirical generalization and allows of exceptions. It is certainly conceivable that a creature might be life possessing but not aware that its life will end. It is also conceivable that a creature might be conscious (in the way that persons are) but just happen not to have in its consciousness repertoire this sort of awareness. Some people might be creatures of this latter sort. I'm not sure. If they were, they might, structurally, be roughly like what Harry G. Frankfurt calls "wantons," that is, creatures who have "first-order desires" but, apart from whether they have any second-order desires, do

not have "second-order volitions." It occurs to me (1) that awareness that one's life will end is an awareness that one's life (one's life itself being a period of time filled with awarenesses of different durations and of different objects) is a certain way or has a certain character, namely, over at some point, and also (2) that, for most of us, this awareness is motivational in certain ways; and that seems to me second-order-like in the way Frankfurt has in mind. Cf. Frankfurt's essay "Freedom of the Will and the Concept of a Person," *The Importance of What We Care About* (Cambridge: Cambridge University Press, 1988). Apart from this possibility that some people lack this form of awareness, many people occasionally conduct their lives as if they lack this sort of awareness, or anyhow as if they do not care much about the information it conveys.

73. Howe's comment on Leo Tolstoy's "The Death of Ivan Ilych," in Irving Howe, ed., *Classics of Modern Fiction* (New York: Harcourt Brace Jovanovich, 1968, 1972), 120.

74. Tolstoy, "The Death of Ivan Ilych," 131.

75. Tolstoy, "The Death of Ivan Ilych," 120–21.

76. Clearly, some people feel the prospect of death more deeply than others, and one might raise philosophical questions about the rationality of how the prospect of death is taken—too seriously in some cases, not seriously enough in other cases. Scott Shane wrote: "Tolstoy always lived at close quarters with his mortality, tormented by thoughts of death, contemplating suicide while at the height of his international fame and literary powers." (In "Was Tolstoy the Same Species as We Are?" in *The (Cleveland) Plain Dealer* [13 March 1989].)

77. I have in mind Albert Camus, *The Myth of Sisyphus* (trans. Justin O'Brien) (New York: Vintage Books, 1955).

78. Camus, *The Myth of Sisyphus*, 41.

79. Camus, *The Myth of Sisyphus*, 12.

80. Intellectual honesty may be a sort of primary virtue for Camus.

81. Camus, *The Myth of Sisyphus*, 41. An alternative word to "defiance," for Camus, is often "revolt." Camus praises "the intelligence's refusal to reason the concrete" at p. 73. "Lucidity" occurs throughout the text, for example, at pp. 15, 70, and 76.

82. Beyond his account of the phenomenological signs of absurdity (*The Myth of Sisyphus*, 10–12), Camus's philosophical analysis yields the view that while we are creatures whose nature is to understand, the world is, at a certain point, opaque to understanding. This mismatch between human beings and their world is definitional of Camus's notion of absurdity. Thus: our "nostalgia for unity, that appetite for the absolute illustrates the essential impulse of the human drama. But the fact of that nostalgia's existence does not imply that it is to be immediately satisfied" (p. 13). "This heart within me I can feel, and I judge that it exists. This world I can touch, and I likewise judge that it exists. There ends all my knowledge, and the rest is construction" (p. 14). "I realize that if through science I can seize phenomena and enumerate them, I cannot, for all that, apprehend the world" (p. 15). Perhaps best of all: "this world in itself is not reasonable, that is

all that can be said. But what is absurd is the confrontation of this irrational and the wild longing for clarity whose call echoes in the human heart" (p. 16). Camus's language is wonderful, but his skeptical metaphysics (setting aside the maxims Camus thinks follow from his metaphysics) is immediately reminiscent of Kant: we can know appearances, but not things in themselves; we can "seize and enumerate phenomena" but not answer ultimate why-questions (for Camus). For both Kant and Camus it is a major fact about persons that their nature is to ask the ultimate why-questions. For Kant, "the empirical use to which reason limits the pure understanding does not fully satisfy the proper calling of reason" (*Prolegomena to Any Future Metaphysics*, intro. Lewis White Beck [New York: The Liberal Arts Press, 1950], 76); but here Kant and Camus appear to part company. Kant carefully sketches how the "calling of reason" can legitimately move beyond the "empirical use" by reference to an understanding of "regulative ideas"; Camus does not do any similar thing and, in fact, writes as if there is no such thing to do.

83. It is not even "romantic and slightly self-pitying," as Thomas Nagel suggests in an essay partly about Camus's view ("The Absurd," *Mortal Questions* [Cambridge: Cambridge University Press, 1979], 22).

84. An important qualification must be added to this rejection of Camus's advice on how to deal with mortality. It is that Camus's defiance maxim is idiosyncratic: it is informed by his skeptical metaphysics, and when defiance is thus informed, it comes out meaning "live without thinking about death" (or about anything else, apparently), so we must observe that there might be some other interpretation of defiance that would meet the need of a human being for a conceptual-cum-normative response to mortality.

85. I have benefited from discussion of the idea of acceptance in this context with Thomas Van Nortwick and from his interpretation of "the tragic perspective," as suggested by Sophocles's *Oedipus at Colonus*, in "The Road to Colonus: Sophocles' Theban Trilogy" (a paper delivered at the annual meeting of the Classical Association of the Midwest and South, Hamilton, Ontario, April 1991).

Chapter 3

1. Could vicious persona moralism ever be justified? Perhaps, but only in special circumstances. The comparison would be with the imaginability of justified violence, rather than, say, with the less difficult justified civil disobedience. The idea of justified vicious persona moralism strains my moral imagination, especially when I remember that moral justification is not necessarily provided by practical necessity. Practical necessity may explain why one does *x* but not morally justify one's doing *x*.

2. Ed. Elizabeth Rapaport (Indianapolis: Hackett, 1978).

3. Mill, *On Liberty*, 9.

4. Here I expand slightly the account of moral personality suggested in "Some Cases" in chapter 1 above.

5. And also by Rawls's remarks about moral personality in *A Theory of Justice*. It is interesting that Mill himself may not have fit this conception of persons. Cf. the view of Mill worked out in Ruth Borchard, *John Stuart Mill, The Man* (London: Watts, 1957).

6. I notice that in Susan Wolf's essay, "Sanity and the Metaphysics of Responsibility," in Ferdinand Schoeman, ed., *Responsibility, Character, and the Emotions* (Cambridge: Cambridge University Press, 1987), the idea of sanity covers not only being in touch with reality as it is but also "the ability to know the difference between right and wrong" (pp. 56–57), from which latter ability flows the sane person's capacity for "self-correction" (pp. 58–59) regarding character. My account here does not include or discuss this additional controversial element. I am aware that each of the four elements I include in the conception of the in-control agent and interpret minimally is a possible subject of extended discussion. Some further thoughts about competent individuals, rationality, and independent thinking appear in chaps. 2 and 4 of my *On Sharing Fate*.

7. In, for example, chapter 3 of *Utilitarianism*, ed. George Sher (Indianapolis: Hackett, 1979).

8. I doubt that this claim is controversial, but of course one cannot be sure. It seems to me plain that the model of the person that Mill works with in *On Liberty* and *Utilitarianism* is that of the in-control agent; otherwise, neither the strong anti-paternalism in the former text nor the insistences in the latter text that the master principle of utility should prevail when secondary moral rules conflict and also over the pressures of the sentiments of self-love and even natural sympathy would make sense. In Kantian moral theory the in-control agent seems suggested by the general themes that the moral life requires that reason constrain inclination and that "ought" implies "can." I find analogs to these Kantian themes in Aristotle's *Nicomachean Ethics*, but, again, my purpose in this discussion is not scholarship regarding the literature of ethical theory.

9. New York: Random House, 1984.

10. Regan, *Earthbound*, 21 (my emphasis).

11. Mill's *Autobiography* (Indianapolis: Bobbs-Merrill, 1957) is more illuminating regarding them than either *On Liberty* or *Utilitarianism*.

12. An interesting externality in this connection—one that may be powerful in its impact on one's sensibility—is information about one's future. In "Opening Pandora's Box," in *Harvard Health Letter* 17:3 (January 1992), the impact of a test for determining with considerable certainty who had inherited the Huntington's gene is described. "Offspring of people with Huntington's disease live with tortuous uncertainty. They watch involuntary movements and progressive dementia overwhelm a loved one, knowing that they have a 50–50 chance of experiencing the same fate." When testing became possible in 1983,

> those who learned they would likely develop the disease were very distressed at first. Twelve months later, however, they were psychologically better off

than they had been prior to testing, although they became worried if they stumbled or felt depressed since they feared those everyday events might signal the onset of Huntington's symptoms. The emotional trajectory for those who got good news was different. They were elated at first but soon fell into a slump when they realized that being free of the Huntington's gene did not confer new powers, change their old habits, or improve their ability to relate to others. . . . Overall there was a similar number of adverse psychological events in the two groups, although one person who got good news did attempt suicide.

13. "Moral Luck," *Mortal Questions* (Cambridge: Cambridge University Press, 1979), 28. Nagel's catalog includes "four ways in which the natural objects of moral assessment are disturbingly subject to luck" and lists ways in which our control of what we do is or can be disrupted, interfered with, conditioned, or canceled. Apart from the constitutional luck I am now concerned with, he also lists "luck in one's circumstances," "luck in how one is determined by antecedent circumstances," and "luck in the way one's actions and projects turn out" (p. 28).

14. These "built-ins," of course, are the built-ins of my nature now; for, as my story above suggests, these built-ins may be the results of negative circumstantial luck and, hence, be different from, or replacements for some former built-ins of my nature. While my nature can change, it has built-ins at any given time.

15. In *The Importance of What We Care About* (Cambridge: Cambridge University Press, 1988), especially the final essay, "Rationality and the Unthinkable," 190. I do not know whether Frankfurt would endorse the use I make of his phrase in this discussion. The "necessities of the will" he has in mind function in a rather positive way, for they "protect the person . . . from succumbing to the influence of radical disturbances of his judgment," whereas the ones I have in mind function in a rather negative way.

16. These terms ("nature's lottery" and "social contingency") are from John Rawls's *A Theory of Justice.*

17. "About 40% of adults describe shyness as one of their persistent personality traits, according to a survey of 10,000 American adults by researchers at Stanford University." Jane E. Brody, "It's Not Easy Being So Shy," *The (Cleveland) Plain Dealer* (20 February 1990).

18. Michael Liebowitz, M.D., "Is There a Drug Treatment for Social Phobia?" *The Harvard Medical School Mental Health Letter* 5:8 (February 1989): 8.

19. "People who are shy at the ages of 8 to 12 remain shy in their 30s, and the temperament can have profound effects on their lives." "Shy Children Grown Up," *The Harvard Medical School Mental Health Letter* 5:12 (June 1989): 6.

20. Owen Flanagan's remarks are suggestive regarding the bearing of constitutional shyness on one's capacity to participate in moral life:

Warmth and a certain minimal level of gregariousness are often considered morally good qualities. But there are many people who are painfully shy.

Furthermore, good evidence suggests that shyness is one of the most heritable personality traits. Persons who are constitutionally shy . . . cannot be expected to develop the traits of warmth and gregariousness in anything like the ideally desirable forms. Exaggerating only slightly, we can say that there is no learning theory for such persons in the domain of gregariousness. . . . It follows that it is psychologically unrealistic for us to expect such persons to develop into the life of the party. Lack of realism aside, it is a commonplace for very shy people to want to be warm and gregarious (and of course they often are with loved ones). They just cannot do it. Furthermore, their not being able to do it is not for lack of knowledge about how nonshy people behave. Many a shy actor has given an excellent portrayal of the warm and convivial sort of character he sometimes wishes he could be. A shy person simply cannot make himself not shy and remain the person he actually is. (*Varieties of Moral Personality* [Cambridge, Mass.: Harvard University Press, 1991], 271–72)

21. In AA, on his own, in a treatment-center after-care program, or with a therapist—or, indeed, all of these.

22. I do not know whether alcoholism is a disease or not. Herbert Fingarette's *Heavy Drinking* (Berkeley and Los Angeles: University of California Press, 1988) argues that the view that alcoholism is a disease is a "myth." Stanton Peele also argues against the disease concept in *The Meaning of Addiction* (Lexington, Mass.: D.C. Heath, 1985) and in *Diseasing of America* (Lexington, Mass.: D.C. Heath, 1989). These books are interesting for their coverage of the research literature and for their attempts to break down what they evidently consider to be a dangerously mistaken conception of alcoholism; but they are unhelpful regarding recovery from alcoholism. They seem negative in their attitudes toward Alcoholics Anonymous, though I do not understand this negativity. AA's recovery program does not require that alcoholism be understood to be a disease. I comment on this point in "About the AA Program" in chapter 5.

23. Or perhaps not: a recent survey by the National Mental Health Association records that "alcoholism was regarded as a personal weakness by 58 percent of those polled and as a health problem by 46 percent." AP report, "Poll Finds That Many View Depression as Weakness," *The New York Times* (12 December 1991).

24. Perhaps this will do as a working account for those who must have some sort of general characterization of alcoholism. The phrase "consistently and over time" is important; many alcoholics manifest episodic control. In one recent account, alcoholism is defined as "preoccupation with acquiring alcohol, compulsive use of alcohol in spite of adverse consequences, and a pattern of relapse to alcohol use in spite of those consequences"; Norman Miller, M.D., and Doug Toft, *The Disease Concept of Alcoholism and Other Drug Addiction* (Center City, Minn.: Hazelden Foundation, 1990), 5. Despite the looseness of its words, my experience suggests that this account hits apt points, though one must remember George E. Vaillant's emphasis in *The Natural History of Alcoholism* (Cambridge, Mass.: Harvard University Press, 1983) on the variety of forms

alcoholism can take. I doubt that an essentialist definition of alcoholism is possible; perhaps some sort of family-resemblances approach to its definition would be possible.

25. *The (Cleveland) Plain Dealer* (13 December 1988).

26. *The (Cleveland) Plain Dealer* (13 December 1988): 5-B.

27. This helpful term is used in Gary Watson's "Responsibility and the Limits of Evil: Variations on a Strawsonian Theme," in Ferdinand Schoeman, ed., *Responsibility, Character, and the Emotions*.

28. A letter to Ann Landers from the mother of a child molester, written in such a way as to regard the son's affliction as a sickness, details the trouble awaiting the child molester who seeks help. In response, Ann Landers notes that there are "not enough trained people to help those among us with psychological problems" and recommends "Molesters Anonymous (a self-help group)." "Help for Child Molesters Available," in *The (Cleveland) Plain Dealer* (5 February 1991).

29. For a helpful short discussion that allows a distinction between "irresponsible gambling" and "pathological gambling," see Jim Mallory, "The Gambling Compulsion Afflicting Ordinary People," in *The (Cleveland) Plain Dealer* (25 August 1989). This piece replies to the piece indicated above in chapter 2, note 2, which suggested that people apparently stuck with a gambling addiction be regarded as "silly." For a helpful short piece about gambling as addiction— written with some medical and treatment authority and touching on its physiological basis, recovery, and some public-policy issues—see Sheila B. Blume, M.D., "Compulsive Gambling: Addiction without Drugs," *The Harvard Mental Health Letter* 8:8 (February 1992). Fyodor Dostoevsky's short novel *The Gambler* in *Four Great Russian Short Novels*, trans. Constance Farnett and Nathan Haskell Dole (New York: Dell, 1959), is a portrayal of pathological gambling written by one who knew it from the inside.

30. See William Saletan and Nancy Watzman, "Marcus Welby, J.D.," *The New Republic* (17 April 1989). An interesting possible illustration of action-addict syndrome might be the jaywalker story in *Alcoholics Anonymous* (New York: Alcoholics Anonymous World Services, 1939, 1955, 1976), 37 ff., though the point of this story in AA's text is, through comparison with the person who can't stop jaywalking even after many serious accidents, to bring out something of the "strange insanity" (p. 38) involved in the condition of the real alcoholic.

31. Detailed in Mill's *Autobiography*.

32. To do so would involve at least working through the items listed in the psychiatrists' *Diagnostic and Statistical Manual of Mental Disorders*.

33. An AP report, "Experts Wrangle over Sex as an Addiction or Disease," in *The (Cleveland) Plain Dealer* (3 November 1988), describes the debate over whether obsession with sex is sin or sickness.

34. Cf. Shari Roan, "Rare Disorder has People Faking Illness Symptoms," *The (Cleveland) Plain Dealer* (20 August 1991).

35. Steven Emond, M.D., "When Symptom Becomes Disease," in *Harvard Health Letter* 16:2 (December 1990): 7.

36. Cf. chap. 5 in Richard Wollheim's *The Thread of Life* (Cambridge, Mass.: Harvard University Press, 1984). Also, see the discussion of fixation on trauma in the two-part piece on post-traumatic stress disorder in *The Harvard Mental Health Letter* 7:8 (February 1991) and 7:9 (March 1991).

37. See the report on the work of David F. Machell, who regards this condition as "a crisis of low self-esteem," given by Carolyn J. Mooney in *The Chronicle of Higher Education* (1 November 1989): A13.

38. *Darkness Invisible* (New York: Random House, 1990), 14–15.

39. A helpful overview of the constitutive calamity of depression is given in Lester Grinspoon, M.D., and James B. Bakalar, J.D., *Depression and Other Mood Disorders* (a "Mental Health Review" published by *The Harvard Mental Health Letter*, 1990).

40. Everyone will have their favorite account of those who possess such qualities. Mine is the account given in "A Man Called Beaver Dick," in Robert B. Betts, *Along the Ramparts of the Tetons: The Saga of Jackson Hole, Wyoming* (Boulder: Colorado Associated University Press, 1978), 107–17. Richard "Beaver Dick" Leigh was an Englishman who became a trapper and guide—a "mountain man"—in the 1870s in frontier Teton country in Wyoming. He was a diarist (though an unconventional grammarian). The essay I cite here contains excerpts from Leigh's diary recording his strenuous yet ultimately doomed efforts to save his wife and children from nature and disease in the isolation of a mountain cabin in December 1870. Leigh is shown to have precisely the combination of inner strength, stamina, and endurance that one would want for one's children. I am grateful to Daniel and Marlene Merrill for calling my attention to this piece.

41. Harry G. Frankfurt, *The Importance of What We Care About*, 190. I think Frankfurt would agree that one must say "if one has it" here. My thought is that one might not have this necessity of the will in one's makeup. To have it in one's makeup is to find the doing of certain things unthinkable.

> Unthinkability is a mode of necessity with which the will sometimes binds itself and limits choice. This limitation may be an affirmation and revelation of fundamental sanity. There are certain things that no thoroughly rational individual would even consider doing. But if a person did somehow *consider* doing them, and even go so far as to *make up his mind* to do them, a basically sane person could not actually bring himself to *do* them. Sanity consists partly in being subject to just such incapacities. (pp. 189–90)

42. In "The Limits of Sainthood," *The New Republic* (18 June 1990): 40.

43. *Self-Consciousness, Memoirs* (New York: Fawcett Crest, 1989), 77.

44. "Personality and Personality Disorder—Part 2," in *The Harvard Medical School Mental Health Letter* 4:4 (October 1987): 4.

45. For a pro and con discussion of the view that early childhood experience is important to the development of adult personality, including personality disorders, see *The Harvard Mental Health Letter* 8:2 (August 1991) and 8:3 (September 1991): the con approach in the former is by Wagner Bridger, M.D.;

the pro approach in the latter is by Jules R. Bemporad, M.D. For a discussion of the bearing of research on the human genome on ethical questions, see Thomas H. Murray, "Ethical Issues in Human Genome Research," *The FASEB Journal* 5 (January 1991). Murray argues that "we must learn not to overinterpret" such research: "The sciences of inequality, with genetics at the forefront, will force us to reinterpret what equal treatment and equal regard mean in an enormous range of contexts. But they need not threaten the ethical core of that commitment" (p. 60). Regarding abuse, see chaps. 5 and 6 of William F. May, *The Patient's Ordeal* (Bloomington and Indianapolis: Indiana University Press, 1991). Let me also acknowledge Claudia Card's paper, "Responsibility and Moral Luck: Resisting Oppression and Abuse," given at the Chapel Hill Colloquium in Philosophy (University of North Carolina at Chapel Hill), 12–14 October 1990; my comments on Professor Card's colloquium paper provided a basis for some of my discussion here.

46. These might be people who have what Susan Wolf calls "sane deep selves," which are selves that "unavoidably *contain* the ability to know right from wrong" and, thus, "unavoidably do have the resources and reasons on which to base self-correction." Wolf comments about those who have such selves:

> it seems that although we may not be *metaphysically* responsible for ourselves—for, after all, we did not create ourselves from nothing—we are *morally* responsible for ourselves, for we are able to understand and appreciate right and wrong, and to change our characters and our actions accordingly. ("Sanity and the Metaphysics of Responsibility," 58–59)

47. *The Will to Believe* (New York: Dover, 1956), 82–83, 88, 171. Cf., too, 100–1.

48. Cambridge, Mass.: Harvard University Press, 1991.

49. Flanagan, *Varieties*, 267.

50. Flanagan, *Varieties*, 268.

51. Flanagan, *Varieties*, 271, 274.

52. Flanagan explains in *Varieties*, pp. 268–75 that he is taking the modularity thesis into ethics, or moral psychology, from work in linguistics and cognitive psychology. He cites work of Noam Chomsky ("On Cognitive Structures and their Development: A Reply to Piaget," in Massimo Piattelli-Palmarini, ed., *Language and Learning: The Debate between Jean Piaget and Noam Chomsky* [Cambridge, Mass.: Harvard University Press, 1980]) and Jerry Fodor (*The Modularity of Mind* [Cambridge, Mass.: MIT Press/Bradford Books, 1983]). He cites, too, Howard Gardner, *Frames of Mind: The Theory of Multiple Intelligences* (New York: Basic Books, 1983). For an interesting short discussion of the legal notion of competence in decision making—a discussion that implicitly treats the self in the modularity fashion and considers the implications for mental-health professionals called to give opinions in court—see Paul Appelbaum, "The Meaning of Competence in Mental Health Law," in *The Harvard Medical School Mental Health Letter* 5:1 (July 1988): 8.

53. Flanagan, *Varieties*, 271.

54. Harry G. Frankfurt, *Importance*, 174–75.

55. Marcus J. Goldman, M.D., "Is There a Treatment for Kleptomania?" *The Harvard Mental Health Letter* 8:5 (November 1991): 8.

56. Dr. Michael Jenike, "Obsessive-Compulsive Disorder," in *The Harvard Medical School Health Letter* 15:6 (April 1990): 5. The last part of this description is interesting. In a *Newsweek* article on obsessive-compulsive disorders (David Gelman, "Haunted by Their Habits," *Newsweek* [27 March 1989]: 72), it is noted that "in France OCD is known as *folie de doute*—the 'doubting disease.' Victims simply don't know how to know."

57. Frankfurt, *Importance*, 174–75.

58. Frankfurt, *Importance*, 21.

59. My thanks to Ira S. Steinberg for exploration in discussion of the idea of the self as, in part, a set of compromises.

60. This suggests that what we count as disorder is to some extent relative to context or to way of life and might be different from community to community. Arthur Kleinman, a psychiatrist and anthropologist, has written interestingly on this theme. See, for example, *Patients and Healers in the Context of Culture* (Berkeley and Los Angeles: University of California Press, 1980); *Social Origins of Distress and Disease* (New Haven: Yale University Press, 1986); *Rethinking Psychiatry: From Cultural Category to Personal Experience* (New York: Free Press, 1988). An instructive short piece by Kleinman is "The Psychiatry of Culture and the Culture of Psychiatry," *The Harvard Mental Health Letter* 8:1 (July 1991).

61. In some of these third-level cases, we may have to institutionalize *T*. It is worth noting here some words at the beginning of Chapter 5 ("How It Works") of AA's "big book," *Alcoholics Anonymous* (New York: Alcoholics Anonymous World Services, Inc., 1939, 1955, 1976). Here, before the Twelve-Step Program is introduced, the chapter speaks of people "who are constitutionally incapable of being honest with themselves" and goes on to say: "There are such unfortunates. They are not at fault; they seem to have been born that way. They are naturally incapable of grasping and developing a manner of living which demands rigorous honesty." These words suggest that a real alcoholic is constitutionally stuck in the manner suggested earlier, but that if the capacity for "rigorous honesty" is intact, there is a way out (via the Twelve-Step Program). If, however, the latter capacity is not intact—if it is blocked or diminished—then recovery, or at any rate Twelve-Step recovery, is not possible. One would in that case be, indeed, an unfortunate. The modularity thesis is compatible with the AA point here and even helpful in understanding it.

62. *Twenty-Four Hours a Day* rev. ed. (Center City, Minn.: Hazelden, 1975), entry for 13 May.

63. *Twelve Steps and Twelve Traditions* (New York: Alcoholics Anonymous World Services, Inc., 1952, 1953, 1981), 92.

64. New York: Atlantic Monthly Press, 1990, 104.

65. In "Pseudo-Psychiatry Debases Justice System," *The (Cleveland) Plain*

Dealer (9 February 1991). Cf. Krauthammer's "Love Thyself and Maybe Then Thy Neighbor," *The (Cleveland) Plain Dealer* (7 May 1989).

66. "A Conspicuous, and Tainted, Compassion," *The (Cleveland) Plain Dealer* (14 May 1989).

67. "In Washington, Everybody Just Keeps Moving On," *The (Cleveland) Plain Dealer* (27 February 1990).

68. "A System that Makes Victims Pay Twice," *The (Cleveland) Plain Dealer* (29 December 1991).

69. This must surely be a major methodological issue for counseling psychologists. For a brief discussion of a recent effort to devise a psychopathy checklist, see "New Test for Psychopathy," *The Harvard Mental Health Letter* 8:7 (January 1992): 7. For an interesting discussion of the complications of dual disorder, see the two-part "Dual Diagnosis," *The Harvard Mental Health Letter* 8:2 (August 1991) and 8:3 (September 1991).

Chapter 4

1. These glib words mask the difficulty that might be involved in *D*'s adoption of such strategies. It is hard to be accurate about one's condition, admit it to oneself, and take on the relevant strategies. The changes involved in doing all this reach to personal identity, that is, one's understanding of oneself, and even to how, where, and with whom one lives one's life.

2. Cambridge, Mass.: The Belknap Press of Harvard University.

3. Rawls, *A Theory of Justice*, ix, 3–11. For the controversy between Rawls and Robert Nozick over the framework, see, for Rawls, *A Theory of Justice*, 290 and 566, but also the essay, "The Basic Structure as Subject," *American Philosophical Quarterly* 14 (April 1977): 160; for Nozick, see *Anarchy, State, and Utopia* (New York: Basic Books, 1974), 32–33, 151, 159, 238, 321.

4. I use a distinctive Kantian notion here and recognize Rawls's respect for the Kantian moral philosophy. Kant wrote: "All imperatives are expressed by an 'ought' and thereby indicate the relation of an objective law of reason to a will which is not in its subjective constitution necessarily determined by this law. This relation is that of constraint" (*Foundations of the Metaphysics of Morals*, trans. and intro. by Lewis White Beck [Indianapolis: Bobbs-Merrill, 1959], 30).

5. Rawls, *A Theory of Justice*, 100ff.

6. Oxford: Clarendon Press, 1980.

7. Cf. Rawls, "The Basic Structure as Subject."

8. Lucas, *On Justice*, 179.

9. Lucas, *On Justice*, 175–76.

10. Cf. Rawls, *A Theory of Justice*, 5–6, 8–10.

11. Lucas, *On Justice*, 6.

12. Lucas, *On Justice*, 18.

13. Lucas, *On Justice*, 18.

14. Cf. Rawls, *A Theory of Justice*, 105–6.

15. Rawls, *A Theory of Justice*, 40–45.

16. Lucas, *On Justice*, 179 (emphasis mine).

17. Lucas, *On Justice*, 170.

18. Lucas, *On Justice*, 181.

19. Lucas, *On Justice*, 181.

20. Rawls, *A Theory of Justice*, 3.

21. Lucas, *On Justice*, 263 (emphasis mine).

22. Lucas, *On Justice*, 18–19.

23. Lucas, *On Justice*, 176.

24. Lucas, *On Justice*, 73.

25. Rawls, *A Theory of Justice*, 333, 334, 339–40.

26. I shall consider the notion of individual-case justice to cover both what Rawls calls "duties of individuals" and what I earlier called (and what may be a subset of duties of individuals) "our general attitudes toward others and ourselves."

27. Rawls, *A Theory of Justice*, 340. I am reminded of a comment of Amartya Sen: "Each principle of social choice selects some facts as intrinsically relevant and others as irrelevant or only derivatively important," in "Individual Freedom as a Social Commitment," *The New York Review of Books* (14 June 1990): 53.

28. Or, to my knowledge, in papers published by Rawls after the appearance of *A Theory of Justice*.

29. New York: Oxford University Press, 1979.

30. Haksar, *Equality, Liberty, and Perfectionism*, 21.

31. Haksar, *Equality*, 66–67. Notice that in the modular view of the self I discussed earlier, some people might suffer constitutional luck that makes them unable to qualify as possessing such potential.

32. Haksar, *Equality*, 84.

33. Haksar, *Equality*, 67.

34. Haksar, *Equality*, 1.

35. Haksar, *Equality*, 71. I wonder, then, how Haksar would characterize those whose potential in this connection is complicated or stifled by the unmanageable internal factors I discussed earlier and is thus something less than "wonderful."

36. Haksar, *Equality*, 95.

37. Haksar, *Equality*, 144. If it is "reasonable to insist" that persons have this duty, this is not so, so far as I can tell, because the duty can be directly inferred from the "wonderful potential." What makes it "reasonable to insist" this is not plain to me.

38. Haksar, *Equality*, 69.

39. Haksar, *Equality*, 69–70. Insofar as Haksar's pragmatic case here recommends setting aside or neglecting differences among persons, it appears to go against Lucas's case for justice individualized discussed above.

40. Cf. Haksar, *Equality*, 20–23 and 70–71.

41. Haksar, *Equality*, 33.
42. Haksar writes: "I shall not prove that . . . perfectionist views are true; it is not possible to do that." *Equality*, 66.
43. Haksar, *Equality*, 280.
44. Haksar, *Equality*, 289.
45. Haksar, *Equality*, 295.
46. Haksar, *Equality*, 291.
47. Haksar, *Equality*, 292.
48. Haksar, *Equality*, 291.
49. Haksar, *Equality*, 297.
50. Haksar, *Equality*, 291.
51. Haksar, *Equality*, 285.
52. Regarding the latter, cf. Haksar, *Equality*, 297.
53. Cf. Haksar, *Equality*, 291.
54. Haksar, *Equality*, 291.
55. Cf. Haksar, *Equality*, 285ff.
56. Haksar, *Equality*, 295.
57. Haksar, *Equality*, 297.
58. Haksar, *Equality*, 297.
59. Haksar, *Equality*, 12.
60. Haksar, *Equality*, 12–13.
61. Haksar, *Equality*, 13.
62. The "reflective equilibrium" vocabulary is Rawlsian. To what degree the approach Haksar uses the vocabulary to refer to is exactly what Rawls uses it to refer to in *A Theory of Justice* may be controversial.
63. The Rawlsian "reflective equilibrium" approach is meant to be justificatory, as I understand Rawls's theory.
64. Assuming that persons are in-control agents tends to keep us from trying to know others well. Of course, even if in a world of modular and differential people I am urged to try to know others well, it does not follow that I will be able to figure out why *J* is the way he or she is.
65. For a short account describing the problems of individualizing the treatment of schoolchildren with dyslexia, see Geoffrey Cowley, "The Misreading of Dyslexia," *Newsweek* (3 February 1992): 57.
66. Perhaps it should be said again that the world of modular and differential people is not necessarily without in-control agents. There may be some people who can meet the terms of the model of in-control agency. Those who can meet those terms do not thereby have a license to impose that model on others.

Chapter 5

1. Let me note again the work of Arthur Kleinman on the bearing of culture on our conceptions of psychological disorder, in the books listed in note 60 in

chapter 3 above. Cf. Edward Shorter, "Historical Changes in Psychosomatic Illness," *The Harvard Mental Health Letter* 9:5 (November 1992).

2. Cf. Lynne McFall's essay, "What's Wrong with Bitterness?" in Claudia Card, ed., *Feminist Ethics* (Lawrence, Kans.: University Press of Kansas, 1991).

3. "Yesterday night, at fifteen minutes after eight, my little Waldo ended his life. . . . I comprehend nothing of this fact but its bitterness. Explanation I have none, consolation none that rises out of the fact itself; only diversion; only oblivion of this and pursuit of new objects." Ralph Waldo Emerson's *Journal* entries for 28 January 1842 and 20 March 1842 in Stephen E. Whicher, ed., *Selections from Ralph Waldo Emerson* (Boston, Mass.: Houghton Mifflin, 1957), 207–8.

4. This is no criticism of the philosophical characterizations. I find very helpful the philosophical discussion of the negative moral emotions in, for example, Herbert Morris's *On Guilt and Innocence* (Berkeley and Los Angeles: University of California Press, 1976).

5. Gerald Dworkin's essay, "Paternalism," in Richard A. Wasserstrom, ed., *Morality and the Law* (Belmont, Calif.: Wadsworth, 1971), discusses tensions, including antiutilitarian features, in Mill's view.

6. A problem arises here, of course. My claim might have to be qualified somehow if our individual is Hitler, but I will let points of this sort pass for the moment. Let us suppose that the individuals we have in mind, pained and baffled by wrongdoing in their pasts, are not moral monsters.

7. Here I find helpful John Rawls's discussion in "The Independence of Moral theory," *Proceedings and Addresses of the American Philosophical Association* 48 (1974–75).

8. Another time-related difference is involved in the contrast between the development of an adequate ethical theory and the development of a how-to-live strategy. There is an urgency to the latter that is not a part of the former. The former may take generations and centuries to occur, but no lives are wasted or souls lost by reason of this leisurely pace. In the latter case the wasting of lives and loss of souls are very much at stake.

9. I have in mind here William James's line of thought in "The Will to Believe," *The Will to Believe* (New York: Dover, 1956).

10. Trans. Thomas W. Higginson, intro. by Albert Salomon (Indianapolis: Bobbs-Merrill, 1948, 1956).

11. New York: Alcoholics Anonymous World Services, Inc., 1939, 1955, 1976.

12. New York: Alcoholics Anonymous World Services, Inc., 1952, 1953.

13. The former of these is more of a collaborative product (among about forty early members of AA) than is the latter. The cofounder of AA with New York stockbroker "Bill W" was Dr. Robert Smith ("Dr. Bob") of Akron, Ohio.

14. Perhaps something stronger should be said. The professional philosophy I have known over a thirty-year period does not seem to me to have in it very many practitioners who would find the subject I attempt to discuss here intellectually worthwhile.

15. Interestingly, Rawls, in *A Theory of Justice*, says that his conception of justice as fairness, as a set of principles for the basic structure of society, allows its members a collective form of reconciliation to the human condition: "should it be truly effective and publicly recognized as such, [it] seems more likely than its rivals to transform our perspective on the social world and to reconcile us to the dispositions of the natural world and the conditions of human life" (p. 512). My general aim in *On Sharing Fate* was to suggest a conception of individual responsibility ("shared-fate individualism") that might operate to reconcile the individual as such (apart from whatever conception of justice guides the basic structure of his or her society) to the human condition. Here I am discussing the possibility of a conception that might serve to reconcile one internally, that is, to oneself, as represented to one by one's understanding of one's own history and, in particular, its negative impact on those one cares for. Perhaps a part of living the life of a human being is dealing somehow with a number of different reconciliation problems.

16. I refer here to the adaptations involved in, for example, Narcotics Anonymous, Gamblers Anonymous, and so on.

17. For example, Herbert Fingarette, "Alcoholism and Self-Deception," in Mike W. Martin, ed., *Self-Deception and Self-Understanding* (Lawrence, Kans.: University Press of Kansas, 1985); and *Heavy Drinking* (Berkeley and Los Angeles: University of California Press, 1988). See, too, Ferdinand Schoeman, "Alcohol Addiction and Responsibility Attributions," in Mary I. Bockover, ed., *Rules, Rituals, and Responsibility: Essays Dedicated to Herbert Fingarette* (La Salle, Ill.: Open Court, 1991) (Fingarette comments on the essay by Schoeman at pp. 176–80 in this volume).

18. Usually in the spirit (torment and exasperation) of John Berryman's famous "extract from Dr. Severance's Journal": "Willpower is nothing. Morals is nothing. Lord, this is illness." *Recovery* (New York: Farrar, Straus and Giroux, 1973), 50. Nothing very technical, relative to the idea of disease, is intended, obviously.

19. The AA literature sometimes refers to alcoholism as an allergy. Herbert Fingarette's writing against the disease conception of alcoholism (in, e.g., *Heavy Drinking*) ends up proposing that it be thought of as a way of life. When increasing drug use—and hence the risk of addiction—became a major concern in the American public discussion after the 1960s, it became fashionable to think of alcoholism, too, as addiction. The disease conception is hardly a new idea, relative to contemporary interest in alcoholism: one of the early American proponents was Benjamin Rush, a physician and signer of the Declaration of Independence. The notion that the suffering alcoholic is simply morally weak has always been at least suspect among thoughtful people, though that has not prevented alcoholics from being the targets of a good deal of anger. For short, informed discussions of addiction, sprinkled with references to alcoholism and AA, see "Addiction—Part 1," *The Harvard Mental Health Letter* 9:4 (October 1992), and "Addiction—Part 2," *The Harvard Mental Health Letter* 9:5 (November 1992).

20. If diseases typically involve involuntary departures from normal functioning, then the helplessness of the suffering alcoholic may contribute to the view that alcoholism is a disease.

21. AA, *Twelve Steps and Twelve Traditions*, 24.

22. As in chapter 1 in this discussion.

23. One cannot overestimate the bewilderment and confusion involved in the sufferer's condition, in my view. Curiously, one's confusion turns one's thoughts to others rather than oneself. When drunk, one does dumb, embarrassing, ugly, funny, and sometimes wrong things. In later encounters with witnesses, one wonders what they think. They laughed at one at the time, or thought one gross, weak, or silly; perhaps they pitied one. What now? What is one to do about that (others' views)?—wondered by one who cannot do anything about that in any case. What is one to do about work?—asked by one who cannot work in any case. How does one get out of this mess?!?—thought by one who is trapped in a life that is a mess.

24. Cf. the informal, yet philosophical, characterization of the connection of this negative phenomenology to the meaninglessness view of life, in William James's *The Will to Believe*, especially pp. 82–83, 88, 171.

25. In AA this condition, this moralized despair, is sometimes called "soul sickness." Cf., for example, *Twelve Steps and Twelve Traditions*, 44.

26. AA, *Alcoholics Anonymous*, 58.

27. *Twenty-Four Hours a Day*, entry for 4 July.

28. Listed as they are for reading out at AA meetings. They occur in the text of *Alcoholics Anonymous*, pp. 83–84, just after the discussion in that book of steps 8 and 9 of the Twelve-Step Program.

29. Cf. AA, *Twelve Steps and Twelve Traditions*, 106. For other sorts of references, see pp. 88, 92, 99, 102.

30. A generality problem seems suggested, for one wonders how far the interpretation of the agency the recovery of which is the aim of the recovery strategy is relative to what I here call "context" and "clientele." I notice the following account of criteria for successful trauma resolution ascribed to "investigators at the Cambridge Hospital Victims of Violence Program in Cambridge, Massachusetts," where the context is rape (both acquaintance rape and stranger rape) and the clientele is women who are victims of rape:

> 1. The victim can recall or dismiss the event at will, instead of suffering from intrusive memories, frightening dreams, troubling flashbacks, and distressing associations. 2. The victim remembers the event with appropriately intense feeling rather than false detachment. 3. Feelings about the rape can be named and endured without overwhelming arousal, dissociation, or numbing. 4. Symptoms of anxiety, depression, and sexual dysfunction, if not absent, are at least reasonably tolerable and predictable. 5. The victim is not isolated from other people but has restored her capacity for affinity, trust, and attachment. 6. The victim has assigned meaning to the trauma and discarded a damaged sense of self, replacing it with a belief in her own strength. Losses

have been named and mourned; self-blame has been replaced by self-esteem and obsessive rumination about the past by realistic evaluation" (Mary P. Koss, "Date Rape: Victimization by Acquaintances," *The Harvard Mental Health Letter* 9 [September 1992]: 6).

31. As indicated in the third of AA's Twelve Traditions defining the nature of AA as a community or organization. Cf. *Twelve Steps and Twelve Traditions*, 10, with discussion at pp. 139–45.

32. These words are pretty anemic for the suffering at stake. They also do not pick up on the isolation the suffering alcoholic experiences. Virginia Woolf writes, in *To the Lighthouse* (New York: Harcourt Brace Jovanovich, 1927, 1955), of a "loneliness which was . . . the truth about things" (p. 301); the *Twelve Steps and Twelve Tradtions* says simply "alcoholism had been a lonely business, even though we had been surrounded by people who loved us" (p. 116). These words reach in the right direction. On the back cover of Norman O. Brown's *Life against Death*, it says grandly that "Brown's thesis is that mankind must be viewed as largely unaware of its own desires, hostile to life and unconsciously bent on self-destruction." I am not sure that mankind must be viewed in this way, but, again, the words reach to the condition of the suffering alcoholic.

33. The words quoted are from the AA Statement of Purpose typically read out at the beginning of meetings. (Copyright by The A.A. Grapevine, Inc., and Alcoholics Anonymous World Services.) It is usually added informally that the sharing here does not extend to advising others on life's problems. Recovering alcoholics sometimes remember that they have not always made effective responses to such problems in their own lives.

34. The features, by and large, that Rawls referred to as "arbitrary from a moral point of view" in *A Theory of Justice*, 15.

35. Anonymity is characterized as "the spiritual foundation of all our traditions," in the last of AA's Twelve Traditions. Cf. *Twelve Steps and Twelve Tradtitions*, 13, with discussion at pp. 184–87.

36. My impression is that intellectuals have an especially difficult time with this aspect of recovery in AA. The notion that one might be able to learn something from someone of different social station, intelligence, educational background, interests, and so on, is hard to absorb. One can be charmed at AA meetings by the sight of persons of very different life circumstances communicating with one another about, say, how to stay in dry places with dry people.

37. In William May's *The Patient's Ordeal* (Bloomington and Indianapolis: Indiana University Press, 1991), the chapter offering discussion of the AA program is titled "The Afflicted Assisting the Afflicted: Alcoholics Anonymous." For a helpful short discussion of self-help groups, with many references to AA as "the oldest and largest" of them, see "Self-Help Groups—Part 1," *The Harvard Mental Health Letter* 9:9 (March 1993), and "Self-Help Groups—Part 2," *The Harvard Mental Health Letter* 9:10 (April 1993).

38. The prayer was originally composed by Reinhold Niebuhr; AA adopted just the first few lines (later lines are more Christian): "God grant me the serenity

to accept the things I cannot change, courage to change the things I can, and wisdom to know the difference." It is interesting that the first and second lines of the prayer are ordered as they are. Some AA members do without the first word of the prayer when it is said at meetings, but that's "legal." The recovery interest in the prayer is in its content and calming effect, not in its theology.

39. In *Alcoholics Anonymous* the Twelve Steps are characterized as a "suggested program of recovery" (p. 59).

40. AA, *Alcoholics Anonymous*, 59–60. Explanation and commentary are given in chapter 5, titled "How It Works," of that work and more fully in *Twelve Steps and Twelve Traditions*.

41. Cf. AA, *Twelve Steps and Twelve Traditions*, 21–24.

42. How long has the typical AA member been involved in heavy drinking? I do not know any statistics on this matter, but experience indicates that the membership of AA is hardly made up only of grizzled old guys living under bridges who have given forty or more years to heavy drinking. I notice that all sorts of people are in the fellowship, and young people, including teenagers, are well represented. Many colleges and universities have meetings on campus. I understand that by the end of the century seventy percent of the AA membership will be people suffering problems with drugs as well as alcohol.

43. These words are also from the AA Statement of Purpose.

44. Of course, a "more credentialed will" need not be the will of God in any theological sense. Moral theory and political philosophy are filled with nonreligious interpretations of the idea of "more credentialed will," including Rousseau's account of the General Will in *The Social Contract*, in *The Social Contract and Discourses*, trans. and intro. G. D. H. Cole (New York: Everyman, 1950), Rawls's account of the principles of justice yielded by deliberations in "the original position" in *A Theory of Justice*, and Kant's account of what it is for maxims to satisfy the categorical imperative in *Foundations of the Metaphysics of Morals*, trans. and intro. Lewis White Beck (Indianapolis: Bobbs-Merrill, 1959).

45. At meetings, but, too, in the chapters on steps 4 and 10 in *Twelve Steps and Twelve Traditions*.

46. As does the commentary on step 7 in *Twelve Steps and Twelve Traditions*. Regarding the philosophical literature, I find Iris Murdoch's discussion of humility very helpful and quite compatible with the use made of the notion of humility in the AA materials. See *The Sovereignty of Good* (London and New York: Ark, 1985), chap. 3, 95. A helpful essay on self-honesty is Mike W. Martin's "Honesty with Oneself," in Mary I. Bockover, ed., *Rules, Rituals, and Responsibility*: *Essays Dedicated to Herbert Fingarette*—also quite compatible, I believe, with the discussion in the AA materials.

47. AA, *Twelve Steps and Twelve Traditions*, 77.

48. For example, in the commentary on steps 8 and 9 in *Twelve Steps and Twelve Traditions*.

49. For example, regarding one's use of alcohol (the amount, the kinds) and providing oneself an adequate supply. The preoccupation of the alcoholic with drinking and supply is often felt in many areas of life.

50. Bill Wilson writes in *Twelve Steps and Twelve Traditions* that "the readiness to take the full consequences of our past acts, and to take responsibility for the well-being of others at the same time, is the very spirit of Step Nine" (p. 87). I am struck by Robert Merrihew Adams's remarks in "Involuntary Sins," *The Philosophical Review*, 94 (January 1985), 16, that the "desire to satisfy one's responsibilities" can be enlisted "in support of the desire to change" and that "to refuse to take responsibility for one's emotions and motives is to be inappropriately alienated from one's own emotional and appetitive faculties." I could see how Adams's remarks might figure in an elucidation of the words of Bill Wilson.

51. AA, *Alcoholics Anonymous*, 58–59.

52. I have often been struck by how unserious the plight of the suffering alcoholic is taken to be in popular culture in America. In fact, without moving into discussion and statistics here, the devastation associated with alcoholism is overwhelming. It is interesting that in the opening deliberately short (4 pages) chapter on step 1 in *Twelve Steps and Twelve Traditions*, there are five matter-of-fact references to death.

53. For discussion of the possibility of naturally occurring remission from alcoholism, see George E. Vaillant, *The Natural History of Alcoholism* (Cambridge, Mass.: Harvard University Press, 1983), chap. 3.

54. I am impressed with how free of theological demands the commentary on step 11 is in *Twelve Steps and Twelve Traditions*, 96–105. There, prayer and meditation are discussed. It is suggested that "in meditation, debate has no place. We rest quietly with the thoughts of someone who knows, so that we may experience and learn" (p. 100). The example of "the thoughts of someone who knows" is the moving prayer of St. Francis:

> Lord, make me a channel of thy peace—that where there is hatred, I may bring love—that where there is wrong, I may bring the spirit of forgiveness—that where there is discord, I may bring harmony—that where there is error, I may bring truth—that where there is doubt, I may bring faith—that where there is despair, I may bring hope—that where there is sadness, I may bring joy. Lord, grant that I may seek rather to comfort than to be comforted—to understand, than to be understood—to love, than to be loved. For it is by self-forgetting that one finds. It is by forgiving that one is forgiven. It is by dying that one awakens to Eternal Life. Amen (p. 99).

The thought we are then especially urged to rest quietly with, is the one toward the end about *self-forgetting* (p. 101). It is reflection on this idea that is considered the point of the meditation. Regarding prayer itself, the commentary urges one to "renew the simple request: 'Thy will, not mine, be done,' " and then adds:

> if . . . our emotional disturbance happens to be great, we will more surely keep our balance, provided we remember, and repeat to ourselves, a particular prayer or phrase that has appealed to us in our reading or meditation. Just saying it over and over will often enable us to clear a channel choked up with anger, fear, frustration, or misunderstanding, and permit us

to return to the surest help of all—our search for God's will, not our own, in the moment of stress. At these critical moments, if we remind ourselves that "it is better to comfort than to be comforted, to understand than to be understood, to love than to be loved," we will be following the intent of Step Eleven (p. 103).

Even in the matter of prayer, then, the point—the how-to-live point—is self-forgetting, "keeping our balance," and managing the emotions that challenge sobriety (anger, fear, frustration, misunderstanding). Pretty consistently, the references to God in the AA materials are glossed in such a way that a theological interpretation is allowed but not required.

55. This is called "service" in AA and needs to be understood in light of traditions 5 and 11. In brief, AA does not ask its members to find drunks and drag them into the fellowship; it asks them to be available to those who ask for help. A "Twelfth-Step call" is initiated by a victim, not by AA.

56. What counts as amends is also unclear in some cases. Honest, sincere apologies may be what is required in certain cases, but other cases may involve much more. In some cases what has happened, in the way of harm or damage, may be such that amends of any ordinary sort will seem hollow.

57. AA, *Twelve Steps and Twelve Traditions*, 113.

58. AA, *Twelve Steps and Twelve Traditions*, 113.

59. The commentary on step 12 in *Twelve Steps and Twelve Tradtions* begins and ends with the words "the joy of living is the theme of A.A.'s Twelfth Step."

60. I have benefited from the discussion of "the God part" in Nan Robertson's *Getting Better: Inside Alcoholics Anonymous* (New York: William Morrow, 1988), chap. 6.

61. Cf. William James, *The Will to Believe* (New York: Dover, 1956), 52: when rationality is inconclusive regarding religious belief, then "passional nature" may govern sensibility, i.e., "we have a right to supplement [the physical order] by an unseen spiritual order which we assume on trust, if only thereby life may seem to us better worth living again." Also, pp. 56–57:

> when I speak of trusting our religious demands, just what do I mean by "trusting"? Is the word to carry with it license to define in detail an invisible world, and to anathematize and excommunicate those whose trust is different? Certainly not! Our faculties of belief were not primarily given us to make orthodoxies and heresies withal; they were given us to live by. . . . It is a fact of human nature, that men can live and die by the help of a sort of faith that goes without a single dogma or definition. This bare assurance that this natural order is not ultimate but a mere sign or vision, the external staging of a many-storied universe, in which spiritual forces have the last word and are eternal—this bare assurance is to such men enough to make life seem worth living in spite of every contrary presumption suggested by its circumstances on the natural plane.

These words from James express something very much at the core of AA's aspirations for its members, and, in fact, Bill Wilson read and was influenced by

James's views, especially the concluding chapter of James's *The Varieties of Religious Experience*. Wilson discusses briefly the influence of James on him in the second chapter of *Alcoholics Anonymous Comes of Age* (New York: Alcoholics Anonymous World Services, 1957), especially 64ff.

62. I enjoy Nan Robertson's term "foxhole humor" in her discussion in *Getting Better: Inside Alcoholics Anonymous*. Joyce Rebeta-Burditt captures some of this humor in *The Cracker Factory* (New York: Macmillan, 1977).

63. Above, in chap. 1, n. 37, I reported George E. Vaillant's account of why AA works for some.

64. I find that responding to another's trouble in this latter way is much more difficult than giving a view on the subject of his or her trouble.

65. AA, *Alcoholics Anonymous*, 58.

66. AA, *Twelve Steps and Twelve Traditions*, 125.

67. AA's colorful jargon, "Stinkin' Thinkin' Leads to Drinkin'," is a wonderful umbrella label for these many ways.

68. AA, *Twelve Steps and Twelve Traditions*, 21.

69. AA, *Twelve Steps and Twelve Traditions*, 106–7.

70. One form, but not the only form. AA does not operate by fear alone.

Works Cited

Adams, Robert Merrihew. 1985. "Involuntary Sins." *The Philosophical Review* 94 (January).

"Addiction—Part 1." 1992. *The Harvard Mental Health Letter* 9:4 (October).

"Addiction—Part 2." 1992. *The Harvard Mental Health Letter* 9:5 (November).

Alcoholics Anonymous. 1976. New York: Alcoholics Anonymous World Services, Inc.

Alcoholics Anonymous Comes of Age. 1957. New York: Alcoholics Anonymous World Services.

Appelbaum, Paul. 1988. "The Meaning of Competence in Mental Health Law." *The Harvard Medical School Mental Health Letter* 5:1 (July).

Aristotle. 1980. *The Nicomachean Ethics*, ed. W. D. Ross. London: Oxford University Press.

Atwood, Margaret. 1976. *Lady Oracle.* New York: Avon Books.

Awalt, L. Christopher. 1991. "Brother, Don't Spare a Dime." *Newsweek* (30 September).

Baier, Kurt. 1972. "Guilt and Responsibility." In Peter A. French, ed., *Individual and Collective Responsibility: The Massacre at My Lai* (Cambridge, Mass.: Schenkman).

Banfield, Edward. 1968. *The Unheavenly City.* Boston: Little, Brown.

Bates, Stanley. 1972. "My Lai and Vietnam: The Issues of Responsibility." In Peter A. French, ed., *Individual and Collective Responsibility: The Massacre at My Lai* (Cambridge, Mass.: Schenkman).

Beck, Aaron J., and Gary Emery, with Ruth L. Greenberg. 1985. *Anxiety Disorders and Phobias.* New York: Basic Books.

Bemporad, Jules R., M.D. 1991. "Effects of Early Childhood Experience." *The Harvard Mental Health Letter* 8:3 (September).

Bentham, Jeremy. 1948. *An Introduction to the Principles of Morals and Legislation.* Oxford: Blackwell.

Berryman, John. 1973. *Recovery.* New York: Farrar, Straus, and Giroux.

Betts, Robert B. 1978. "A Man Called Beaver Dick." *Along the Ramparts of the Tetons: The Saga of Jackson Hole, Wyoming.* Boulder, Colo.: Colorado Associated University Press.

Black, Claudia. 1981. *It Will Never Happen to Me!* Denver, Colo.: M.A.C. Publications.

191

Blume, Sheila B. 1992. "Compulsive Gambling: Addiction without Drugs." *The Harvard Mental Health Letter* 8:8 (February).

Borchard, Ruth. 1957. *John Stuart Mill, The Man*. London: Watts.

Bowie, Norman E. 1979. "Welfare and Freedom." *Ethics* 89 (April).

Bradley, F. H. 1927. "My Station and Its Duties." *Ethical Studies*. Oxford: Clarendon.

Brazaitis, Thomas J. 1988. "Pease's Office Door is Open." *The (Cleveland) Plain Dealer* (20 March).

Bridger, Wayne, M.D. 1991. "Early Childhood and Its Effects." *The Harvard Mental Health Letter* 8:2 (August).

Brody, Jane E. 1990. "It's Not Easy Being So Shy." *The (Cleveland) Plain Dealer* (20 February).

Brown, Norman O. 1959. *Life against Death*. New York: Vintage Books.

Camus, Albert. 1955. *The Myth of Sisyphus*, trans. Justin O'Brien. New York: Vintage Books.

Care, Norman S. 1987. *On Sharing Fate*. Philadelphia: Temple University Press.

Card, Claudia. 1990. "Responsibility and Moral Luck." Paper delivered at Colloquium in Philosophy, University of North Carolina at Chapel Hill (October).

Cohen, Richard. 1991. "A System that Makes Victims Pay Twice." *The (Cleveland) Plain Dealer* (29 December).

Conrad, Joseph. 1957. *Lord Jim*. New York: Bantam Books.

Cowley, Geoffrey. 1992. "The Misreading of Dyslexia." *Newsweek* (3 February).

Dostoevsky, Fyodor. 1959. *The Gambler* (1866). In *Four Great Russian Short Novels*, trans. Constance Farnett and Nathan Haskell Dole. New York: Dell.

Drabble, Margaret. 1989. *A Natural Curiosity*. New York: Viking Penguin.

"Dual Diagnosis: Part 1." 1991. *The Harvard Mental Health Letter* 8:2 (August).

"Dual Diagnosis: Part 2." 1991. *The Harvard Mental Health Letter* 8:3 (September).

Dworkin, Gerald. 1971. "Paternalism." *Morality and the Law*, ed. Richard A. Wasserstrom. Belmont, Calif.: Wadsworth.

Emerson, Ralph Waldo. 1957. *Journals. Selections from Ralph Waldo Emerson*, ed. Stephen E. Whicher. Boston: Houghton Mifflin Co.

Emond, Steven, M.D. 1990. "When Symptom Becomes Disease." *Harvard Health Letter* 16:2 (December).

Epictetus. 1956. *The Enchiridion*, trans. Thomas W. Higginson, intro. A. Salomon. Indianapolis: Bobbs-Merrill.

"Experts Wrangle over Sex as an Addiction or Disease." 1988. AP report. *The (Cleveland) Plain Dealer* (3 November).

Everett, Arthur, Kathryn Johnson, and Harvey Rosenthal. 1971. *Calley*. New York: Dell.

Falk, W. D. "Morality, Self, and Others." 1963. *Morality and the Language of Conduct*, eds. Hector-Neri Castañeda and George Nakhnikian. Detroit: Wayne State University Press.

Feinberg, Joel. 1980. "Legal Paternalism." *Rights, Justice, and the Bounds of Liberty*. Princeton: Princeton University Press.

———. 1986. *Harm to Self*. New York: Oxford University Press.

Fingarette, Herbert. 1985. "Alcoholism and Self-Deception." *Self-Deception and Self-Understanding*, ed. Mike W. Martin. Lawrence, Kans.: University Press of Kansas.

———. 1988. *Heavy Drinking*. Berkeley, Calif.: University of California Press.

———. 1990. "We Should Reject the Disease Concept of Alcoholism." *The Harvard Medical School Mental Health Letter* 6:8 (February). Reprinted in Lester Grinspoon and James B. Bakalar, eds., *The Harvard Medical School Mental Health Review*: "Alcohol Abuse and Dependence." President and Fellows of Harvard College.

Flanagan, Owen. 1991. *Varieties of Moral Personality*. Cambridge, Mass.: Harvard University Press.

Foot, Phillippa. 1970. "Morality and Art" (a bound lecture). *The Proceedings of the British Academy*, 56.

Frankfurt, Harry G. 1988. *The Importance of What We Care About*. Cambridge: Cambridge University Press.

Gelman, David. 1989. "Haunted by Their Habits." *Newsweek* (27 March).

Goldman, Marcus J., M.D. 1991. "Is There a Treatment for Kleptomania?" *The Harvard Mental Health Letter* 8:5 (November)

Golding, Martin P. 1984–85. "Forgiveness and Regret." *The Philosophical Forum* 16 (Fall-Winter).

Goleman, Daniel. 1991. "Imagined Ugliness an Illness." *The (Cleveland) Plain Dealer* (8 October).

Goodman, Ellen. 1988. "Why Didn't She Just Get Out of There?" *The (Cleveland) Plain Dealer* (13 December).

Goodwin, Donald W. 1986. *Anxiety*. New York: Oxford University Press.

Grafton, Sue. 1988. *"E" is for Evidence*. New York: Bantam Books.

Grinspoon, Lester, M.D., and James B. Bakalar, J.D. 1990. *Depression and Other Mood Disorders*. A "Mental Health Review," published by *The Harvard Mental Health Letter*.

Haksar, Vinit. 1979. *Equality, Liberty, and Perfectionism*. New York: Oxford University Press.

Hammer, Richard. 1971. *The Court Martial of Lt. Calley*. New York: Coward, McCann and Geoghegan.

Hart, H. L. A. 1961. *The Concept of Law*. London: Oxford University Press.

Hobbes, Thomas. 1957. *Leviathan*, ed. and intro. Michael Oakeshott. Oxford: Blackwell.

Honoré, A. M. 1980. "Law, Morals, and Rescue." In Joel Feinberg and Hyman Gross, eds., *Philosophy of Law*. Belmont, Calif.: Wadsworth.

Howe, Irving. 1978. "The Right Menace." *The New Republic* (9 September).

Hume, David. 1962. *An Enquiry Concerning the Principles of Morals*. In L. A. Selby-Bigge, ed., *Hume's Enquiries*. Oxford: Clarendon Press.

———. 1970. *Dialogues Concerning Natural Religion.* In Nelson Pike, ed., *Hume: Dialogues Concerning Natural Religion.* Indianapolis and New York: Bobbs-Merrill.

Ignatieff, Michael. 1988. "Modern Dying." *The New Republic* (26 December).

———. 1990. "The Limits of Sainthood." *The New Republic* (18 June).

James, William. 1982. *The Varieties of Religious Experience.* New York: Penguin.

———. 1956. *The Will to Believe.* New York: Dover.

Jenike, Michael, M.D. 1990. "Obsessive-Compulsive Disorder." *The Harvard Medical School Health Letter* 15:6 (April)

Kant, Immanuel. 1950. *Prolegomena to Any Future Metaphysics,* intro. Lewis White Beck. New York: The Liberal Arts Press.

———. 1959. *Foundations of the Metaphysics of Morals,* trans. and intro. Lewis White Beck. Indianapolis: Bobbs-Merrill.

Kierkegaard, Soren. 1985. *Fear and Trembling.* Harmondsworth, Middlesex, England: Penguin Books.

Kleinman, Arthur. 1980. *Patients and Healers in the Context of Culture.* Berkeley and Los Angeles: University of California Press.

———. 1986. *Social Origins of Distress and Disease.* New Haven: Yale University Press.

———. 1988. *Rethinking Psychiatry: From Cultural Category to Personal Experience.* New York: Free Press.

———. 1991. "The Psychiatry of Culture and the Culture of Psychiatry." *The Harvard Mental Health Letter* 8:1 (July).

Kolnai, Aurel. 1978. *Ethics, Value, and Reality.* Indianapolis: Hackett.

Koss, Mary P. 1992. "Date Rape: Victimization by Acquaintances." *The Harvard Mental Health Letter* 9 (September).

Krauthammer, Charles. 1989. "Love Thyself and Maybe Then Thy Neighbor." *The (Cleveland) Plain Dealer* (7 May).

———. 1991. "Pseudo-Psychiatry Debases Justice System." *The (Cleveland) Plain Dealer* (9 February).

Landers, Ann. 1988. "Mentally Unstable Walk a Thin Line." *The (Cleveland) Plain Dealer* (27 January)

———. 1991. "Help for Child Molesters Available." *The (Cleveland) Plain Dealer* (5 February).

Liebowitz, Michael, M.D. 1989. "Is There a Drug Treament for Social Phobia?" *The Harvard Medical School Mental Health Letter* 5:8 (February).

Locke, John. 1963. *The Second Treatise of Government.* In Peter Laslett, ed., *Locke's Two Treatises of Government.* Cambridge: Cambridge University Press.

Lucas, J. R. 1980. *On Justice.* Oxford: Clarendon Press.

Lukes, Steven. 1973. *Individualism.* Oxford: Blackwell.

Mallory, Jim. 1989. "The Gambling Compulsion Afflicting Ordinary People." *The (Cleveland) Plain Dealer* (25 August).

Martin, Mike W. 1991. "Honesty with Oneself." In Mary I. Bockover, ed.,

Rules, Rituals, and Responsibility: Essays Dedicated to Herbert Fingarette. La Salle, Ill.: Open Court.

Marx, Karl. 1963. "Alienated Labour." In T. B. Bottomore, ed., *Karl Marx: Early Writings.* New York: McGraw-Hill.

May, William F. 1991. *The Patient's Ordeal.* Bloomington and Indianapolis: Indiana University Press.

McFall, Lynne. 1987. "Integrity." *Ethics* 98 (October).

———. 1990. *The One True Story of the World.* New York: Atlantic Monthly Press.

———. 1991. "What's Wrong with Bitterness?" In Claudia Card, ed., *Feminist Ethics.* Lawrence, Kans.: University Press of Kansas.

McInerney, Peter K. 1985. "Person-Stages and Unity of Consciousness." *American Philosophical Quarterly* 22 (July).

———. 1991. "The Nature of a Person-Stage." *American Philosophical Quarterly* 28 (July).

Mill, John Stuart. 1978. *On Liberty,* ed. Elizabeth Rapaport. Indianapolis: Hackett.

———. 1979. *Utilitarianism,* ed. George Sher. Indianapolis: Hackett.

———. 1957. *Autobiography.* Indianapolis: Bobbs-Merrill.

Miller, Arthur. 1949. *Death of a Salesman.* New York: The Viking Press.

———. 1957. "Introduction to the Collected Plays." In Miller, *Arthur Miller's Collected Plays.* New York: Viking Press.

Miller, Norman, M.D., and Doug Toft. 1990. *The Disease Concept of Alcoholism and Other Drug Addiction.* Center City, Minn.: Hazelden Foundation.

Moore, Barrington, Jr. 1978. *Injustice: The Social Bases of Obedience and Revolt.* White Plains, N.Y.: M. E. Sharpe.

Mooney, Carolyn J. 1989. "A Crisis of Low Self-Esteem." *The Chronicle of Higher Education* (1 November).

Morris, Herbert. 1976. *On Guilt and Innocence.* Berkeley: University of California Press. See especially "Persons and Punishment" and "Shared Guilt."

———. 1987. "Nonmoral Guilt." In Ferdinand Schoeman, ed., *Responsibility, Character, and the Emotions.* Cambridge: Cambridge University Press.

———. 1988. "The Decline of Guilt." *Ethics* 99:1 (October).

Murdoch, Iris. 1985. *The Sovereignty of the Good.* London: Ark.

———. 1973. *An Accidental Man.* London: Penguin.

———. 1982. *Nuns and Soldiers.* London: Penguin.

Murphy, Jeffrie G. 1973. "Marxism and Retribution." *Philosophy and Public Affairs* 2 (Spring).

Murray, Thomas H. 1991. "Ethical Issues in Human Genome Research." *The FASEB Journal* 5 (January).

Nagel, Thomas. 1979. *Mortal Questions.* Cambridge: Cambridge University Press. See especially "The Absurd," "War and Massacre," and "Moral Luck."

———. 1980. "The Limits of Objectivity." In Sterling M. McMurrin, ed., *The Tanner Lectures on Human Values* 1. Salt Lake City: University of Utah Press, and Cambridge: Cambridge University Press.

"New Test for Psychopathy." 1992. *The Harvard Mental Health Letter* 8:7 (January).

Nozick, Robert. 1974. *Anarchy, State, and Utopia.* New York: Basic Books.

"Opening Pandora's Box." 1992. *Harvard Health Letter* 17:3 (January).

Original Constitution. 1839. Oberlin College Alumni Association.

O'Neill, Onora. 1975. "Lifeboat Earth." *Philosophy and Public Affairs* 4 (Spring).

Pears, David. 1984. *Motivated Irrationality.* Oxford: Oxford University Press.

"Personality and Personality Disorder—Part 2." 1987. *The Harvard Medical School Mental Health Letter* 4:4 (October).

Peele, Stanton. 1985. *The Meaning of Addiction.* Lexington, Mass.: D. C. Heath.

———. 1989. *Diseasing of America.* Lexington, Mass.: D. C. Heath.

"Pilot's Nightmare Becomes Reality." 1987. *The (Cleveland) Plain Dealer* (27 October).

Pincoffs, Edmund L. 1966. *The Rationale of Legal Punishment.* New York: Humanities Press.

"Poll Finds that Many View Depression as Weakness." 1991. AP report. *The New York Times* (12 December).

"Post-traumatic Stress: Part 1." *The Harvard Mental Health Letter* 7:8 (February).

"Post-traumatic Stress: Part 2." *The Harvard Mental Health Letter* 7:9 (March).

Rawls, John. 1971. *A Theory of Justice.* Cambridge, Mass.: Belknap Press of Harvard University Press.

———. 1974–75. "The Independence of Moral Theory." *Proceedings and Addresses of the American Philosophical Association* 48.

———. 1977. "The Basic Structure as Subject." *American Philosophical Quarterly* 14 (April).

Rebeta-Burditt, Joyce. 1977. *The Cracker Factory.* New York: Macmillan.

Regan, Tom. 1984. "Introduction." In Regan, ed., *Earthbound.* New York: Random House.

Roan, Shari. 1991. "Rare Disorder Has People Faking Illness Symptoms." *The (Cleveland) Plain Dealer* (20 August).

Robertson, Nan. 1988. *Getting Better: Inside Alcoholics Anonymous.* New York: William Morrow.

Rousseau, Jean-Jacques. 1950. *The Social Contract.* In *The Social Contract and Discourses,* trans. and intro. G. D. H. Cole. New York: Everyman.

———. 1954. *The Confessions,* trans. J. M. Cohen. Harmondsworth, England: Penguin Books.

———. 1982. *The Reveries of the Solitary Walker,* trans., preface, notes, and interpretive essay, Charles E. Butterworth. New York: Harper Colophon.

Royko, Mike. 1990. "In Washington, Everybody Just Keeps Moving On." *The (Cleveland) Plain Dealer* (27 February).

Saletan, William, and Nancy Watzman. 1989. "Marcus Welby, J.D." *The New Republic* (17 April).

Sartre, Jean-Paul. 1951. "Existentialism is a Humanism." In Walter Kaufman, ed., *Existentialism from Dostoevsky to Sartre*. New York: Meridian Books.

Schoeman, Ferdinand. 1991. "Alcohol Addiction and Responsibility Attributions." In Mary I. Bockover, ed., *Rules, Rituals, and Responsibility: Essays Dedicated to Herbert Fingarette*. La Salle, Ill: Open Court.

"Self-Help Groups—Part 1." 1993. *The Harvard Mental Health Letter* 9:9 (March).

"Self-Help Groups—Part 2." 1993. *The Harvard Mental Health Letter* 9:10 (April).

Sen, Amartya. 1990. "Individual Freedom as a Social Commitment." *The New York Review of Books* (14 June).

Shakespeare, William. 1936. *The Tempest*. In William Aldis Wright, ed., *The Complete Works of William Shakespeare*. Philadelphia: Blakiston.

Shane, Scott. 1989. "Was Tolstoy the Same Species as We Are?" *The (Cleveland) Plain Dealer* (13 March).

Sher, Kenneth J. 1991. *Children of Alcoholics*. Chicago and London: University of Chicago Press.

Shorter, Edward. 1992. "Historical Changes in Psychosomatic Illness." *The Harvard Mental Health Letter* 9:5 (November).

"Shy Children Grown Up." 1989. *The Harvard Medical School Mental Health Letter* 5:12 (June).

Steinberg, Ira S. 1968. *Educational Myths and Realities*. Reading, Mass.: Addison-Wesley.

Steinbock, Bonnie. 1985. "Drunk Driving." *Philosophy and Public Affairs* 14 (Summer).

Styron, William. 1990. *Darkness Invisible*. New York: Random House.

"Tax on $100 Billion Illegally Escaping." 1979. AP report. *The (Cleveland) Plain Dealer* (17 July).

Thomas, Laurence. 1989. *Living Morally*. Philadelphia: Temple University Press.

Tolstoy, Leo. 1972. "The Death of Ivan Ilych." In Irving Howe, ed., *Classics of Modern Fiction*. New York: Harcourt Brace Jovanovich.

Twelve Steps and Twelve Traditions. 1953. New York: Alcoholics Anonymous World Services, Inc.

Twenty-Four Hours a Day, rev. ed. 1975. Center City, Minn.: Hazelden.

Updike, John. 1989. *Self-Consciousness, Memoirs*. New York: Fawcett Crest.

"Unbathed Couple Baffles Society." 1979. AP report. *The (Cleveland) Plain Dealer* (24 July).

Vaillant, George E. 1983. *The Natural History of Alcoholism*. Cambridge, Mass.: Harvard University Press.

———. 1990. "We Should Retain the Disease Concept of Alcoholism." *The Harvard Medical School Mental Health Letter* 6:9 (March).

Van Nortwick, Thomas. 1991. "The Road to Colonus: Sophocles' Theban Trilogy." Paper delivered at the annual meeting of Classical Association of the Midwest and South, Hamilton, Ontario (April).

Vatz, Richard E., and Lee S. Winberg. 1989. "Gamblers Aren't Sick, Just Silly." *The (Cleveland) Plain Dealer* (5 July).

Walsh, W. H. 1970. "Pride, Shame, and Responsibility." *The Philosophical Quarterly* 20 (January).

Watson, Gary. 1987. "Responsibility and the Limits of Evil: Variations on a Strawsonian Theme." In Ferdinand Schoeman, ed., *Responsibility, Character, and the Emotions*. Cambridge: Cambridge University Press.

Wittgenstein, Ludwig. 1969. *On Certainty*, ed. G. E. M. Anscombe and G. H. von Wright, trans. Denis Paul and G. E. M. Anscombe. New York: Harper.

Will, George F. 1989. "A Conspicuous and Tainted Compassion." *The (Cleveland) Plain Dealer* (14 May).

Williams, Bernard. 1981. *Moral Luck*. Cambridge: Cambridge University Press. See especially "Persons, Character, and Morality" and "Moral Luck."

Woititz, Janet Geringer. 1983. *Adult Children of Alcoholics*. Pompano Beach, Fla.: Health Communications, Inc.

Wolf, Susan. 1987. "Sanity and the Metaphysics of Responsibility." In Ferdinand Schoeman, ed., *Responsibility, Character, and the Emotions*. Cambridge: Cambridge University Press.

Wolfe, Alan. 1992. "The New American Dilemma." *The New Republic* (13 April).

Wollheim, Richard. 1984. *The Thread of Life*. Cambridge, Mass.: Harvard University Press.

Woolf, Virginia. 1955. *To the Lighthouse*. New York: Harcourt Brace Jovanovich.

Zilboorg, Gregory. 1954. *The Psychology of the Criminal Act and Punishment*. New York: Harcourt Brace.

Index

About the Author

Norman S. Care is professor of philosophy at Oberlin College. He was educated in music at Indiana University and in philosophy at the University of Kansas, Yale University, and Oxford University. His areas of interest in teaching and writing are moral theory, moral psychology, political philosophy, environmental ethics, and aesthetics. He is the author of *On Sharing Fate* (1987) and coeditor of a number of collections, and has published essays and reviews in journals in philosophy, law, and education and in magazines of social comment. In 1991 Professor Care received a Teaching Excellence and Campus Leadership Award from the Sears-Roebuck Foundation. His research and writing have been supported over the years by a Fulbright Fellowship, and grants from the American Council of Learned Societies, the National Endowment for the Humanities, and Oberlin College.